THE SICKLY
STUARTS

*With love, I dedicate this book to
my wife, friend, and paediatric consultant,
Professor Grace E.F. Holmes*

THE SICKLY STUARTS

THE MEDICAL DOWNFALL OF A DYNASTY

FREDERICK HOLMES

SUTTON PUBLISHING

This book was first published in 2003 by
Sutton Publishing Limited · Phoenix Mill
Thrupp · Stroud · Gloucestershire · GL5 2BU

This paperback edition first published in 2005

British Library Cataloguing in Publication Data
A catalogue record for this book is available from the British
Library.

ISBN 0 7509 3292 9

Typeset in 11/12.5 Photina.
Typesetting and origination by
Sutton Publishing Limited.
Printed and bound in Great Britain by
J.H. Haynes & Co. Ltd, Sparkford.

Contents

Preface

In 1991 I took sabbatical leave from my university post as Professor of Medicine to enrol in graduate courses in Modern British History, and it was my great fortune to begin with a colloquium on the Stuart period taught by the late Professor John P. Kenyon. Though wary of older students with peculiar vocations for history, he kindly took me on and over the next several years, until his retirement from academic life, we developed a warm friendship. Fascinated by the Stuarts, I took more of his courses when free from my regular duties as a consultant physician at our university hospital. Professor Kenyon helped me realize two important truths, first, that I should not consider, even for a minute, transferring from medicine to history to make my living, but second, that as a seasoned physician with some background in history, I could see and evaluate medical data in primary and secondary source material better than most historians. In our discussions about the rise of Parliament in the seventeenth century I came to the realization that the aggregate medical problems and medical misadventures of the English Stuart monarchs and their family members brought this dynasty down, so that Parliament rose to fill the vacuum created. In 1998 I received a Master's degree in History from the University of Kansas using this theory as my thesis. Thus, I owe a considerable debt to Professor Kenyon and to his successor, Professor Jonathan C.D. Clark, current occupant of the Hall Chair in Modern British History at the University of Kansas, and also to the other members of my thesis committee, Professors Rose Greaves, Robert Hudson, and John Sweets.

In writing the medical histories of members of the Stuart family I sought primary source materials as I could find them, looking particularly for the writings of their physicians, but often finding clues in letters and reports of those unbiased by the medical knowledge of the day, for example in the *Calendars of State Papers*. The best and most accurate source for obstetrical details proved to be Professor Sir John Dewhurst's book, *Royal Confinements: A Gynaecological History of Britain's Royal Family*, published in 1980 and still the benchmark authority for obstetrical information about British royalty. In the text I have made reference to and quoted extensively from Professor Dewhurst's work.

Surprisingly, nearly all of the English Stuart monarchs had post-mortem examinations and the observations of the surgeons and physicians who performed them were often particularly cogent and helpful. Where several versions or translations were available, I have chosen the most complete and accessible one for citation, verifying it with the original when possible. In most chapters of this book the post-mortem examination is the pivot or fulcrum for the text transition from medical history to interpretation of the meaning of medical events, in historical context. My friend and colleague of many years, Francis E. Cuppage, Emeritus Professor of Pathology at the University of Kansas Medical Center, was very helpful in the interpretation of these post-mortem reports, written so many years ago. When dates or the sequence or timing of events were not clear I referred to entries in the *Dictionary of National Biography* for the last word, and used this source extensively for minor characters in the Stuart family and for prominent seventeenth-century physicians. However, the latter were also located in *William Munk's Roll of the Royal College of Physicians of London* for specific biographical details and in Elizabeth Lane Furdell's recent book, *The Royal Doctors 1485–1714: Medical Personnel at the Tudor and Stuart Courts*.

I ask the reader to be patient with my historical interpretations, I have tried to keep them to a minimum, in consideration of my modest background in British history of the seventeenth century. I have attempted to expunge this treatise of confusing medical jargon, but have left enough medical words to improve colour and meaning where applicable. The text is meant to be medically accurate, to the standard of a paper published in a peer-reviewed medical journal, but easily understood by the lay reader without a medical background.

Two caveats must be mentioned, disclaimers of a sort, offered here to defend the two weaknesses of this study. First, there is always arrogance in making diagnoses on another physician's patient, particularly at a remove of time. A trite phrase in medicine tells us that diagnostic accuracy is always certain through the 'retrospectoscope'. As I hope I will show, the physicians who attended the Stuarts were thoughtful and competent men, who displayed great skill and wisdom in caring for their patients. Over the years, the more I have read of their personal accounts and the medical records of the Stuarts the more I yearn to talk with them, physician to physician. I sincerely believe I would be the richer for such an experience. They were physicians, not doctors in the generic sense, because their training and competence were certified by the Royal College of Physicians, as mine has been endorsed by the American College of Physicians. Second, while the medical diagnoses I have made in the Stuarts are defensible, within the scheme of *certain*, *possible*, *doubtful* and *uncertain meaning*, as will be explained at the end of the first chapter, my diagnosis of delusional disorder in Charles I is less easily defended. I have not had training in psychiatry so I function at the edge of my competence in this assessment of Charles I, some might say past the edge. However, I have tried to find a way to understand the appalling failure of Charles I as a monarch, and this diagnosis fits him quite nicely, in my thinking.

Of the 111 years from the time James VI, King of Scotland, came to the throne of England in 1603 until the death of the last Stuart monarch, Queen Anne, in 1714, a Stuart sat on the throne of England for only 93 years, while others ruled England for 18 years during this period. In fact, the Stuart dynasty came to an end three times, in 1649, 1688, and 1694, before it finally ended with the death of Queen Anne in 1714. The sickly Stuarts were simply unable to sustain their rule of England.

Acknowledgements

The research for this study was spread over many years and I was particularly fortunate to have at hand the rich library resources of the University of Kansas, including the Clendening History of Medicine and Dykes libraries on the medical school campus in Kansas City, and the Anschutz, Malott, Spencer (Rare Books), and Watson libraries on the main university campus in Lawrence. When possible I made forays to London to use the British Library, both old and new, and the library of the Royal Society of Medicine. My debt to the librarians of all of these wonderful places is greater than I could ever acknowledge. I must also recognize with gratitude my secretary, Mrs Linda Taylor, who typed and revised this manuscript many times, and my clinic nurse, Mrs Donna Lawrence, who often eased the pressures of my practice so that I could slip briefly back to the seventeenth century to see my patients there, the Stuarts. The idea for the title, *The Sickly Stuarts*, came from Professor Jane Ohlmeyer, then at Aberdeen University. To describe a seminar I gave at her university in 1999 she cleverly condensed the history of the English Stuarts into three words. I thank my daughter, Julia McMorrough, for her drawings of the Stuarts which appear at the beginnings of the texts of the biographical chapters. These are composites, created largely from images in the collection of the National Portrait Gallery. Finally, I am ever grateful to my wife and paediatric consultant, Professor Grace E.F. Holmes, who frequently saw me off to seventeenth-century London and then joined me there occasionally to help me understand the medical problems of the Stuarts as children; I could not have put into proper focus the childhood problems of James I, Charles I, or William, Duke of Gloucester, without her direction and insight. In recent years Professor Jonathan C.D. Clark has been both a friend and a mentor. Finally, I want to thank my faculty colleagues from the University of Kansas, Professor Susan Kemper, Dr Kristine Williams, and Dr Janet Marquis, for including me in the study of the linguistic aspects of the dementia of King James I and allowing me to cite this work in the chapter on his rule.

ONE

The Sad End of the Stuart Dynasty

A nne Stuart, Queen of Great Britain and Ireland, awoke on Thursday morning at Kensington Palace with a terrible headache. She was confused and it was difficult for her to gather her thoughts. The harsh words of the meeting of her Council were still ringing in her ears, a meeting which did not resolve the difficult question of whom she should name Lord Treasurer. An interminable meeting, begun on Tuesday and lasting until the small hours of Wednesday morning. Her confusion alarmed her bedchamber women, who immediately called her personal physician, John Arbuthnot, and promptly he was at her bedside. After examining her carefully, he consulted with his colleagues, Drs Hamilton, Lawrence, Shadwell, and Sloane, and it was agreed that she should be bled and cupped. Mr Ayme, her surgeon, performed these procedures early that Thursday afternoon and found that her blood was dark and thick, not a good sign, indicating that she was plethoric, possessed of too much blood, a very unusual finding in a woman. Though still fuzzy-headed throughout the rest of that afternoon, by evening she seemed better, only to awaken at three o'clock on Friday morning, sick to her stomach and needing to vomit. Finally, feeling much better, she slept until awakened by the morning light streaming into her bedroom, her head felt fine and she asked to have her hair combed. However, suddenly confused after she sat up, she found herself unable to read the dial of her clock, again frightening her bedchamber women. Her physicians were called immediately and they came in haste. After brief deliberation they concluded she had had a stroke, so she was bled once more.

Just two miles away, at Whitehall, her Council assembled and tried again to resolve the question of who should become Lord Treasurer. At Kensington Palace, Anne became increasingly confused and gradually lapsed into stupor and then coma as Friday wore on. The Council finally chose Charles Talbot, Duke of Shrewsbury, the man who was certain to effect the Hanoverian succession should Anne die, a man experienced in government but threatening to many in Parliament. All that remained to make their choice official was for Queen Anne to speak with him and present him with his staff of office. Although all but one of her physicians were loath to admit the fact, clearly Anne was dying, and there was little hope for her survival. Quickly the Council went to the Kensington sick room of their sovereign to tell her of their choice of Shrewsbury, presuming she would then speak with him and give him the staff. History tells us that Anne rallied long enough to thank her Council for their fine choice, and telling Shrewsbury to use his office for the good of her people, she handed him the staff of office of Lord Treasurer. In fact, Anne was not mentally competent at this juncture, she was likely incapable of coherent speech and did not give the staff to Shrewsbury, rather he took it from her still hand. Worsening on Saturday, Queen Anne died early on Sunday morning, the first day of August 1714, and so also died the Stuart dynasty.

In taking the staff of office, Shrewsbury took the government of Britain and the Stuart crown as well, guaranteeing that both would go to George, Elector of Hanover, as Parliament and King William III had decided in the Act of Settlement of 1701, more than a year before Anne even became queen. The real heir to the Stuart throne, James Francis Edward Stuart, Anne's 26-year-old half-brother, languished in France. He and his line were forever excluded from their rightful claim to rule England, or Britain as it was now constituted. The contrast between the settlement of the throne on the death of Queen Elizabeth, the last Tudor, and Queen Anne, the last Stuart, could not have been greater. Elizabeth, with no heir at all and keeping her own counsel to her very last breath, by the most subtle statecraft and through the agency of her chief minister, Robert Cecil, nonetheless allowed James Stuart, King of Scotland, to be named her successor. Her Parliament had little or no part in this decision. Somehow, between the death of Elizabeth in 1603, and the death of Anne in 1714, the monarchy had lost power and Parliament had gained it. While it might be imagined that Parliament grew in strength throughout the seventeenth century because right was on their side and Englishmen were successful in their demand to rule themselves, this in fact is only part of the picture, and perhaps the smaller part. In reality, the Stuarts were a sickly lot who were sapped of their strength and vitality by disease and disability during the four generations their six monarchs ruled England. The power of the Stuarts and the English monarchy slowly faded throughout the long seventeenth century as the Stuarts were brought down by a variety of medical problems and Parliament simultaneously increased in power to fill the void.

Few monarchies have survived to the twenty-first century and where they exist, kings, queens, emperors and other potentates usually reign as figureheads of parliamentary governments of one sort or another. Yet, in the seventeenth century, monarchs ruled with almost absolute authority. Parliaments of any sort were few, and holding the idea that a king must be accountable to those he governed, with or without a parliament, was likely to get one jailed and given an appointment with the executioner. In attempting to understand the transition that occurred over the 400-year period from 1600 to 2000 we instinctively fall into the trap of popular modern views of history. We imagine that the power of monarchy could be reduced over time only from below, from the people governed, either by slow and steady erosion or by revolution. While there is obviously truth in this belief, there was another force that crippled some ruling houses, and that force was disease and disability. A weakened vessel is less able to withstand pressure than a strong one, and monarchs weakened by illness are less able to resist demands for power from their parliaments and people than healthy monarchs. An extension of this principle is that a succession of sick monarchs from a reigning family further magnifies this effect. The rise of parliamentary power in England during the seventeenth century was made possible by the progressive weakening of the House of Stuart by disease and disability.

Early modern European states functioned most efficiently when led by strong monarchs who curbed and focused the powers of local magnates, all the while keeping an eye on foreign adversaries and essentially representing their kingdoms in their very persons, projecting an image of strength and control. Focusing on English history, a good example of such a ruler would be the first Tudor, Henry VII, who ended the Wars of the Roses and welded England into a strong bureaucratic entity, keeping his country prosperous and at peace during his reign of more than twenty years. A careful manager, he was in possession of intelligence, guile and stamina, ruling his subjects with considerable skill and possessing a clear mind until his death at the age of fifty-two. That he was thin to the point of being gaunt, had a chronic cough, and frequently coughed up blood is interesting but seemingly not important when one evaluates his effectiveness as a ruler. In fact, Henry has variously been diagnosed as having had tuberculosis, asthma, and bronchitis, but until shortly before the end of his life his illness, or illnesses, did not significantly diminish his vigour nor compromise his image as a king in control of his country and its relations with other states. Henry left a strong central government to his son and namesake, Henry VIII, as well as peace with other European powers and even a surplus in the royal treasury. England was fortunate with Henry VII because his chest condition was a nuisance for him rather than a disability. In early modern times one had to hope and pray that the monarch would live a long and healthy life, aptly expressed in the words, 'Long Live the King'.

Staying healthy in early modern times depended much more on luck than it does now. But although balancing the fate of a kingdom on a single life entailed risk, nonetheless it was a strategy that could bring great benefit to a state. A clever and apparently healthy monarch who reigned for decades gave his or her state great stability – examples include the 38-year reign of Henry VIII, the 44-year reign of Elizabeth I and the remarkable tenure of the Bourbon Sun King, Louis XIV, who ruled France for seventy-two years. But lives might end suddenly and unexpectedly, truncating the rule of monarchs who seemed to have made a good start and who had promise: the six-year reign of Edward VI and the five-year reign of Mary I are good examples. Edward came to the English throne in 1547 at the age of nine years and was just beginning to exert personal authority when, shortly after his fifteenth birthday, he sickened and died of rapidly progressive pulmonary tuberculosis. Mary's luck was little better, she inherited the English throne at the age of thirty-seven on the death of Edward and died, possibly of ovarian cancer, in 1558 at the age of forty-two. It must be mentioned that the old canard that Edward and Mary suffered from congenital syphilis is untrue, neither showed the stigmata of this disease in their portraits and neither had any of its common manifestations, for example compromise of sight or hearing. The brief reigns of Edward and Mary were each followed by lessened political stability and a weakened English ship of state. That ship was saved by Elizabeth who had a good compass to right its course and who jettisoned dangerous cargo and trimmed sails, in a sense, as surely and adeptly as had her grandfather, Henry VII. It was propitious for England that Elizabeth enjoyed good health and that she did not suffer disability. In fact she was able to reverse whatever damage may have been done to monarchy in England by her two weakened Tudor predecessors, her half-brother and half-sister.

In spite of the medical problems of Edward and Mary, the Tudors as a family ruled firmly and well for 118 years, leaving a strong and stable England to their Scottish relatives, the Stuarts. In retrospect, the Stuarts were a weak bridge between the Tudors and the Hanoverians. In fact, had Cromwell accepted the crown when it was offered to him, the Stuart dynasty would have come to an end after the rule of just two monarchs. During the seventeenth century, while the power of monarchy in England declined, by contrast monarchs of her continental rivals, France, Spain, and Austria, reigned with undiminished power, and in the case of Louis XIV, monarchical power might be said to have increased. The Stuart family lessened the overall power of the monarchy in England because of their enfeeblement, both individually and collectively. For example, in contrast to Elizabeth, the final Tudor, Anne, the last Stuart, was the sickliest and most disabled of her family. She had no ability even to sustain their rule by providing an heir, let alone consolidate or improve their fortunes. One can see irony in the facts that Elizabeth had no interest in marriage, was never pregnant and, thus, had no heir, whereas Anne was eager to have children, was pregnant seventeen times but also left no heir. Elizabeth was a healthy woman throughout her reign of forty-four years, while Anne was physically disabled for all of her short eleven-year reign. The contrast between these two queens and the dynasties they represented could not be more clear.

For the purposes of presenting the argument that it was disease and disability that brought down the Stuarts, disease is defined as illness, ailment, malady, or disorder of body or mind, and disability is want of ability, inability, incapacity or impotence. Most of the Stuarts' deficiencies can be identified as medical problems and medical diagnoses can be adduced to identify and explain these problems. Viewing the Stuarts from a distance of three to four hundred years means that medical diagnoses of that distant time will often have to be converted to modern terminology and are then qualified as *certain, possible, doubtful* or of *uncertain meaning*. Thus, a medical problem for which there is an objective finding or classic description that allows a specific diagnosis can be called *certain*; for example, the lung cancer of King George VI or the angina pectoris (heart pain) of the Scottish surgeon and physiologist, John Hunter can be considered *certain* diagnoses. When symptoms or signs strongly suggest a particular diagnosis but objective confirmation is lacking, the designation *possible* must be used. For example, central nervous system syphilis causing mental decline and death in Lord Randolph Churchill or otosclerosis causing deafness in Ludwig van Beethoven are both *possible* diagnoses. Diagnoses which cannot be substantiated in the light of modern medical practice and thinking must be identified as *doubtful*. For example, the diagnosis of porphyria, made in George III and Vincent van Gogh, is an attractive and appealing idea, but viewed as highly unlikely when seasoned modern physicians examine the evidence. Finally, interesting symptoms or signs of illness that do not readily suggest a specific diagnosis or syndrome must be placed into the category of *uncertain meaning*; a good example would be the ague of previous centuries, or leprosy as mentioned in the Bible.

This diagnostic yardstick of *certain, possible, doubtful* and of *uncertain meaning* can be used to measure the medical problems of the English Stuart monarchs, as well as various of their family members whose lives were important to the Stuart dynasty. More complicated schemes than this four-level one have been devised but they are really too subtle for the medical data of history, which are scant at best.

The Stuart dynasty began in Scotland in 1316 with the birth of Robert Stuart, grandson of Robert the Bruce. He was an unlikely king, coming to the throne of Scotland at the advanced age of fifty-five years, but he ruled Scotland well as Robert II from 1371 until his death in 1390, at the age of seventy-four. Through land acquisition and patronage for his sons he made the Stuart family powerful in Scotland. The dynasty ended seventeen Stuarts and nearly five hundred years later in France in 1807, with the death of Henry Benedict Stuart, Cardinal Duke of York and grandson of James II, the last Stuart king to rule England. Henry Benedict was a good and gentle man who made little pretence of wanting to regain the throne of England. At the time of his death he was Dean of the College of Cardinals in Rome. The earlier Stuarts (James I through to James V) ruled and managed the quarrelsome Scots with some facility but the last three members of the dynasty, James Francis Edward, Charles Edward and Henry Benedict, never ruled any territory at all, and are remembered only for mismanaged attempts to regain the throne of England. They simply disappeared from British history as exiles in continental Europe.

The Stuarts appear to have functioned well as a ruling family before England was given to them, but the ignominious exile to the continent of the last three Stuarts stands in stark contrast to the optimistic Scottish beginning. One could characterize the Stuart family in England as slowly deflating, as its political power diminished.

Real power in Europe in the seventeenth century was held by the Habsburgs, who ruled Austria and Spain, and the Bourbons who ruled France. Stuart-governed England was a peripheral and junior partner of the day, occasionally involved but never politically dominant in any sense. One might consider the Swedes in the north and the Dutch in the United Provinces across the Channel from England junior even to the English, although Gustavus Adolphus of Sweden shook the foundations of Habsburg power in the Thirty Years War and William of Orange made life difficult for the Bourbons up to the War of the Spanish Succession. The Habsburgs and Bourbons were obsessed with having strong men on their thrones and Salic Law guaranteed that Habsburg and Bourbon thrones would be occupied by males only, a distinction that separated them from England and

Scotland, where a queen might reign alone. During the period of Stuart rule in England, three Bourbon men ruled France, four Habsburg men ruled Spain and six Habsburg men ruled Austria. The Bourbon rulers of France, Henry IV, Louis XIII, and Louis XIV, held the throne of their country in a firm grip and ruled with authority – their power actually increased throughout the seventeenth century. In spite of ever-closer inbreeding in the Spanish Habsburgs, with its consequences of mental enfeeblement, and the ever-lengthening jaw of the Austrian Habsburgs, this family held firmly onto its thrones. Today, a Bourbon – Juan Carlos – is the King of Spain, and the heir to the lapsed Habsburg thrones, Dr Otto von Habsburg, lives in Germany, near Munich. While the Stuart family did not actually come to an end until the death of Henry Benedict Stuart in 1807, one might wonder whether the dynasty might have survived and still be ruling Great Britain today had disease and disability not significantly compromised the Stuarts' dominance of English political life and directly affected their ability to produce viable heirs. Appendix I and Appendix II compare the reigns of Stuart, Habsburg, and Bourbon monarchs.

In contrast to the Habsburgs, inbreeding was not really a problem for the Stuarts, theirs was a much larger gene pool than that of their continental counterparts. The first Stuart King of England, James I, could be said to have had a family tree in which the branches were only slightly thinned above him, while the descendants of the first Habsburg, Charles V, had a family tree that gave very little shade at all. James's parents, Mary Queen of Scots and Henry Stuart, Lord Darnley, shared a grandmother in Margaret Tudor, daughter of Henry VII, but they did not share a grandfather, though both were descendants of James III of Scotland. By definition this is considered consanguinity, but it can scarcely be identified as inbreeding of any significance, equating instead to something between a second and third cousin union.[1] Mary Stuart and William of Orange were first cousins, they shared two grandparents, but as they had no offspring this did not affect the Stuart line. Whether or not this relationship contributed to Mary's relative sterility is moot.

Besides James I, the only other Stuarts who produced heirs to the throne of England were Charles I and James II. The mother of Charles's heirs was Henrietta Maria, daughter of Henry IV of France, the first Bourbon king, a strong monarch and organizer of the government of France. The mother of James II's daughters Mary and Anne, both of whom became Stuart queens, was Anne Hyde, daughter of Edward Hyde, Duke of Clarendon. Neither of these women were related to their husbands. The mother of James II's final and fateful contribution to the Stuart family, James Francis Edward Stuart, was Mary of Modena, again not related to her husband in any way. James II's last contribution would have been James III but, unfortunately for the Stuart line, he entered the race for succession late and, as a Roman Catholic, was wearing the wrong colours. The Stuarts cannot be considered inbred to any significant degree and aside from smallpox, the scourge of the world at that time, there was no important single recurrent medical problem or disease that haunted them or brought them down. To comprehend how sickness and infirmity sapped them, one must carefully examine their individual medical records.

In performing this analysis, it is important to have an understanding of court medical practice of the time. Most of the letters, diaries, case notes, and other reports of various kinds, which, taken together, constitute the medical records of the individual Stuarts, were generated by court physicians. Kings and queens were served by large numbers of physicians, surgeons and apothecaries. None of these were members of the aristocracy and so they were not actual members of the court but rather employees of a sort, or at best, experts paid on a retainer basis. In reviewing household rosters of the English court one finds the physicians, surgeons and apothecaries heading up these lists, but sharing them with tailors, grooms, plumbers, bakers and scullery maids, among others. Many court physicians probably never saw the monarch and only a select few were involved in the day-to-day health concerns of the court. Sudden or serious illness might enlarge the inner circle of attending physicians but only for the duration of the monarch's indisposition. With but few exceptions, the Stuarts chose their personal physicians and various consultants from among the best available to them – most were fellows of the Royal College of Physicians.

The Royal College of Physicians was founded by Thomas Linacre and chartered by Henry VIII in 1518 as the College or Commonality of the Faculty of Medicine of London. It adopted its present name in 1682. For the sake of order, the name Royal College of Physicians will be used throughout this book, for events prior to and after 1682. To distinguish it from other colleges of physicians, it is now usually known as the Royal College of Physicians of London. Dominating medical practice in seventeenth-century London, with influence in other parts of England, this was for the most part a guild of Oxford and Cambridge graduates. Its members were the social and educational elite of medical practice and few court physicians were not associated with the Royal College of Physicians. For centuries the Royal College of Physicians controlled medical practice in London by granting membership and fellowship to the men they thought properly educated and bringing to justice quacks and charlatans. Surgeons then occupied somewhat lower positions on the social and educational scale than they do today, as they were still allied with barbers in the Company of Barber-Surgeons. The charter for the Royal College of Surgeons, first of London then of England, would not be granted until 1800. Drug dispensing in London was controlled by the Society of Apothecaries, whose members assumed a direct medical role in many cases. The common people were served medically by a variety of practitioners, some honest and capable, but many quacks of the worst kind. Childbirth in all levels of society was the realm of midwives, the best of whom were licensed by bishops. Male physicians and surgeons occasionally assisted with difficult births. For example, male physicians of the Chamberlen family invented the obstetric forceps and kept them secret throughout the seventeenth century. Beyond childbirth, midwives often advised women, even the well born, about gynaecological problems not associated with childbirth. They were also consulted about illness in babies and children. At its best, the practice of medicine, from fellows of the Royal College of Physicians down to midwives, was eclectic but successful. The remedies and treatment methods that seemed to work were adopted by the medical community and those that did not were discarded; science, per se, had little to do with medical practice.

Science and medicine as we now know them did come together for the first time in the seventeenth century, but while most eminent physicians were interested in the new science, it cannot be said that medical practice was, by current standards, scientific or directly affected by science. Even the best physicians were still strongly influenced by Galen, the second-century Greek physician who defined the philosophy of medicine for more than 1,000 years. The most famous medical scientist of all time, William Harvey, who described the circulation of the blood in 1616, observed that his personal interest in science actually kept some prominent patients from consulting him. It can be acknowledged that science did begin to influence medical practice towards the end of the seventeenth century but not substantially. It was still comfortable for doctor and patient alike to feel that all was in the hands of God, that all were accountable to God and must therefore accept without query the occurrence of disability or disease.

In seventeenth-century Europe it was also generally accepted that kings were accountable only to God, and certainly not to those whom they governed. James I, the first Stuart monarch of England, is often remembered for his elegant publications which elaborated on this theme, *Basilikon Doron* and *A Trew Law of Free Monarchies*. Interestingly, these were first published in the 1590s, before he became King of England, and therefore antedated his encounters with the long-established English Parliament. James's peers on the continent were not constrained by parliaments. France did have a parliament of sorts, the Estates General, but it met only twice, once in 1614 and then again in 1787. Spain had virtually no middle class and no parliament, and Austria would not even recognize a governmental bureaucracy until Empress Maria Theresa established one in the eighteenth century. At the beginning of the seventeenth century, the English Parliament was a relatively light counterweight to monarchical power, but it was a counterweight nonetheless.

This English Parliament was a well-established institution with a tradition dating back to the thirteenth century and it was the only authority available to the monarch when taxes needed to be raised. But Parliament did not have an independent existence. It was called and either prorogued (recessed) or dismissed by the monarch at his or her pleasure. Parliament existed to create laws and raise money by taxes. The monarch could govern quite well without it, in fact governing was much easier when Parliament was not in session. When James I came to rule England in 1603, Parliament met infrequently for relatively brief periods and controlled only part of the royal purse. Its acts could be vetoed by the monarch, or statutes could be applied quite unevenly by his or her government (dispensing powers) or not applied at all (suspending powers). Freedom of speech within Parliament was by no means assured, members were occasionally arrested and even sent to The Tower for remarks made in parliamentary sessions. Yet by the end of Stuart rule, marked by the death of Queen Anne, Parliament had gained considerable power at the expense of the monarchy. Parliament met regularly, for all intents and purposes annually, it enjoyed real freedom of speech, convened and dismissed itself, did not allow the monarch to apply its laws selectively and never saw another royal veto after Queen Anne's 1708 veto of the Militia for Scotland Bill. Parliament held the royal purse in strong hands and opened it carefully and reluctantly. The Convention Parliament of 1689 stopped the monarch's dispensing and suspending powers, ending the autonomy of the English monarchy for all time. It also defined England as a Protestant kingdom to be ruled by a Protestant prince, putting an end to James II and all Roman Catholics' aspirations to the throne.

The change in the balance of power between the monarch and Parliament during Stuart rule was neither gradual nor by the evolution of law. Rather, Parliament gained power each time Stuart rule faltered because of sickness and infirmity. Thus the course of change was uneven and sometimes even reversed for certain periods.

James I was temperamentally unsuited to rule in partnership with Parliament and momentum for change built within Parliament during the final years of his reign, when his previously sharp mind was clouded by dementing illness. Mentally compromised, he then allowed the self-serving George Villiers, Duke of Buckingham, essentially to rule in his stead. The fate of the Stuarts had already been compromised by this time, for in 1612 James's eldest son, Prince Henry, had died of typhoid fever at the age of eighteen. Henry was a strong and vigorous young man who would have made a very able monarch. Upon James's death, parliamentary antipathy was directed towards the weak young King Charles I, James's second son, and Charles's mentor, the aforementioned Buckingham. The contest between Parliament and this feeble king, disabled by a lack of guile and a delusional belief in his divine right to rule, led directly to Parliament's victory over Charles and the end of the monarchy in 1649. Charles might be said to have died a surgical death; he was beheaded.

In some respects, Prince Henry's death may have been the greatest medical tragedy to befall the Stuart family, for Henry was everything that Charles was not. Indeed he was everything his father was not. Physically strong, imposing and self-assured, he would have been a strong monarch, probably more than a match for the machinations of Parliament.

The Sad End of the Stuart Dynasty

Parliament's victory over the Stuarts in 1649 set the stage to prove that England could be ruled without a monarch. The Restoration in 1660 seemed to reinstate the balance of power between monarch and Parliament to the status quo of 1603, although the relations of Charles II with Parliament were not always smooth. It could be argued that Charles II was a strong and successful monarch because he ruled without Parliament during the final five years of his reign. In a sense, he enjoyed the status and power of his grandfather, James I. However, by 1660 the vigour of the Stuart house had already been considerably diminished and Parliament had emerged with the upper hand. As Christopher Hill states, 'It is significant for the future history of England that the Convention Parliament of 1660 was not summoned by the King: it summoned him.'[2]

Whether or not Charles II can be adjudged a strong monarch, he proved mortal and made his own untimely contribution to the catalogue of disease and disability in the Stuart family. The sudden and unexpected death of Charles II in 1685 from acute and chronic mercury poisoning brought his brother James II to the throne, essentially dropping the monarchy from the frying pan into the fire. Two medical events ended James's brief three-year reign, the birth of his son and heir, James Francis Edward Stuart in 1688, which galvanized Parliament against him, and his three-day nosebleed at Salisbury, which led him to abandon the field of battle against the invading William of Orange. His subsequent flight to France a month later left the Stuart throne vacant. The Convention Parliament of 1689 put James II's daughter Mary Stuart and her husband, William of Orange, onto the throne of England. By that time Parliament was in a far more powerful position than it had ever been before. Mary's death from smallpox in 1694 left William to rule England alone for eight years. He was not a Stuart and got on rather well with Parliament, as did his successor, his sister-in-law, Anne Stuart. Parliament at the beginning of the eighteenth century was an entirely different organization from what it had been at the beginning of the seventeenth century. It met regularly, was the master of its own affairs and kept a tight grip on the royal purse and prerogatives. Anne was disabled by systemic lupus erythematosus during her reign and she had less and less impact on the affairs of Parliament as her physical disability increased. Her death, alone and without heir or even consort, brought down the curtain on an empty stage.

At the time of Anne's death, first the Privy Council then the Regency Council wrote urgent notes to George Elector of Hanover, arranging his hurried trip to London to take the throne of Britain as George I. This succession had been assured by Parliament, acting in concert with William of Orange, during the 1690s and finalized in the Act of Succession of 1701. As George was the great-grandson of James I through James's daughter Elizabeth and granddaughter Sophia, he had Stuart blood, albeit in a direct female line. It was enough to get him the throne, but in the name of Hanover, not Stuart. The man with a direct link through the male line, James Francis Edward Stuart, now known as the Old Pretender, who would have preserved the Stuart name and dynasty, waited in France for an English throne that was never to be his. His family had survived the Civil Wars of the 1640s, but it barely survived the Glorious Revolution of 1688.

England's Civil Wars and Glorious Revolution, which were devastating events for the monarchy at the time, pale into insignificance when compared with the French or the Russian Revolutions. These destroyed royal families and abruptly ended royal rule in France and Russia. The Stuarts were not destroyed in a single event but died a lingering death, and Parliament grew ever stronger as they grew ever weaker. It seems likely that the survival of a generally popular and functioning British monarchy in the twenty-first century is in part a consequence of the gradual lessening of the monarchical power of the Stuarts in the seventeenth century.

Succinctly put, the six English Stuart monarchs can be ranked as follows: they score two out of six for lack of innate ability (Charles I and James II), two out of six for queen as monarch (Mary II and Anne), and three out of six for lack of an heir (Charles II, Mary II, and Anne). Dementia, a fixed delusion, mercury poisoning, a harmless nosebleed, acute haemorrhagic smallpox and systemic lupus erythematosus brought them down, one after the other. The rule of the Stuarts was suspended three times before it finally ended in 1714 with the death of Queen Anne. The first time was in 1649 when the 46-year struggle between Parliament and the first two Stuarts culminated in the beheading of Charles I. James II absconded in 1688 to suspend Stuart rule a second time and the death of Mary II from smallpox put a halt to Stuart rule in 1694. Although not significantly inbred, the Stuarts were sickly. In fact, throughout the seventeenth century, enfeeblement defines Stuart rule better than accomplishment. In the following chapters it shall be shown exactly how disease and disability brought down the Stuart dynasty.

TWO

Disease and Physicians in Seventeenth-century England

On the first day of December 1623, Theodore de Mayerne sat down to consolidate his notes on James Stuart, whom he identified not as King of England or of Scotland, but as the King of Great Britain. He meant to record the complete medical history of this colourful 57-year-old man, whom he had known since 1612 when he attended the death by fever of his eldest son, Henry Frederick, Prince of Wales, at the tender age of eighteen.

James Stuart had a complicated medical history, it took several hours to get all of the details organized and recorded, and the 50-year-old Swiss physician did not finish his writing until well into the evening. He observed that James had been bright and interesting, but that of late his mind was failing him and he had great difficulty keeping to any topic of conversation for more than a few minutes. In fact, there were so many things going wrong with James that it was a wonder he could function at all. After finishing his exhaustive account of James's health, from birth to the present, de Mayerne wrote a summary that included more questions about his famous patient than answers. James Stuart was an entire collection of chronic diseases, and although de Mayerne knew how to describe them, he recognized that he did not have the means to change most of them. James rarely took the advice of his physicians in any event, even that of de Mayerne for whom he had considerable respect, for James regarded his encounters with his medical advisers as disputations not consultations. De Mayerne finished his long treatise by signing his name, noting himself to be the king's primary physician.

England had been kind to this Huguenot physician; he particularly enjoyed living in London which was a growing and vibrant city with a medical community much more open to new ideas than Paris, where he had practised before. Clearly London was Europe's most interesting city, it was the place to live if you wanted to enjoy both a scholarly life and a substantial income from medicine.

James would surely not live much longer, given his many medical problems, and his son, Charles, not cut of the same cloth as his father, might not prove much of a monarch. However, these Stuart times in England were good times to be a physician; both the city and the country were growing and there were plenty of patients willing to pay well for their medical care.

During the Stuart years, England's population slowly increased from 4 to around 5 million and London expanded rapidly. Its population tripled from 200,000 to about 600,000. With more than 10 per cent of England's population in 1700, London had become the largest city in Europe. It was a young city, with at least a third of its citizens just children. For all of England, life expectancy ranged from 33 to 39 years during the seventeenth century, and the infant mortality rate – deaths during the first year of life – was about 250 to 300 per 1,000 live births, hence 25 to 30 per cent. London repeatedly outgrew what little infrastructure it could create; ordinary people lived in crowded dwellings, buying water from vendors who got their supplies from questionable sources. There was no sewage system, and slops and rubbish were thrown onto the narrow streets. The rich lived in large houses, so at least they did not have to suffer cramped conditions. However, epidemic diseases swept through the abodes of rich and poor alike.

Even if one survived the birth process and the first month or so of life, malnutrition, measles, diphtheria, whooping cough, bronchitis and pneumonia were ever-present dangers during early childhood regardless of social status. The various diseases of filth, such as typhoid fever, rotavirus infection and shigellosis, claimed the lives of many babies and infants. In the best of circumstances, about two out of every three babies born were still alive at five years old. However, the chance of getting from the age of five to adulthood was actually fairly good. Women married in their mid-twenties and, without effective birth control, each fertile woman could expect to have six to eight pregnancies. The chance of a woman dying in childbirth was about one in a hundred. Well-bred women had more pregnancies than poor women because they could afford wet nurses and did not suffer from the period of relative infertility associated with breast-feeding. Family structure patterns were different – becoming a widow or widower at a relatively young age was unfortunately frequent, so blended families or second wives raising the children of a deceased first wife were commonplace. Children, uncles and aunts were numerous but living grandparents much less common. Older children and adults were at constant risk of death from accidents. Without antibiotics to treat infections and immunization to prevent tetanus, a simple flesh wound might lead to death. Acute disorders within the abdomen were beyond the reach of surgeons, and simple problems like acute appendicitis and acute gall bladder infection often killed the patient. Caesarean sections were very rarely attempted. When they were done it was usually in desperation to get a live baby when the mother was already dead. No woman is known to have survived a Caesarean section until well into the eighteenth century.

Tuberculosis was ubiquitous in the time of the Stuarts, virtually everyone was eventually infected with the tubercule bacillus, typically during childhood from a family member or neighbour who was chronically afflicted. Most people's tuberculous infections naturally healed but some progressed slowly over months or even years to death. Tuberculosis affecting the lungs and associated with generalized wasting was known as consumption or phthisis, and was a common medical problem. Tuberculosis affecting the lymph glands of the head and neck was called scrofula. It was believed that this latter affliction could be cured and even prevented by a touch from the reigning monarch, known as touching for the King's Evil. Most of the Stuart monarchs enjoyed this rare physical contact with their subjects, particularly Queen Anne, who had frequent touching ceremonies for hundreds of her grateful subjects at a single session. Most physicians believed that the touch of the sovereign had value in curing or preventing scrofula. Of course, there was a general feeling that consumption and scrofula might somehow be contagious, although they were also presumed to be heritable. Lacking the unifying concept of a micro-organism, they were considered separate diseases and were sufficiently common that they were accepted as part of everyday life, as endemic rather than epidemic diseases.

Epidemic diseases were known to one and all and were easily recognized. Smallpox and plague were the most feared, as their visits were associated with great likelihood of death. Although the concept of germs and micro-organisms was yet to be recognized, nonetheless contagion was understood very clearly and the wealthy were always ready to leave London for the countryside to escape epidemics. Ordinary folk and the poor also understood the concept of contagion, but were much less mobile and not often free to flee in the face of epidemic illness.

The most infectious epidemic disease was smallpox, which occurred frequently and periodically in population centres when the number of those not previously infected, mostly babies and children, reached a critical mass. In seventeenth-century Europe, virtually everyone would eventually suffer smallpox, with the chance of death being about one in five.

For those who survived, immunity was lifelong – one did not suffer smallpox twice. Physicians' knowledge of smallpox was so great that we can only dimly appreciate the medical sophistication of discussions among physicians about diagnosis and prognosis in individual patients, as most of these men would have seen hundreds of cases of the disease. Smallpox was known in China and India nearly 4,000 years ago and, in fact, there is an ancient Chinese proverb that says your child is not truly yours until he has survived smallpox. Smallpox was described in the sixth century in France and Italy, and by the sixteenth century it had been transported from Europe to Central and South America.

Treatment of smallpox was by either the 'hot method' developed in Arabia or the 'cold method' proposed by Dr Thomas Sydenham, prominent in medical circles in London in the late seventeenth century. These two methods involved either keeping the unfortunate patient as hot as possible or as cold as possible and, as there is no physiological basis for either treatment, neither would have altered the course of this terrible disease. Smallpox was officially eradicated from the world in 1979 and, barring use in terrorist warfare, should never be seen again. In 1701, just seven years after the death from smallpox of Mary II, the Chinese practice of inoculating non-immune subjects with pus from a smallpox patient, to cause a mild case which would give future immunity, was reported in England. The Turkish experience of the same preventive measure was described in 1706, and the first two Britons to be inoculated were the sons of the British Embassy secretary in Turkey. In 1717 Lady Mary Wortley Montagu wrote her famous letter to a friend, Miss Mary Crisswell, about smallpox inoculation, advocating its use in England. Because the Latin name for this disease is variola this practice was called 'variolation'. It was in 1796 that Dr Edward Jenner used pus from a closely related animal disease, cowpox, the Latin name for which is vaccinia, to 'vaccinate' James Phipps and thereby induce immunity to smallpox.

Disease and Physicians in Seventeenth-century England

Bad as smallpox was in the seventeenth century, plague was worse. Now known to be caused by the bacteria *Yersinia pestis* and spread by rats and their fleas, plague visited England much less frequently, but its effects on the population were devastating. London was particularly vulnerable because it was both a seaport and a densely settled urban centre. Plague epidemics occurred in London in 1603, 1609, 1624, 1636, and 1665. The chance of dying once infected was at least one in two and once an epidemic was in full swing, probably approached a rate of four in five. In a fifteenth-century epidemic of this 'Black Death', the population of Europe was reduced by a quarter.

Diseases associated with war and crowding, such as the several forms of typhus, were recognized by their skin manifestations and probably brought back from the continent periodically to cause small epidemics. Influenza also visited Europe regularly but it was identified as a disease not likely to cause death. The Sweating Sickness, which swept through England five times from 1485 to 1551, was remembered and anticipated but did not occur in the seventeenth century. It was possibly caused by a Hantavirus but the true cause will probably never be known.[1] The infectious diseases of childhood, particularly measles, diphtheria, and whooping cough, regularly marched through the population and each small epidemic took the lives of some children, particularly those weakened by malnutrition and diseases such as rickets. Diphtheria, a bacterial infection of the throat, could kill three or four children in a family in just a few days, through strangulation by closure of the trachea.

Rickets, a bone deformity in young children caused by lack of sunlight and vitamin D absorption through the skin, was common in English cities. Rickets also occurred in the countryside but less commonly. In most respects, life in the countryside was safer in every way imaginable. For example, less overcrowding meant fewer epidemic illnesses, drinking water was less likely to be polluted and food was more plentiful. True famine was rare in England during the seventeenth century, but it did occur regionally when crops failed, or occasionally when too much common land was enclosed and kept from people by large landowners. Enclosure had taken about half of the common land by 1700 and would continue relentlessly until 1800, when almost no common land remained in England.

While famine was rare, the diet of ordinary people was monotonous, whether in town or countryside, and depended on the local and seasonal availability of various foodstuffs. In regard to diet, as well as most other health-related factors, it was better to be rich than poor.

There is no question that the aristocracy ate better and lived longer than those of the lower social orders but there were other differences in their lives and health as well. Women of noble status married younger, often in their teens, because of the importance of dynastic considerations, family alliances, and the preservation and enlargement of wealth. Proper selection of wet nurses guaranteed adequate nutrition for well-born babies, and the older members of the family enjoyed a much better diet, rich in meat and game, a diet that would have included even non-seasonal fruits and vegetables for some. Life expectancy for young aristocrats was about forty years, with survival into old age not unusual.

Acute illness associated with fever, usually called ague, was a common problem in the seventeenth century and physicians were skilled in recognizing it and had a feeling for prognosis in individual cases. Some physicians even had skill in treating agues, although without an understanding of micro-organisms they were without the means to appreciate fully what they saw or to understand the pathology of it. Shrewd physicians knew that fevers in otherwise healthy people were likely to be self-limited and that uneventful recovery was to be expected, with or without treatment.

Treatment of illness was empiric, that is to say, medicines were directed against symptoms. For example, salicylates were to be found in a variety of herbal sources, particularly willow bark, and were used by some to reduce fever, as we today use the common salicylate, aspirin. The seventeenth century saw the introduction of Jesuits' Bark into Europe, actually one of the first specific medicines known to humankind. This preparation of the bark of the cinchona tree from Peru contains quinine, which kills malarial parasites and is used to this day for that purpose. Initially quite expensive, 'The Bark' was popular with London's physicians because it could actually cure some agues, specifically those caused by malaria. Physicians became quite skilled at classifying, and perhaps over-classifying, the agues they saw. For example, a tertian ague was a fever recurring every other day and a quartan ague was one occurring periodically with two-day respites. Malaria caused by the parasite *Plasmodium vivax* can cause a tertian fever and that caused by the parasite *Plasmodium malariae* can cause a quartan fever. Quinine could cure, or at least put into remission, either one of these infections. However, although quinine might temporarily seem to reduce the fever of a patient with, for example, typhoid fever or a simple urinary tract infection, it was not curative as it was with malaria, although it might have been assumed to be curative if the patient recovered.

In a population where the mean and median ages were close to twenty, as opposed to our times when they are about forty, a large middle-aged and elderly population suffering chronic disease was not to be found. Arthritis was as common then as now and when acute was usually thought to be gout, an affliction known since the time of Hippocrates, and studied carefully and described with great clarity by Thomas Sydenham. Chronic pains in bones and joints were often attributed to gout as well or simply labelled as rheumatic. Pathology as a concept of altered anatomy or physiology, whether applied to bones and joints or to other body parts, was only just beginning to be appreciated by seventeenth-century physicians.

Although William Harvey first described the circulation of blood and the heart's part in this phenomenon in his Lumleian Lectures to the Royal College of Physicians in

1616, physicians of his time had no basic understanding of diseases of the heart or blood vessels. Characterized by grossly swollen legs, dropsy was a disease long recognized and it was usually caused by what we now know as congestive heart failure, although liver failure and kidney failure could produce dropsy as well. As with gout, the dropsical patient was often the subject of jest and cartoons. In fact, the seventeenth-century physician had no way to separate primary diseases of the heart, kidneys, or liver, and treatment was not effective in any event.

It was not until 1775 that the English physician, William Withering, proved that foxglove leaf, *Digitalis purpurea*, was the active ingredient in the herbal tea used with great success to treat dropsy in Shropshire. Today this medicine is known as digitalis and, in a purified form, it is still used to treat heart failure. In the eighteenth century, foxglove might have relieved the oedema of heart failure but it would not have affected the oedema of kidney or liver disease.

Blindness, deafness, epilepsy and lameness from a variety of causes were all very common, and limb paralysis from previous polio was often seen. An appreciation of the functions of the brain and nerves was slow in developing. Thomas Willis, a physician and Sedlian Professor at Oxford during the seventeenth century, studied the anatomy of the nervous system extensively but was not able to do much more than describe diseases of the nervous system; he had no ability to devise rational treatment. And while the brain was associated with thinking, mental disorders were not even separated and classified at that time.

Madness in all its forms was a part of daily life. Most sufferers were cared for by their families without any understanding of the nature or treatment of this group of illnesses, although there were some institutions for the insane. The most famous asylum, London's Bethlehem Hospital, was founded in 1247 and known familiarly as Bedlam. It was moved to Moorfields in 1676 and its name has become a modern metaphor for noisy disorder.

What we now call dental hygiene was almost totally lacking from seventeenth-century life. Missing teeth were the rule in almost any adult mouth and dentistry was largely confined to tooth extraction to cure the ache of abscessed teeth. Dentists were vaguely related to surgeons and found even lower on the social scale. Many other medical practitioners, particularly those of modest education and qualification, knew when and how to pull teeth.

Hospitals were already part of London life. St Bartholomew's Hospital had been founded in 1123, and many hospitals received the poor as patients with all due charity, although those with contagious diseases were usually, and wisely for the time, barred from admission. Separate hospitals called pest houses were reserved for patients with smallpox and plague. Accident victims could be taken to hospitals in London where physicians and surgeons were in regular attendance. In fact, it was a mark of professional status in London for a physician or surgeon to have a hospital position and to see patients in regular clinics there. These physicians saw both the rich and the poor, although the rich might more often be seen in the comfort and convenience of their own homes.

Physicians and surgeons, or any practitioners or doctors, were not likely to have had anything resembling modern consulting rooms and surgeries. Indeed, some even saw their patients in coffee houses or taverns, and surgeons could operate almost anywhere. There was no technology in existence, beyond relatively simple surgical instruments. The only laboratory test in routine use was inspection of a flask of urine, noting colour and clarity, although in 1694 Thomas Willis was the first to note that the urine of diabetics 'is wonderfully sweet, like Sugar or hony'.[2] In spite of these limitations some physicians were expert at diagnosis and prognosis even though they had very little in the way of effective treatment. Surgeons were adept at treating limb and body surface conditions, and some were even able to invade the urinary bladder to remove stones. Physicians, surgeons, apothecaries and midwives of the seventeenth century all merit admiration and respect because the best of them were actually quite effective in spite of their lack of scientific knowledge.

In a recent compendium, Professor Elizabeth Lane Furdell has identified more than 300 practitioners of medicine, surgery and midwifery, as well as apothecaries, who served the Tudor and Stuart monarchs. About half of this number could be considered physicians, by virtue of membership or fellowship in the Royal College of Physicians. The principal or initial medical degrees of these physicians, when known, fall very roughly in thirds among Cambridge, Oxford and continental universities. To facilitate acceptance by the Royal College of Physicians and, thus, medical practice in London, Oxford and Cambridge were generous in awarding their own degrees to some exemplary continental medical graduates, thus giving them the added cachet of two doctoral degrees.[3] An even more recent review of the medical care of English monarchs, written in a more light-hearted vein by Raymond Lamont-Brown, finds seventeenth-century medical practitioners of all stripes to be a generally colourful lot, with great contrast between the competent and the incompetent.[4]

Medical practice, the medical problems of the Stuart family and the affiliation of science with medicine in the seventeenth century can perhaps be best appreciated by examining the lives of prominent competent physicians who worked and practised in London. A reasonably complete list of physicians who attended the Stuarts can be found in Appendix III. This complete list of medical luminaries is too long to consider, but it is possible to choose seven who represent and define medicine at this time, their working lives spanning the entire period of Stuart rule. They range from the most famous medical scientist of all time, William Harvey, to one of the most successful practitioners, Richard Mead. The other five physicians are Sir Theodore Turquet de Mayerne, a chemist and a superb clinician; Thomas Sydenham, a soldier who took up a career in medicine rather late in life and whose classic description of the manifestations of gout is taught to medical students to this day; Richard Lower, a very successful practitioner with an excellent London practice who was also a cardiovascular physiologist of first rank; John Radcliffe, perhaps the best diagnostician of his day, an iconoclast, and a great philanthropist; and John Arbuthnot, a warm and caring physician, a close friend of Jonathan Swift and the physician most loved by Queen Anne, the last of the Stuart rulers. All of these men attended various members of the Stuart family as personal physicians. Interestingly, they started their lives at different points on the social scale and their widely varied interests and activities beyond medicine make them interesting examples of Stuart times. They represent the best face of medicine of their time and, with their vast experience and wisdom, would have little difficulty conversing with physicians of modern times about patients and illness. The importance of these men to the sickly Stuart family cannot be overstated. Brief examination of their lives and practice provides the best possible introduction to the story of the decline of the House of Stuart.

THEODORE DE MAYERNE

James I, although not always the best judge of men, was indeed fortunate in his choice of Theodore Turquet de Mayerne to be his principal physician. De Mayerne served James faithfully and well, and also assumed responsibility for the care of family members, including Queen Anne, Prince Henry, Charles I and some members of his family, among them Charles II. De Mayerne was born to a well-connected Protestant family at Mayerne, near Geneva, in 1573. He pursued medical studies at the universities in Heidelberg and Montpelier, attaining an MD degree in 1597, and then moved on to Paris where he quickly acquired a reputation as a teacher. He thought and lectured as a chemist, as he would throughout his medical career, and alarmed the dominant Galenist physicians of Paris with his ideas that specific diseases might have specific chemical remedies. He was a follower of the iconoclastic scientist of the early sixteenth century, Paracelsus (Theophrastus Bombastus von Hohenheim), whose assault on Galenist principles and inquiries into chemistry began a revolution in medicine. After skirmishing with his adversaries through pamphlets, letters, and other published works, de Mayerne was ostracized by the medical hierarchy of Paris in 1603 and forced to cease his lecturing and his practice of medicine there. In about 1606, he treated a young English gentleman and was influenced by him to visit London, a place he found very much to his liking. The medical community there was much more open to his views about chemistry and medicine. He obtained an MD degree from Oxford University in 1606 by incorporation, a courtesy and recognition of his training and eminence. Then, for reasons not clear, he returned to Paris for five years before finally relocating his practice to London in 1611. After his second arrival in London de Mayerne quickly became a very successful consultant physician, and at a meeting of the Royal College of Physicians in June 1616, he was unanimously elected to fellowship and received into the college at a special gathering, such was the great respect he enjoyed among London physicians. His clinical notes on James I and other notables survive, including Lord Rochester, who probably had colon cancer, and the daughter of Lord Monteagle, who suffered from epilepsy. Reading de Mayerne's clinical notes – from the Sloane manuscripts in the British Library – is illuminating for any modern doctor. They are clear, well-written descriptions of the thorough medical histories he obviously obtained first hand from his patients, and of his meticulous physical examinations of these patients. His writings are so precise and accurate that they could be placed among twenty-first-century medical records and be easily appreciated and understood. De Mayerne's long summary of the medical problems of James I is a fine example of the quality of his work.

King James was wary of physicians, perhaps for good reason, but apparently thought well of de Mayerne as he sought his help with medical problems a number of times during the second half of his reign. As a fellow of the Royal College of Physicians, and in keeping with his background in chemistry, de Mayerne participated in the preparation of their pharmacopoeia (description of drugs in common use) in 1618. His medical practice in London continued until his death in 1655 at the grand age of seventy-seven. In caring for members of three generations of the Stuart family, his relationship with the Stuarts generally was as a friend and family physician. Although he attracted some criticism for his treatment of Henry Frederick, Prince of Wales, before the prince's death in 1612, de Mayerne wisely participated in the post-mortem examination of the young princes's body, which put to rest the suspicion that he had been poisoned. In fact, de Mayerne is remembered as an early and vigorous proponent of the post-mortem examination. He enjoyed such a reputation as a wise physician that patients from the continent frequently journeyed to London to consult him and he was knighted by King James in 1624.

Throughout his years of practice in London, de Mayerne nevertheless returned to the continent frequently, often for long periods, and maintained a separate residence near Lausanne. His interests in chemistry were broad and he is remembered for extensive work with pigments, particularly those used in enamels. He even compounded cosmetics for some of his female patients. Theodore de Mayerne wrote and published case reports to the end of his days and must be regarded as one of the great medical innovators of the seventeenth century, never wavering from his belief that specific diseases could be treated with specific chemicals. At his death in 1655, his body was interred with that of his second wife and several of his children in St Martin's-in-the-Fields in London. After his early problems with his peers in Paris he seems to have found ways to relate positively with physicians in both England and France – there are no later records of discord or dissension and he was widely respected, even admired, in spite of his quite revolutionary views that left the doctrines of Galen behind.

De Mayerne knew James I well and his observations about the king, medical and otherwise, provide some of the best objective biographical material on James available. Well placed in London society, de Mayerne was more a physician than a clinical scientist but he seems to have been able to hold his own with peers who were deeply committed to finding out how the human body actually worked, for example William Harvey.

WILLIAM HARVEY

Also a physician to three generations of the Stuart family – from James I to Charles II and James II – William Harvey was, by contrast with de Mayerne, more interested in science than the actual practice of medicine. Despite this he attended the Stuarts for their medical problems faithfully and well, even following Charles I in the Civil Wars as the king's political fortunes faded. Although quite well connected, Harvey did not have much interest in court or national politics generally. He knew the Stuarts well, however, every bit as well as de Mayerne. Most of de Mayerne's papers have survived but, sadly for history, most of Harvey's papers were destroyed in disasters during his own lifetime.

As a native Englishman William Harvey is an interesting contrast to de Mayerne. Harvey was born to a family of small landholders in 1578 in Folkestone in Kent, where his father, Thomas, was a local magistrate. As de Mayerne was a chemist, Harvey was a physiologist, moving beyond anatomy to study how the body actually worked. De Mayerne studied the body from the outside, Harvey studied it from the inside. Harvey entered Gonville and Caius College at Cambridge without a scholarship when he was fifteen years of age, and he graduated with a bachelor's degree in 1597 at nineteen. Wishing to study medicine, he went to the continent and eventually enrolled in the university at Padua, the most famous medical school of the time. Padua was the institution where Andreas Vesalius had been Professor of Anatomy and one of the first dissectors of human cadavers, ultimately challenging the Galenists in 1643 with his magnificent treatise, *De Humani Corporis Fabrica*. Hieronymus Fabricius, who further perfected the dissection of cadavers, succeeded Vesalius at Padua and was one of Harvey's professors. It was Fabricius's studies of the valves in veins that started Harvey thinking about the flow of blood in the human body. Harvey graduated with an MD degree from Padua in 1602 and then returned to Cambridge, receiving another MD degree there by incorporation, recognizing his excellent continental education, in the manner that de Mayerne had been recognized. Soon Harvey was professionally established in London, augmenting his position by marrying Elizabeth Browne, daughter of Dr Lancelot Browne, a well-known physician who had attended Queen Elizabeth I. By 1604 Harvey was a candidate of the Royal College of Physicians and in 1607 he became a fellow. In 1609 Harvey began his long association with St Bartholomew's Hospital, starting as assistant physician and then becoming physician before the year was out. Once each week, for many years, he conducted a clinic at the hospital, seeing mostly poor and ordinary folk.

In 1615, Harvey was made the Lumleian Lecturer of the Royal College of Physicians, a position of great eminence for a 37-year-old physician in London. On 17 April 1616 he made the first public presentation of his new and revolutionary understanding of the circulation of blood in the human body. He drew on a wealth of direct experimental evidence he had amassed over years of dissection of animals. In addition, he had conducted personal experiments as simple and obvious as putting tourniquets on his own arm to show the direction of blood flow in superficial veins. Harvey solved the problem the Galenists had always ignored, how the blood got from the circulation of the right side of the heart and the lungs to the left side of the heart and the rest of the body, the four chambers of the beating heart holding the blood and then propelling it outward through arteries to see it return again through veins. While others had solved part of the puzzle of blood circulation, William Harvey was the first person to understand and describe the entire process. It was twelve years before Harvey published his work, using a printer in Frankfurt in 1628. Today that publication is perhaps the most famous medical book of all time, *Excercitatio Anatomica de Motu Cordis et Sanguinus in Animalibus*.[5] At the time it drew general acclaim throughout Europe, even though a few traditionalist physicians of the school of Galen were opposed to his new understanding of the circulation of blood. It is the measure of the importance and timeliness of his discovery that by the year of his death, 1657, both Harvey and his views were universally accepted. It is tragic that many of his personal papers were lost when his house was ransacked during the Civil Wars. Most of those few saved were burned when the building that housed the Royal College of Physicians was destroyed in the Great Fire of London in 1666.

Harvey was a prodigious worker, maintaining an active medical practice during his entire professional life in addition to his scientific research. A physician to James I over the last seven years of James's life, he was constantly involved in the affairs of the Royal College of Physicians and medical politics generally. Harvey opposed medical quackery and there seemed no medical curiosity that escaped his notice. For example, he published an account of the autopsy of Tom Parr, the oldest man in England, who died at an alleged age of 152 years. He had a keen interest in embryology and published an elegant account of the development of the chick embryo, once again using commonplace and simple methods to understand basic scientific principles.

Harvey seems not to have been much interested in politics beyond those of medicine, but in the Civil Wars he accompanied King Charles I as his physician and was at the Battle of Edgehill, allegedly protecting the future Charles II and James II from the Parliamentary forces. In those years he was able to work at Oxford University and was, for a period, warden of Merton College. He lived again in London for the last decade of his life, dying at the age of seventy-nine years. Harvey was buried at Hempstead in Essex and reburied in 1883 in the Harvey Chapel of Hempstead Church.

That William Harvey was the greatest medical scientist of all time is widely accepted. He was certainly a capable physician as well, giving competent medical service to the Stuarts in good times and bad. Because Harvey was interested in how the body actually worked he can be called a basic scientist, in comparison to a clinical scientist, a physician principally interested in the interactions of the human body and disease.

Also a physician to the Stuarts, and generally regarded as the greatest clinical scientist of all time, Thomas Sydenham followed Harvey not as a student or disciple, but as an innovator who found ways to perform research with clinical data.

THOMAS SYDENHAM

Thomas Sydenham was first a soldier, not a physician, and he was a different sort of man than either de Mayerne or Harvey. Born in 1624 to a prosperous Dorset family with Puritan sympathies, he and his four brothers were officers in the Parliamentary army during the Civil Wars. Two brothers died in combat and his mother was killed by a Royalist in 1644. Sydenham himself was both wounded and made a prisoner of the Royalist forces for some months. In 1642, between periods of military service, he was briefly a student at Oxford and in 1647 returned to study for several years thereafter, although he may have seen further military service during this time. Sydenham's Oxford University education was apparently never quite completed. Nonetheless, he was granted a Bachelor of Medicine degree in 1648 and by 1655 was practising medicine in Westminster. During the Cromwell years he was active in politics and stood for Parliament on at least one occasion, although apparently he did not serve.

During the late 1650s and perhaps into the 1660s, Sydenham was a medical student at Montpelier, the medical school de Mayerne had attended in France. In his mid-thirties by this point, he was very much a mature medical student, presumably trying to complete the education he had started twice and, because of the Civil Wars, never quite finished. Sydenham returned to London and completed the examinations of the Royal College of Physicians, being licensed by them in 1663. At the age of 40 he was, finally, an established physician with a practice in Pall Mall. Still seeking to complete a full medical education, he eventually received an MD degree from Cambridge in 1676, at the age of fifty-two, but he never achieved full fellowship in the Royal College of Physicians. Ill health complicated Sydenham's life still further, as he suffered from gout and stones in his urinary tract, and he died in 1689 at sixty-five years of age. He was buried in St James's Church in Westminster.

In spite of his spotty education, lack of a fellowship in the Royal College of Physicians and poor health, Sydenham was a towering medical presence in London and is remembered as one of the most accomplished clinicians of his times. He has often been called the 'English Hippocrates'. He was not interested in dissection or the other basic scientific pursuits of his London colleagues, rather he was obsessed with observation of the patient and collection of clinical data. He made a number of quite original observations on plague and other epidemic diseases, so that today he would be known as an epidemiologist as well as a physician. Sydenham devised the cold method of treating smallpox, a radical departure in his time, and he described a movement disorder associated with rheumatic fever in children, which was later named after him as Sydenham's chorea. His description of gout, of which he was a long-time sufferer, is so clear and cogent that it has never been improved upon. In fact, it is used in the teaching of medical students to this day, in the very words he wrote:

He goes to bed and sleeps well, but about two o'clock in the morning, is waked by the Pain, seizing either his great Toe, the Heel, the Calf of the Leg, or the Ankle; this Pain is like that of dislocated Bones, with the Sense as it were of Water almost cold, poured upon the Membranes of the part affected, presently shivering and shaking follow with a feverish Disposition; the Pain is first gentle, but increased by degrees – till – towards Night it comes to its height, accompanying itself neatly according to the Variety of the bones of the Tarsus and Metatarsus, whose Ligaments it seizes, sometimes resembling a violent stretching or tearing of those ligaments, sometimes gnawing of a dog, and sometimes a weight; more over, the Part affected has such a quick and exquisite Pain, that it is notable to bear the weight of the cloths upon it, nor hard walking in the Chamber.[6]

Though Sydenham lacked both a university connection and fellowship in the Royal College of Physicians, he nonetheless enjoyed the friendship of many of the notables of his day, including the philosopher-physician, John Locke, and the famous chemist, Robert Boyle. Two prominent physicians of the next generation of accomplished clinicians, Hans Sloane and Thomas Dover, considered him a mentor. Sydenham wrote his six medical treatises in English but they were translated by others into Latin, the language of their publication, and are regarded today as seminal clinical works. Sydenham's great contribution to medical science was to focus directly on the patient, and to make actual patient care and direct clinical observation respectable and useful to his brother physicians. His influence was immediate and widely acknowledged; for example, a contemporary, Richard Lower, made a transition from productive basic scientist at Oxford to accomplished London clinician, a transition surely eased by the clinical climate of which Sydenham was the principal mover.

RICHARD LOWER

A physician and scientist who is not as well known as his peers but who belongs in the first rank of Stuart-era clinicians and scientists is Richard Lower, born in Cornwall in

1631 of a good family, and educated at Westminster School. Lower studied and pursued research at Oxford for some years, receiving his Bachelor of Arts degree there in 1653, his Master of Arts degree in 1655, and his MB and MD degrees in 1665, the latter two being earned degrees, not given him by incorporation, as they were in the cases of de Mayerne and Harvey. Lower had the good fortune to work with accomplished chemists at Oxford, including Robert Boyle and Robert Hooke. He also worked with Thomas Willis, who was one of the first physician-scientists to study the central nervous system. In 1666, just after the plague, Lower followed Willis to London and set up a practice near Covent Garden. Soon he was one of London's most eminent physicians, with a large and lucrative practice, and was associated with the Royal Society and the Royal College of Physicians. In fact Lower was a prime mover in the Royal Society, which was first chartered in 1662 by Charles II, himself an amateur chemist. Lower died in 1691.

Lower's contributions to the science of medicine were numerous and of the greatest significance. He was the first person to understand the function of the lungs in changing oxygen-poor venous blood to oxygen-rich arterial blood, and his treatise on pulmonary physiology, *Tractatus de Corde*, is considered one of the classics of medical science. At Oxford he had experimented with transfusion of blood between dogs and, although not the first to try blood transfusion between humans, he is remembered for being the first to transfuse human blood in England, in an experiment performed at the Royal Society in 1667. Today, Lower is recognized for being a major force in founding the scholarly discipline of cardiovascular physiology. He understood the structure and function of the heart as a muscular organ, and was able to produce dropsy, heart failure, in animals by experimental means. In a sense, Lower was a scientist of accomplishment equal to Harvey and a clinician of ability equal to Sydenham. He was physician to Charles II but his politics – he was a Whig – put him at cross purposes with some of his medical peers. In many ways he was not unlike the remarkable man who followed him – John Radcliffe, a paradigm of clinical excellence who cared little for political correctness.

JOHN RADCLIFFE

It is not possible to consider seventeenth-century medicine, particularly in relation to the Stuart family, without examining the life and career of John Radcliffe, the cranky and irascible physician who cared very little for learning or science but who seemed to know everything about the practice of medicine, except how to get along with his colleagues and patients. Radcliffe was born in Wakefield in 1650. His father was master of the local house of correction and his mother from a family of some means. Radcliffe spent his childhood years at Wakefield Grammar School and is thought also to have attended Northallerton Grammar School. A very bright student, he matriculated at University College, Oxford, in 1666, and made his way easily with his sharp mind and quick wit, thoroughly enjoying the ambience of the place. Radcliffe received a Bachelor of Arts degree in 1669, an MA degree in 1672, an MB degree in 1672, and finally, his MD degree in 1675. All of his degrees were earned, none were received by incorporation. Radcliffe began a medical practice in Oxford and continued to be associated with the university, although he made no effort to respect the professional niceties of the community. In spite of his excellence as a clinician, he got on poorly with his colleagues, particularly those senior to him. In 1684 he moved to London and established a practice in Bow Street; the death of Richard Lower in 1691 was said to have enlarged his practice quite remarkably. Radcliffe was made a fellow of the Royal College of Physicians in 1687.

In the thirty years that he practised in London, John Radcliffe became immensely wealthy by the standards of the day. He was a prominent public figure known for his brilliance as a physician but feared, and often held in contempt, for his strong Jacobitism, foul temper, sharp tongue and utter disdain for the leading lights of the city. Despite his attitude towards them, the rich and prominent citizens of London always called for him when they were seriously ill, or at least when they thought they were seriously ill. He is alleged to have refused to see Princess Anne (not yet the queen) because he said she 'only had a fit of the vapours', and is alleged to have told William of Orange, who had asthma and dropsy, that, 'I would not have your three kingdoms for your two legs'. Radcliffe was often involved in politics, both medical and national, was a governor ofSt Bartholomew's Hospital and served twice in Parliament, from different constituencies. His generosity was, even in his time, legendary. He gave substantial gifts to the Church throughout his life and large gifts of property to Oxford. His name is attached to some of these gifts – of particular note is the Radcliffe Infirmary. After suffering a stroke in 1714, Radcliffe died at his country home. He was buried in St Mary's Church in Oxford. Never having married, he left no family.

John Radcliffe is important in the medical history of Stuart times because he was a physician of rare clinical acumen and sagacity. It was for that reason that he was physician to a number of members of the Stuart family, including Princess Anne as early as 1686. Radcliffe attended Queen Mary at the time of her death from haemorrhagic smallpox, and managed the asthma of Anne's husband, Prince George of Denmark. He often attended William of Orange and was physician to Anne's son, William, Duke of Gloucester. Anne's relationship with John Radcliffe was a stormy one but even when he was out of her favour, he was regularly consulted by her other physicians. His absence from Anne's deathbed in 1714 led to his vilification by one and all when it was reported that he had refused to attend her in her final illness. In truth, he was himself too sick to go to London at that time and it was ultimately understood that neither Anne nor her physicians had actually summoned him to attend the queen when she needed him most. Radcliffe said he would have gone to his queen, sick or not, had she called him to her.

Queen Anne had a number of competent physicians with whom she enjoyed good relations, in contrast to her difficulties with John Radcliffe. By the end of the seventeenth century the medical establishment of London had become well organized, and there were capable physicians in ample numbers to serve the aristocracy and the wealthy. One of the most accomplished and interesting of these was Richard Mead, a man whose achievements matched his amiability.

RICHARD MEAD

The direct successor to Radcliffe was the smooth and urbane Richard Mead, essentially a very well-educated Radcliffe without the rough edges. Mead was the eleventh child of a Stepney minister and was born in 1673. He was educated privately in the classics and by the age of eighteen was studying classical subjects at the University of Utrecht, before going on to the University of Leyden to study medicine. He completed his studies at the great medical school at Padua, receiving an MD degree there in 1695 at the age of twenty-two. Mead had the richest and broadest education of all the great English physicians of his time. He retained a life-long interest in antiquities, amassing a large library which fetched more than £5,000 at his death. During his career, he identified the insect cause of the skin disease scabies, and studied and wrote on topics as varied as viper envenomation, solar and lunar influences on humankind, the illnesses of biblical figures, and practical clinical topics. Mead ultimately acquired an MD degree from Oxford in 1707, probably by incorporation.

By the age of thirty, Mead was a fellow of the Royal Society and by forty-three years of age, he was a fellow of the Royal College of Physicians. Throughout his long professional life he held a number of offices in these two eminent bodies. Mead began his medical practice in Stepney in 1696 in the house where he was born. He moved several times over the early years of his practice, even living for a while in the house of his patron, Radcliffe, before finally settling in an elegant house on Great Ormond Street, at the site of the present Hospital for Sick Children. His medical practice in London extended across more than fifty years and he died after a brief illness a wealthy and well-loved man, at the ripe old age of eighty-one. Dr Samuel Johnson wrote of him, 'Dr Mead lived more in the sunshine of life than almost any man.'

Mead's first royal patient was probably Queen Anne, whom he attended in her final illness, causing some distress to his medical colleagues when he predicted that she would not survive. Subsequently, he attended everyone in London who was anyone, finally being principal physician to George II. In addition to his recognition as a cultured man of learning, Mead clearly was respected for his vast clinical experience and his ability to focus the slowly growing science of medicine at the patient's bedside. For example, he is noted for describing the importance of keeping the abdomen compressed when large volumes of fluid are removed in the treatment of ascites – the accumulation of fluid within the abdomen as a consequence of heart or liver failure. Since Mead, every junior doctor who has tapped a belly swollen with fluid is in his debt for the wisdom that shifting large volumes of fluid from the patient's body must be done with all due care, with vascular collapse possible if caution is not exercised.

Mead was conservative in the care of his patients and had good clinical sense; he knew when to intervene and when to let nature take its course. Mead represents the ideal physician, the one who has a thorough knowledge of both his patients and their diseases and, by his presence at the bedside, brings calm and order. Queen Anne found him a much more acceptable medical adviser than Radcliffe and, in many ways, a fine companion to her favourite physician, John Arbuthnot.

JOHN ARBUTHNOT

The final physician who illustrates the Stuart age of medicine and who was the favourite physician of Queen Anne, is John Arbuthnot, a Scot. Arbuthnot was born in 1667 in Kincardineshire, the son of an episcopal minister who was displaced from his church at the time of the Glorious Revolution. Arbuthnot studied medicine at Marischal College in Aberdeen, at University College at Oxford, and finally at St Andrews, from which he received a doctor's degree in 1696. He then left Scotland for London to create a new life for himself. A man of many interests and considerable energy, he began his new life in London as a mathematics teacher, and soon acquired a reputation as a writer of treatises in both science and literature, as well as a composer of church music. By 1710 he was a fellow of the Royal Society and, as a scientist, was among the first persons to recognize the fact that more male than female babies are born, speculating on the meaning of this peculiar biological phenomenon. Not much is known about his medical practice until he suddenly achieved royal favour, attending Prince George, consort of Queen Anne, as he suffered an acute asthma attack while at the horse races at Epsom. Arbuthnot's quick reactions at Epsom led to his appointment as physician extraordinary to Queen Anne in 1705 and within a few years he had become Anne's favourite. He was a fellow of the Royal College of Physicians by 1710, its censor in 1723 and Harveian Orator in 1727. Arbuthnot was known as a jovial man with a large family and a happy home, although sadly only four of his many children reached adulthood. He was a prolific writer but rather careless with what he wrote. It is thought that he made kites of some of his papers for his children, and he seemed to have little concern about public recognition of his authorship. In spite of this casual participation in the world of letters he was a member of the famous Scriblerus Club, an intimate of Alexander Pope and William Congreve, and enjoyed a long and close friendship with Jonathan Swift. His writings, particularly his satires, are generally acknowledged to be of high quality and it is likely that he could have been just as successful as an author as he was a physician.

With the death of Queen Anne in 1714, John Arbuthnot lost his place at court. Nevertheless, he continued an active medical practice with patients who included the leading literary figures of the day and many others of status and importance. He wrote on medical themes rather more than in the earlier years of his life, considering such topics as diet, the importance of clean air to humans, and management of common diseases. None of these were seminal works of the quality of the writings of Harvey or Lower, for example, but they were useful and had a fairly wide circulation. A satirist of rare ability, Arbuthnot most famously published the *History of John Bull* in 1712, memorializing forever the essence of the Englishman. His health was poor in the last ten years of his life – by his reckoning he had a large stone in his right kidney – and he had continuing intestinal problems as well, which may have been diverticulitis. He died at sixty-seven in his house in Cork Street.

Arbuthnot served Anne well as did all the fellows and members of the Royal College of Physicians in London whom the Stuarts chose as their medical advisers. In understanding how the Stuart family was served by this medical community it can be observed that they had available to them the best of the physicians of cosmopolitan London, men who were well educated, most often at either Oxford or Cambridge, and who had usually had additional education and training at Europe's best medical schools. There were some exceptions, particularly in the time of James I when Scottish physicians served the court, as did the occasional quack who caught James's attention. One such quack was Leonard Poe, a specialist in venereal diseases who was largely ignorant of medicine and who was several times disciplined by the Royal College of Physicians. For the most part, however, those physicians who served the Stuarts were seasoned clinicians, skilled as diagnosticians, whose direct clinical experience made them expert at prognosis. Skilled surgeons and experienced apothecaries were also at the monarch's beck and call, and the general style of practice was one of liberal consultation of peers, particularly when serious illness was being addressed. The inability to treat many of the diseases these men saw was a reflection of the limits of medical science of their time. It is unfair to judge physicians of the past, particularly those who cared for royalty, by saying that they did more harm than good. They did the best that they could with the limited means they had available, and the careful and conservative ones, as illustrated in the seven examples above, actually benefited their patients quite considerably.

The competence of seventeenth-century physicians can be illustrated by considering their quick recognition and thoughtful use of the world's first antibiotic, quinine. In modern times it is often imagined that antibiotic therapy of infectious disease was not possible until Gerhard Domagk found the first sulfa drug and Alexander Fleming discovered penicillin, both in the 1930s. In fact the world's first antibiotic was quinine, available in seventeenth-century Europe in the bark of the cinchona tree brought back from South America. In the same manner a modern antibiotic would be quickly adopted and used by the medical community, 'The Bark', as it was known in seventeenth-century medical slang, was tried and its use quickly perfected by English physicians. Of course it only cured malarial fevers, the true agues of the seventeenth century, but it did give physicians of the Stuart era one of the first specific medicines they would know, and they used it wisely and well, even discovering and describing its unwanted side-effects. Of the Stuart monarchs, at least Charles II and Anne were given 'The Bark' and this was done at some risk to the physicians themselves, for it was a new drug and every action of every royal physician was under the scrutiny of the royal patient and the court.

It is very difficult to be a physician to a monarch or national leader because political considerations always loom as large as illness and disease. If the nation is represented by the person of the leader then sickness of the body of the leader may be seen as sickness of the body politic. Aspects of this fascinating paradox have been studied by Jerrold Post and Robert Robins, a psychiatrist and an historian respectively, in their book, *When Illness Strikes the Leader: The Dilemma of the Captive King*. They crystalize their thinking as follows: 'Especially in a closed society, where the alternative to power may be death, the mortally wounded king and desperate court increasingly become locked into a mutual dependency in which neither trusts the other but each needs the other to survive – the syndrome of the captive king and his captive court.'[7]

In this charged political arena the physician must stay focused on the royal patient and his or her welfare, despite the fact that both the patient and the court are interpreting the meaning of illness to their own advantage, probably exercising what is now known as damage control. Consequently, as seen by Post and Robins, medical data from royal illnesses in the past are particularly difficult to interpret and understand, for court medical bulletins usually have sufficient political spin to cast medical events in less than accurate terms. From the viewpoint of a court or a government, in consideration of serious illness of their leader, the fewer bulletins issued and the less said the better. Thus, health data on leaders, from any time in history, are usually sparse and often misleading. Consequently, historians are likely to assume that national leaders enjoyed relatively good physical and mental health, a presumption often not consistent with medical reality. There is no political theory relating health, and lack of health, to events in the lives of national leaders. Often there is no clear way to relate disease and disability to political fact.

In order to understand the undesirable impact of disease and disability on the political performance of the Stuart monarchs, each of the six will be considered individually in turn, with his or her medical history constructed from primary sources and examined in detail. Important members of their families will also be considered in the same light but in less detail. The political consequences of disease and disability in the Stuarts will be identified with care to avoid overstatement, recognizing that accurate political information is much more easily obtained than accurate medical information.

The greatest problem for historians in evaluating the medical problems of the past is getting the diagnoses right. The first requisite for making a correct medical diagnosis in either the present or the past, is to have medical training. Because few historians have medical degrees, faulty perceptions of illness and infirmity in historical figures are common. For example, most historians accept without question that the last Stuart monarch, Anne, suffered from gout, because this diagnosis has been associated with Anne for three centuries. By contrast, any modern physician presented with Anne's complete medical history will discount this accepted diagnosis of gout immediately, instinctively proceeding to other possible diagnoses to explain her recurrent rheumatic problems.

The second requisite for making a correct medical diagnosis is to have sufficient medical data. Unfortunately, in considering persons from times past, it is not always possible to find enough data to make definite diagnoses. Consequently, diagnoses made in historical figures must be qualified, that is, the degree of certainty of a particular diagnosis must be determined. So, diagnoses made during each monarch's life, and as accepted or made by subsequent historians, biographers, and physicians, should be sorted into the scheme of *certain, possible, doubtful* and of *uncertain meaning*, as previously described. When appropriate, new and original diagnoses may be presented, within the scheme of *certain* and *possible*.

It is clear in the scrutiny of the medical problems of each of the Stuarts that their physicians performed well and generally followed the advice of Hippocrates, 'First, do no harm!' No Stuart monarch died as a result of medical misadventure, and none of them would have been saved by a modern X-ray or surgical operation. Beginning with James I, they were a sickly lot, not inbred to a significant degree, but slowly weakening as a ruling family, each illness sapping the strength of their dynasty until it ended with the sickest member of all, Queen Anne.

THREE

James VI of Scotland, I of England

A FINE BEGINNING, A POOR ENDING

James was of medium height and weight but appeared larger because he wore bulky clothing, padded to protect him from the daggers of possible assassins. James's doublets were stuffed with cloth and his breeches made in plates of thick cloth, according to the accounts of Sir Anthony Weldon. And James was timorous, wary of strangers. His large eyes constantly followed those in his presence, making some sufficiently uncomfortable that they avoided being in the same room with him if they could. Considering his harrowing childhood in Scotland and the Gunpowder Plot of 1605, which nearly ended his English reign just as it was beginning, James had good reason to be fearful.

As Weldon remembered, sharing a meal with James meant that his companions had to overlook the king's sloppy eating habits, particularly his protruding tongue which gave the impression that he ate liquids rather than drank them, slobbering his drink down his chin and onto his clothing.

James never washed his hands, he only wet his fingertips and rubbed them dry with his napkin. His tongue seemed too large for his mouth and his speech was far from clear.

Walking with James was awkward because his legs were very weak. Invariably he leaned on the man next to him, propelling him in a circuitous path, all the while fiddling with his codpiece as he walked. Weldon thought the leg weakness was the result of foul play in James's childhood, or, more likely, when his mother, Mary Queen of Scots, was carrying him in her womb.

In concluding his unflattering physical description of James it is interesting that Weldon did give him faint praise, stressing James's greatest gift to England, Scotland, and Ireland during his reign, namely peace. 'In a word, take him altogether and not in peces, such a King I wish this Kingdome never have any worse, on the condition, not any better; for he lived in peace, dyed in peace, and left all his Kingdomes in a peaceable condition, with his own Motto, Beati pacifici.' This paraphrased description is taken from Sir Anthony Weldon's book of 1650, *Court and Character of King James the First*, and James's motto, *Beati Pacifici*, is Latin for 'Blessed are the peacemakers'.[1]

James Stuart took pleasure in being King of Scotland and, in spite of being timorous, he ruled his native country with confidence and authority. He was a shrewd and successful monarch, but he was ambitious and had his eye on a larger prize, he wanted to be King of England. His claim to the English throne was not strong but, to his credit as a planner and skilled politician, the throne did become his in 1603 when the aged Queen Elizabeth died without heir. During the years he reigned in Scotland, James thought deeply about being a monarch and ruling a country, and he came to possess considerable knowledge about this subject. His two publications dealing with kingship, *A Trew Law of Free Monarchies* and *Basilikon Doron*, contain both philosophical musings and practical advice about the character of a ruler and how he should function. Given his insight, his years of experience in Scotland, and his considerable intelligence and ambition, there was every reason to expect that he and his heirs would rule England firmly and well for many generations. Sadly, this would not be the case.

At the beginning of his reign as King of England, James could never have imagined that he would end his days a sick and demented failure, with his crown passing to the least able of his children, Charles, who would later be executed by his subjects. Furthermore, he could never have conceived of the possibility that both of his grandchildren who would eventually rule, Charles II and James II, would die Roman Catholics and one would actually abandon the throne. In a final irony, the two great-grandchildren who followed them as rulers of England and Scotland, Mary II and Anne, would be women who left no heirs. No one could have foreseen that the Stuart dynasty would prove to be such a weak link between the Tudors and the Hanoverians.

Generally speaking, the Tudors, from Henry VII through to Elizabeth, had welded England into a national entity, given it stability and kept stronger European powers from invading or dominating their island kingdom. The Tudor monarchy maintained ascendancy over the Church and Parliament, allowing neither much independence. Thus, the English throne that James received in 1603 was relatively strong and secure. James died in 1625 at fifty-eight years of age, sick and senile, and the monarchy that he left to his second son, Charles, was considerably diminished. James has been characterized as having three faults: he failed to realize his own poverty, he had a great love for his favourite, and he was lazy. Although, initially he was an effective monarch, both in Scotland and in England, he ended his long reign weak in body and mind, diminishing the very throne on which he sat.

James's parents were a strange couple by any measure. At the time of their marriage his mother, Mary Queen of Scots, was a 22-year-old widow and the dowager queen of France. His father, Henry Stuart, Lord Darnley, was an immature nineteen-year-old Scottish lad of no particular accomplishment, with modest intellectual endowment and the pawn of anyone who sought to use him. Henry Stuart is a puzzling figure, apparently giving this ruling house nothing but its surname and first monarch. He was the son of the Earl of Lennox, an English sympathizer, and spent a brief time at the French court when Mary was Queen of France. Tall and thought by many to be handsome, he shared a grandmother with Mary, Margaret Tudor, daughter of Henry VII. However, his grandfather was Archibald Douglas, Earl of Angus (Margaret Tudor's second husband) while Mary's grandfather was James IV of Scotland (Margaret's first husband). In February 1565, Darnley was introduced to Mary, who found him attractive and a good dancing partner. Mary, also tall, was actively looking for a husband and Darnley was a man she could look up to, at least in a physical sense. In March Darnley became sick with the measles and Mary appointed herself his nurse; apparently love bloomed as the measles faded. There were rumours of a secret marriage arranged by her Italian secretary, David Rizzio, and then on 29 July 1565 they were officially married at Holyrood, in a Catholic ceremony, just five months after they met.

Mary and Darnley, deemed cousins by the Catholic Church, applied to the Pope for dispensation to marry, although in fact this dispensation did not reach them until months after the wedding. As they did not share a grandfather, their genetic relationship was somewhere between that of second and third cousins, as previously mentioned, and while this might be considered consanguineous, it cannot be considered inbreeding of importance by modern understanding of genetics. The marriage of Mary and Darnley was short and eventful; Darnley was not given the power of a monarch of Scotland, in part because of his age but mainly because of Mary's reluctance to share her power. The following September Mary took off enough time from the maelstrom of Scottish politics to cooperate with Darnley in the conception of James. Throughout most of her pregnancy Mary was estranged from Darnley, and in March 1566, Darnley joined James Morton, James Ruthven and other Scottish Protestant troublemakers in a conspiracy against David Rizzio, Mary's accomplished secretary. Darnley's participation in the murder of Rizzio gives credence to the notion that he – and others – suspected Rizzio to be the father of Mary's unborn child. The murderers are said to have threatened Mary by putting a dagger to her breast, apparently to frighten her into an early labour and loss of her pregnancy. Shortly thereafter, a reconciliation of sorts took place between Mary and Darnley and, in her eighth month of pregnancy, she persuaded him to help her escape from the Scottish lords who were confining her. The two of them rode 25 miles at night to Dunbar on the east coast, quite a feat for a woman late in pregnancy.

Shortly thereafter, Mary was back in Edinburgh again and on 19 June 1566, James was born to Mary at Edinburgh Castle after a long labour culminating in a normal birth. The baby arrived in the world with a caul, a covering of amniotic membrane from the placenta over his face, nothing of medical significance, but thought to presage good fortune and protection from drowning. Darnley was still in favour with Mary at the time and was nearby during the labour and birth. In what must be one of the great affirmations of history, Mary announced to her husband, 'My Lord, God has given you and me a son, begotten by none but you . . . here I protest to God, as I shall answer to Him at the great day of judgement, this is your son and no other man's son.'[2] In the matter of James's paternity it seems likely that Mary was telling the truth – James bears a strong resemblance to Darnley when portraits of the two are compared. There is a fine description of the infant James by Sir Henry Killigrew, '[I] was brought to the young Prince, sucking of his nurse, and afterwards saw him as good as naked, I mean his head, feet, and hands, all to my judgement well proportioned and like to prove a goodly Prince.'[3] Darnley's influence in James's life, however, seems to have been minimal; it is likely that he rarely saw James and that Mary kept the two of them apart.

Darnley did not live with Mary after the birth of James and did not even attend his elaborate baptism, in a Catholic service at Stirling, although he was living there at the time. Still under suspicion for the murder of Rizzio, he was in a precarious position and was distressed to learn that his co-conspirators, Ruthven and Morton, had been pardoned of Rizzio's murder. Darnley wisely decided to leave Scotland but was taken ill, the illness variously described as a febrile disease and as a poisoning. This brought what seemed to be another reconciliation with Mary, who sent her physician to see him and visited him herself. Sadly for Darnley, his illness ruined his plan to board a ship leaving Scotland, because Mary's apparent concern for him concealed her romantic involvement with James Hepburn, Earl of Bothwell. Early in the morning of 10 February 1567, the house in which Darnley was staying, on the grounds of the Kirk o-Field in Edinburgh, was blown up in an explosion so great that the adjacent church was damaged. The bodies of Darnley and his servant were found 40 yards from the wreckage of the house. Murder was suspected, with an explosion to cover it. Bothwell, thought to be the perpetrator of this foul deed, was indicted, tried, and acquitted in short order. Within three months he had divorced his wife and, in a Protestant ceremony, married the recently widowed Mary. It could be observed that James was part of Mary's dowry, a very valuable possession, as he was the heir-at-law to the throne of Scotland. Although his mother's marriage did give James the protection of a powerful Scottish noble, it did not place him in a stable home with a loving stepfather.

To say that James was born into a dysfunctional family would be an understatement; he did not know his father and any enjoyment of the bond between mother and baby was brief indeed. Well before his first birthday, Mary fled to England without him and lived there in captivity until her death at the instigation of Elizabeth when James was twenty years old. James was crowned King of Scotland on 24 July 1567 at the age of thirteen months. Without mother or father, without even the anchor of a brother or sister, he was shunted around Scotland in four separate regencies and looked after by several different families. There was little in the way of love and affection in the life of this boy, and James expressed bad feelings about his childhood until his dying day. In modern terms James could be described as a pitiful foster child whose father had been murdered by his mother and whose mother was in prison in a distant country. James grew up alone and his emotional growth and development were surely compromised by his detachment from what little family he could claim to be his.

James did not walk until he was about five years of age (reports of the exact age vary) and the accepted explanation for this is that he had weakened legs from rickets, caused by the tainted milk of a drunken wet nurse. James had measles and smallpox as a child but was apparently otherwise quite healthy until he reached adulthood, except for his persistently weak legs. He is not often described as being in the company of other children, rather he seems to have been a bookish boy who spent long periods alone. His education was supervised by the Scottish scholar George Buchanan, a dark and forbidding presence in James's life. Buchanan was the moderator of the General Assembly of the Church of Scotland and had a deep hatred for the Catholic Church and for James's mother. He never missed an opportunity to tell James about her wickedness. In adult life James remembered Buchanan as a harsh man and a fierce taskmaster.

James was a bright and capable student, using Latin and French with equal facility as early as eight years of age. His weak legs made running and the usual sports of boys difficult for him, but he found riding horses very much to his liking, an activity encouraged by his various surrogate parents. James did have a fondness for some of his surrogate family members and at least part of the time his behaviour was that of a normal boy. Illustrative of this is a letter, written in his own hand at the age of nine years to his foster-mother, Annabel, Countess of Mar. He thanks her for a gift of fruit and, as any normal little boy would do, asks for more.

Lady Minny [Minny is a familiar Scots word for mother],

This is to show you that I have received your fruit and
thanks you therefore, and is ready for mee [more] when
ye please to send them, and shall gif [give] as few by me
as I may. And I will not trouble you farther till meeting
which shall be as shortly as I may, God willing. And so
fare ye well as I do, thanks to God.

JAMES R[4]

James's lonely childhood progressed to a lonely
adolescence. In his early teens he developed a strong
attachment to his much older male cousin from France, Esme
Stuart, who had journeyed to Scotland to visit him. The visit
lengthened to a stay of several years because they became
close friends, and Esme has always been regarded as
instrumental in giving James a view of the wider world,
particularly the arts. James clearly had an adolescent crush
on him and many consider this the beginning of James's lifelong interest in handsome young men.

Esme arrived in Scotland as an agent of the French court.
Not all of the Scottish lords were at ease with his close
association with James, although Esme even became a
Protestant while in Scotland. Attesting to his attachment to his
cousin, James ultimately made him the Duke of Lennox.
However, the Scottish lords, led by William Ruthven, Earl of
Gowrie, were threatened by his influence on James and they
alleged the likelihood that he would convert James and
Scotland to Catholicism. In an episode now called the Ruthven
Raid, in August 1582 they gained control of the sixteen-year-
old James to keep him from Esme, essentially making him their
captive for a year. James was finally released in June 1583 only
after Esme had been forced to return to France, where he died
that same year, still a Protestant.

Esme Stuart was loved by James and was probably the only
family member with whom James formed any real emotional
attachment. Esme's banishment to France and his subsequent
death seem to have been the spur for James to use the power

of his Scottish throne to stand up to the Scottish nobles, so that when James escaped from his captivity by Ruthven, just past his seventeenth birthday, he was his own man and quickly became the master of Scotland.

By the time he reached his early twenties, James Stuart had surrounded himself with lords of a moderate political stance and sat firmly on his Scottish throne. He enjoyed riding and hunting and began to write, activities that gave him pleasure for the rest of his life. In 1587 his mother, Mary Queen of Scots, was put to death at Fotheringay Castle in Northamptonshire. James and Mary had corresponded over the years but it is difficult to know how close he felt to his mother. Unlike his response to the later deaths of his young son, Henry, and his wife, Anne, there is no evidence that Mary's death caused James either depression or the bouts of diarrhoea and gastrointestinal distress (probably psychosomatic) that marked periods of stress later in his life. In his communications with Queen Elizabeth he carefully counterbalanced his feelings about his mother's death with the deference he owed Elizabeth, so that he remained in consideration as her successor for the throne of England. Mary was buried at Peterborough Cathedral and when James became King of England, he had her body reburied at Westminster Abbey. Elizabeth, and the throne of England, were never out of James's mind, and Elizabeth exerted considerable influence on his life, even in respect to his marriage.

James needed a queen and his choice was made only after Elizabeth had given her approval, keeping him waiting, perhaps, to assert her dominance over him. The choice, Anne, fifteen-year-old second daughter of King Frederick II of Denmark, did not suggest an alliance of importance in European political affairs, but neither did it complicate the relations of either England or Scotland with the major continental powers. James and Anne were married by proxy not long after his twenty-third birthday. James then went to Denmark to claim his bride – the only time in his life he ever left Britain – and the two were properly married in November 1589. Their return to Scotland was delayed by bad winter weather and they did not arrive until the spring of 1590, whereupon they were married yet another time. Anne took up her duties as Queen of Scotland. While apparently not a Nordic beauty, she was noted to have pretty blonde hair and very fair skin, typical of her origins in the Lutheran northland of the European continent.

All things considered, Anne was probably a good wife for James. She complemented him with possession of the social graces and social interests he lacked and she enlivened the Jacobean court with her presence. Anne has been described as frivolous but not unkind or particularly selfish, and she did not dabble much in politics. In spite of speculation that she was a secret Roman Catholic, she did not disturb religious affairs in either Scotland or, later, England and she died a Protestant in 1619 at forty-four years of age.

Anne bore James seven children. The first, Henry, Prince of Wales, was born in 1594, more than four years after their marriage. With no effective birth control in the sixteenth century, Anne may have had earlier pregnancies ending in miscarriage, but there is no record of such. In 1596 she gave birth to Elizabeth, who became the wife of Frederick, Elector Palatine. Ultimately this couple became the grandparents of George of Hanover who, under the Act of Settlement of 1701, was crowned George I, King of Great Britain and Ireland in 1714, when the Stuart dynasty came to an end. Anne's third child was a daughter, Margaret, who died in infancy. Charles was the fourth child. Born in 1600, he succeeded his father to the thrones of Scotland and England. Robert was born in 1601, Mary in 1605, and Sophia in 1607. Unfortunately, all three of these children died in infancy. Anne seems to have been a good mother and she fought hard to remain close to her eldest son, Henry Frederick, despite the court custom that he should not be part of her household. Henry's untimely death in 1612, at the age of eighteen, was very hard for Anne and James to bear.

James ruled Scotland as a shrewd and canny monarch. He was more than a match for the wily Scottish nobles as his handling of the Gowrie Conspiracy illustrates. In August 1600, James was attacked at Gowrie house and in the struggle both John Ruthven, Earl of Gowrie, and his brother, Alexander, were killed. James claimed to his dying day that he was kidnapped by the Ruthvens but others said that he had arranged the whole affair to justify their elimination. They were, of course, the very family that had kidnapped him in 1582. However one views these incidents in James's life, it is very obvious that he acquired a useful measure of guile as he matured and became a clever and resourceful ruler. By his mid-thirties James was known throughout Europe as a wise king, secure on his Scottish throne.

If James had a pivotal event in his life then it was surely coming to the throne of England when he was thirty-six years old. Queen Elizabeth died on 24 March 1603 but there had been no certainty that James would succeed her. The shrewd Elizabeth kept all guessing about a successor until her death, although she had quietly arranged matters so that James would be chosen. James's actual blood relationship to Elizabeth was distant; her aunt, Margaret Tudor, was his great-grandmother. For several years, James had been in confidential contact with Robert Cecil, chief minister to Elizabeth, and it was Cecil who paved his way to the English throne. Once James was crowned, Cecil became his chief secretary and, ultimately, his lord treasurer.

James learned of his good fortune from Robert Carey who rode for 60 hours, day and night, from London to Edinburgh to tell him that he had become King of England. James wasted no time in going south to claim his throne, leaving Edinburgh for London on 5 April. His queen and children joined him later and James and Anne were crowned King and Queen of England in August 1603.

It is of some medical interest that James fell from his horse on the way to England and broke his clavicle but it healed without event and, as he was always wont to observe, without much assistance from his physicians. In fact, in spite of his weak legs, James was a good physical specimen in his early thirties, and in many ways he took his good health for granted. However, he abhorred tobacco, the new fad of his time, imported in ever increasing quantities from the New World. In his famous polemic against the use of tobacco, he was remarkably prescient in writing about smoking as, '. . . a custom loathesome to the eye, hatefull to the nose, harmefull to the braine, dangerous to the lungs, and in the black stinking fume thereof, nearest resembling the horrible Stygian smoake of the pit that is bottomlesse'.[5]

James followed a good diet and prided himself on eating simple meals; he enjoyed fruits and vegetables and was never corpulent. Several of James's contemporaries describe him as being fond of alcoholic drinks, particularly wine, but to his credit, drunkenness is not mentioned, so it is unlikely that he abused alcohol. He rarely drank water or other watery beverages and by his own later description his urine was usually quite concentrated. During his early middle age, James enjoyed relatively good health, athough he had occasional bouts of abdominal pain often associated with passing dark or bloody urine, and sometimes accompanied by fever. He also had episodes of jaundice, particularly at times of stress. Theodore de Mayerne, describing himself as James's first (principal) physician, reviewed this part of James's medical history quite carefully and wrote the following in his thorough evaluation of 1623:

. . . kidneys warm, disposed to generate sand and gravel . . . urine generally normal and sufficient. Often sandy sediment after a time. Sometimes friable calculi [stones] or rather agglutinated grains of sand are sifted out . . . many years ago, after hunting and long riding, he often had turbid urine and red like Alicant wine (which are His Majesty's words), but without pain . . . July 12, 1613, bloody urine, with red sand, soon faeculent and with thick sediment. Ardor urinae, pain in the left kidney; frequent vomiting and other nephritic symptoms. . . . The same, but worse, August 17. In

1615, October, the same symptoms. His accustomed flux [diarrhoea] relieved all these paroxysms. Afterwards the evil often renewed, and in some of the accessions calculi or rather concoctions were ejected, and soft sand adhering together with imperfect cohesion, and then the attack came to an end.[6]

Actually, James passed stones in his urine a number of times throughout his middle years of life; sometimes these episodes were associated with fever but most often only with bloody urine and flank pain. He became accustomed to these episodes; the pain, when it occurred, was usually in his left flank and was of varying severity, sometimes keeping him from attending to his duties for several days at a time. His physicians had a fairly clear understanding of the nature of the problem and dealt with it as they could and as James would allow them. When an episode of pain and bloody urine commenced there was little to do but wait for the stone to pass. James was philosophical about his medical problems and took delight in testing his physicians on what they might think of a particular symptom or problem, before adding his own interpretation which he regarded as correct and final. However, slowly he began noting problems for which there were no ready answers. His weak legs ached more and more, and the pain seemed to be settling in his joints.

De Mayerne's notes suggest that arthritis and swelling of both feet were occurring as early as 1616. His description is long but very clear and it shows the sort of interaction James enjoyed with his physicians.

Pains many years since invaded first the right foot, which had an odd twist when walking, and from a wrong habit of steps had a less right position than the other, and grew weaker as he grew older. Afterwards occurred various bruises from knocking against timber, from frequent falls from horseback, from the rubbing greaves and stirrups and other external causes which the King ingeniously discovered, and exactly noted, that he might baffle the accusation of internal disorder on the part of his physicians.

Pain of his right foot used to afflict him most often: not the toes, not the joint of the foot with tibia, but underneath the external malleolus [the lateral bump of the ankle]. All the same I have observed that the whole foot has more often swelled and so much weakness from pain remained, that for several weeks he had to give up usual exercises and was compelled to stay in bed or in a chair. At last, in the year 1616, this weakness continued for more than four months with oedematous swelling of the whole skin of both feet. In following years it happened that the pain went on to joints of other parts, the great toe of the left foot and the malleoli to both knees and shoulders and hands, more often with swelling. The pain is acute for the first two or three days. By night it rages now worse now milder: weakness succeeds, which is neither subdued nor disappears till after a long course of days.

The evolution of James's arthritis was gradual, with intermittent pain in the joints of his feet, more the right than the left, and occasional episodes of swelling and inflammation of these joints. Finally this arthritis extended to the knees, hands, and shoulders, again with swelling and inflammation. Given James's weakened legs, the added factor of arthritis made walking extremely difficult at times, and he was occasionally laid up for days or weeks with this problem, which worsened and grew more frequent as he aged.

Although James could not be described as an attentive and devoted husband, nonetheless he and Anne had an efficient marriage that saw to the nurture of their children, and together they fulfilled the expectations of the English court. There is no record of James having an interest in other women and Anne accepted his fascination with handsome young men, apparently without fear that it would compromise their own relationship. Anne was a steadying influence for James during the first sixteen years of his rule of England, and most particularly upon the death of their son, Henry, in 1612.

Anne enjoyed good health until she was about thirty-seven years of age when she was thought by her physicians to have gout and eventually dropsy, that is legs swollen with oedema. It can be stated with certainty that she did not have gout because, as Hippocrates observed 2,500 years ago, women do not get gout before menopause. She presumably had arthritis of some other cause but it is not possible to take the diagnosis much further because primary source material is not available. Anne was too young for the arthritis of ageing, osteoarthritis, so an active inflammatory arthritis is the likely culprit. In consideration of her notable leg swelling, she could even have been suffering from one of the uncommon rheumatic diseases. James visited her several times in the months of her decline prior to her death, but when she died on 2 March 1619, he was not present. When her body was opened, the abdominal organs were described as being shrunken, particularly her liver.[7] The opening of a body after death was roughly akin to an autopsy and was usually performed by a surgeon, most often in the company of physicians. The medical significance of Anne's shrunken liver is moot, although it might be observed that she did not die with congestive heart failure because in that event her liver would have been swollen. Her cause of death cannot be determined from the data available, but James missed her, and he rapidly became unable to sustain the order in his life that had been maintained before her death.

In fact, James became very depressed after the death of his queen and was subsequently quite ill late in March. He is reported to have had severe abdominal pain and to have passed three stones with his urine while travelling near Royston; de Mayerne has summarized this illness quite succinctly:

. . . 1619, after the queen's death, pain in joints and nephritis with thick sand. At Royston continued fever, bilious diarrhoea, watery and profuse throughout the illness. Hiccough for some days. Aphthae [small whitish ulcers] all over the mouth and fauces [back of the throat] and even the oesophagus. . . . Fainting, sighing, dread, incredible sadness, intermittent pulse. Nevertheless, it is to be noted as to this intermission of pulse in the King that it was frequent. Nephritis [kidney infection or inflammation], from which, without any remedy having been administered, he excreted a friable calculus [stone], as was his wont. The force of this, the most dangerous illness which the King ever had, lasted for eight days. Remedies were used with success.

In another primary source, a letter from the noted London gossip John Chamberlain to his friend Sir Dudley Carlton, then English ambassador at The Hague, it is noted that James had fever, irregular pulse, vomiting, diarrhoea, and hiccough during this illness.[8] Although James recovered from this serious episode, he never regained the physical strength or mental sharpness of his former years. It was a complicated illness and it is difficult to link the variety of symptoms and signs he suffered; a single diagnosis will not account for all of them. However, an intermittent irregular pulse raises the ominous possibility that James suffered a serious heart rhythm disturbance, such as atrial fibrillation, itself known to be a cause of strokes.

The final six years of James's life were a sad last chapter of a reign that had begun well. With difficulty, James had managed the Addled Parliament of 1614, then he lost control of the Parliament of 1621. The Thirty Years War on the continent placed a great strain on both Parliament and king and caused increasing concern about England's foreign affairs, particularly the aggression of Spain towards the Protestant Germanic states. The *Commons Protestation* of 1621, a statement by members defining their rights and privileges vis-à-vis the monarch, affirmed the privileges of Parliament and attacked James and his royal prerogatives directly. James personally tore this document from the *Common's Journal* after he had ended the parliament late in December. King James had a smoother relation with his last parliament, in 1624, although by this time his son Charles and George Villiers, Duke of Buckingham, were meddling ineffectively in the proceedings of Parliament, a state of affairs that would cause James, and ultimately Charles, great trouble.

The handsome and charming George Villiers first came to the attention of James in 1614 when Villiers was twenty-two years of age. In the fourteen subsequent years until he was stabbed to death by John Felton, Villiers rose from genteel obscurity to become a very wealthy man, arguably the most powerful man in England. As James's mental faculties began to fade, the star of this young opportunist rose ever higher in the Jacobean court until, finally, he dominated both the court and the king.[9] As irony would have it, George Villiers had a wife, small children, and a large extended family who moved in with James after the death of Queen Anne, when the relationship of James and Villiers was at its most intense. James eventually found the invasion of his solitary domestic situation disquieting and towards the end of his life, when he was tiring of George, he tried without success to evict the large, noisy Villiers family. But it was too late, he lacked the necessary force and guile to get rid of George and his pesky relations and so they remained in the king's household to the end of his life, providing companionship and company he neither wanted nor enjoyed.

It was Queen Anne who had interested James in Villiers, when she was seeking to distract him from his deepening fascination with his previous reckless favourite, Robert Carr. This was probably a sincere, perhaps even desperate, effort on the queen's part to rescue her husband from the growing political liability of Carr, who had a penchant for causing state problems. However, James had evidently not learned to be wary of handsome, but unprincipled, young men and he foolishly ennobled Villiers, making him a gentleman of the bed chamber in 1615, viscount in 1616, earl in 1617, marquess in 1618, and the Duke of Buckingham in 1623.

In the last few years of James's life, Villiers's influence stretched from day-to-day matters of government to the negotiation of foreign policy. He even had a say in the political education of Charles, Prince of Wales. There is no doubt that Villiers was clever and devious, but he could never have accomplished such swift advancement and acquisition of power had James been in full possession of his mental faculties. James had survived from an early age in a dangerous Scottish world and had become the King of England, not by luck but by careful planning and manoeuvring. Undoubtedly, in his younger years, James would have handled Villiers more appropriately, no matter how blinded by love he might have been. Villiers set out to exploit his intimate relationship with the demented and befuddled king and came to dominate James in ways that no woman could ever have managed, his malign influence exerted until the very end of James's life.

James died at a country house called Theobalds on Sunday 27 March 1625, after an illness of several days characterized by fever and diarrhoea. He was attended by William Harvey and other court physicians – Theodore de Mayerne was on the continent and not present. Harvey was probably the only physician to have a clear idea of what was happening to James but, unfortunately, any notes he may have kept have been lost. In addition to the gastrointestinal symptoms, James had difficulty swallowing and speaking, and he may also have suffered weakness in one side. His was a pitiful end; by all accounts he lay dying in a bed of his own excrement.

George Villiers and his mother insisted on participating in James's medical care and, surreptitiously, when his attending physicians were at supper, they placed a medicinal plaster on his chest and gave him a potion to drink. After James's death, there was widespread belief that the Villiers, mother and son, had poisoned the king. James's physicians were incensed that unqualified interlopers had been treating their patient. They were eager to attach the blame for their monarch's death to Villiers and, in fact, one of James's physicians of many years, Dr George Eglisham, published a pamphlet in 1626 publicly accusing Villiers and his mother of poisoning King James.[10]

POST-MORTEM EXAMINATION OF JAMES VI/I

Two days after James's death, a post-mortem examination was performed by William Walton, a surgeon, who received £50 for his services. Walton's report shows him to have been astute and experienced; his observations are very useful in defining some of James's medical problems, particularly his failing mind. The extant record of this post-mortem examination is found in a letter from William Neve to Sir Thomas Holland, dated 5 April 1625, and the most accessible secondary source is Geoffrey Keynes's *Life of William Harvey*.

> The King's body was about the 29th of March disbowelled, and his harte was found to be great but soft, his liver fresh as a young man's; one of his kidnys very good, but the other shrunke so little as they could hardly find yt, wherein there was two stones; his lites [lungs] and gall blacke [gall bladder], judged to proceed of melancholly [dark bile]; the semyture [skull] of his head soe stronge as that they could hardly breake it open with a chissell and a saw, and so full of braynes as they could not, uppon the openninge, keep them from spillinge, a great marke of his infinite judgement. His bowels were presently put into a leaden vessel and buryed; his body embalmed.[11]

Using these autopsy data it is possible to understand many of the medical events of James's life more fully, and then to appreciate their effects on his ability to rule. Some of the findings are minor and merely interesting, not of consequence but deserving of comment, others are of great significance in defining James's disability. As with any autopsy, what was not found is often as important as what was found.

James's nearly lifelong trouble with abdominal pain and bloody urine, occasionally accompanied by particulate matter in his urine and fever, is explained by the small damaged kidney containing two stones, which squares nicely with his long history of kidney stone disease. In all likelihood these stones and the tissue around them contained bacteria, because the fever that often accompanied James's stone problems certainly represented both acute and chronic kidney infection.

Among other matters, this finding negates and lays to rest the presumption of Dr Ida Macalpine and her colleagues that James and his mother had acute intermittent porphyria. Macalpine's work was published in the *British Medical Journal* in 1966[12] and 1968,[13] and later in a popular book, written with her son, Richard Hunter, entitled *George III and the Mad-Business*.[14] Most seasoned physicians have long regarded the Macalpine/ Hunter theory that the Hanoverians, particularly George III, and the Stuarts extending back to Mary Queen of Scots were afflicted with the metabolic disease acute intermittent porphyria as a very doubtful diagnosis. Unfortunately this idea has had a life of its own and it is generally believed that these English royal houses were rife with porphyria, culminating in the very entertaining film, *The Madness of King George*. For the person who wishes to understand the truth of this matter, it is worth examining the correspondence in the *British Medical Journal* following the publication of Macalpine's papers and the benchmark medical textbook on porphyria by Dr Geoffrey Dean, *The Porphyrias: A Story of Inheritance and Environment* (second edition, published in 1971).[15] Dean patiently and carefully refutes the Macalpine diagnosis of acute intermittent porphyria in the royal houses of Europe. James did not have porphyria. Nor, for that matter, did any of the Stuarts or Hanoverians.

The clinical description of de Mayerne and the autopsy report of Walton provide a clear description of chronic kidney stone disease. The mention of bloody urine without pain after vigorous horseback riding is very interesting. Vigorous exercise can cause haematuria (blood in the urine) even in the absence of stones in the kidneys but stones bouncing around in the calyces (the large ducts which collect urine from the kidneys) could also cause abrasion and bleeding. James certainly had kidney stone disease and also certainly had recurrent acute kidney infections. The medical term for kidney infection is pyelonephritis, and the acute episodes of pyelonephritis were laid against a background of chronic kidney infection, chronic pyelonephritis. There were bacteria in and on the stones in James's kidneys and even if antibiotics had been available at that time, it would have been difficult, perhaps impossible, to eradicate this chronic infection.

It is now well known that a single small damaged kidney can lead to hypertension. In James's time, hypertension could not have been diagnosed or even understood because William Harvey's great medical classic, *Excercitatio Anatomica de Motu Cordis et Sanguinis in Animalibus*, was not published until 1628, three years after James's death. An understanding of the circulatory system was necessary even to imagine excessive blood pressure within the arteries and therefore the fundamental concept of hypertension. Of course hypertension is a very common disease and James could also have had hypertension unrelated to the small damaged kidney. The large heart, carefully noted at this autopsy, lends credence to the possibility of long-standing hypertension and hypertensive cardiovascular disease, including hypertensive disease of the arteries of the brain. Strokes, large and small, are the very hallmark of hypertensive cerebrovascular disease.

Finally, his brain was swollen, not from his large intellect of course, but from a recent stroke and subsequent oedema (swelling) of the brain. The brain does not protrude when the skull is opened at autopsy unless there is acute damage to its substance, usually the cerebral cortex, or there is a mass within the bony confines of the skull. No mass, tumour, blood or blood clot was described by the surgeon. This swelling would have obscured the scar of a stroke he might have suffered in 1619, when his heart rhythm was intermittently irregular, and perhaps also the small scars of lesser strokes suffered subsequently. Of course, Surgeon Walton would not have known to look for evidence of previous small strokes but, without the swelling, he might have been able to see asymmetry and evidence of brain damage, although he would not have referred to it as stroke or vascular injury in those days.

From fifty-two years of age, the time of his serious illness after the death of Queen Anne, James began markedly to lose both his physical vigour and mental sharpness. He lost interest in the affairs of state, his sound judgement became progressively clouded and his political skills seemed to wither. These late failings in James have been identified by many eminent scholars over the years. On top of his illness in 1619 when he may have had atrial fibrillation (with its strong association with strokes) it appears that something else may have been a determining factor in this phase of his decline. Three men who spent years studying James recognized his gradual loss of faculties, each seeing it through the lens of his own expertise. The late eminent Stuart historian, John P. Kenyon, described him as 'prematurely old'.[16] His medical biographer, Archibald Goodall, a Scottish surgeon, noted, '. . . one can only suggest that early arteriosclerosis had impaired his mental processes'.[17] The editor of James's letters, G.P.V. Akrigg, called him 'burned out nervously and weakened physically in the several years before his death . . . the last six years of his reign were to bring ignominious failures which would discredit James in the eyes of foreign observers and of his own subjects'.[18] There is still further significant and impartial evidence that James had mental compromise in the latter years of his reign. In 1623, Alvise Valaresso, a Venetian ambassador in England, noted in a letter home that James was reduced to 'profound lethargy and stupid insensibility'.[19] John Chamberlain wrote in 1624 that James's speeches were cloudy and in need of interpretation and explanation.[20]

Thus, it is incontrovertible that James suffered increasing mental compromise in the latter years of his life. This intersection of historical, medical, literary and even diplomatic opinions raises obvious questions: what happened to James, what launched his physical and mental decline, and how can this decline best be understood in medical terms? Recently, corroboratory evidence of James's mental decline from 1619 onwards has been developed from analysis of letters written by him throughout his life and made available to scholars through the collection of Professor Akrigg.[21] There is a sudden and definite change in syntax beginning just before his 1619 illness and then a long steady decline in the quality of his written material until the time of his death. By modern research standards this is diagnostic of the intellectual deterioration of dementia. Dr Kristine Williams, myself, Professor Susan Kemper and Dr Janet Marquis have analysed the letters James wrote personally. By accepted methods of linguistic scholarship, attention being focused directly on syntax and grammar and using standardized methods of computer data management and analysis, we have shown that there are statistically significant changes over time in James's letters during the period 1604 to 1624. The linguistic tests used included mean length of utterance, mean clauses per utterance and type token ratio. These changes in facility with language are certain documentation of dementing illness in James.[22]

Dementia is a syndrome, not a specific disease. The usual cause of this syndrome is Alzheimer's disease, first described by Alois Alzheimer at the beginning of the twentieth century and now recognized as the most common cause of dementia in the world. Typically, Alzheimer's disease begins in the seventies or eighties and is slowly but steadily progressive; it can occur in younger patients but does so very rarely, and then it is most often familial. We can eliminate Alzheimer's disease as a cause of James's dementia because he was too young and we know that it was not familial because none of the other Stuarts was demented.

Syphilis must also be proposed as a cause of James's dementia. A gift from the New World to the Old, syphilis invades the central nervous system in some of its chronic sufferers and, among other symptoms, causes compromise of judgement and eventually dementia. Though now uncommon due to the widespread use of antibiotics, central nervous system syphilis was once the most common cause of dementia in the world; it has variously been termed dementia paralytica, general paresis and general paresis of the insane. More common in men than women, the time from diagnosis to death is about three years and vascular disease of the brain and stroke can occur in the late stages. James could have been infected with syphilis earlier in his life, perhaps by one of his paramours, and it could have developed, over the years, to become central nervous system syphilis. However, this seems unlikely, as central nervous system syphilis is usually associated with a tremor and, despite his neuromuscular problems, James never suffered from a tremor. Additionally, James did not show the relentless downhill course of dementia that one would associate with central nervous system syphilis and the course of his dementing illness is too long, so this must be considered a doubtful diagnosis.

Dementia is a terrible disability, especially for one who wields executive authority. Paradoxically, the sufferer will almost certainly be blissfully unaware of his problem, because all of the higher functions of the brain are usually affected, that is, memory, orientation, personality, intellect and judgement. It is recent memory that usually appears to fade first, but demented patients often instinctively develop quite wonderful defences to cover this loss of knowing what they had to eat for breakfast or whether or not they took the dog for a walk before bedtime. When asked specific questions about, for example, the breakfast menu, a demented patient would most likely reply: 'The same thing I always have every morning'.

A seventeenth-century monarch was constantly surrounded by functionaries and servants so orientation to time and place would not have been a problem for James, the rhythm of court in familiar surroundings carried him along from hour to hour, day to day. His personality did change, however, and he is noted to have become querulous and childish in the last years of his life, a caricature of himself, as it were. Sadly, his intellect and his judgement deteriorated along with his memory, and of course his speeches and writing make this quite clear. Sadder still, this developing vacuum was smoothly filled by George Villiers, from about the time of Anne's death and James's illness in 1619, until his own death in 1625.

To understand the extent of Villiers's influence on James in his dotage, it is pertinent to examine James's attraction to men. History is replete with examples of ruling men being brought down by calculating women, through love, lust or a combination of the two. Samson had his Delilah, Bill Clinton his Monica Lewinsky, and other examples abound. That James loved Villiers is beyond dispute, and reading the letters to his young paramour makes this quite clear. Villiers was 'Steenie', while James called himself 'Dad' or even 'husband' and addressed Villiers as 'Sweet heart'. James was remarkably informal in much of his correspondence, even when dealing with important matters of state. For example, he almost always addressed his chief minister, Robert Cecil, Earl of Salisbury, as 'My little beagle'. However, his letters to Villiers are far more intensely personal and even display the peevishness of a lover.[23] The other two men whom James loved earlier in his life, Esme Stuart and Robert Carr, must be seen in the same light as Villiers.

Whether or not James's relations with Villiers, Stuart, and Carr had a physical aspect to them will probably never be known. For the purpose of understanding the hold George Villiers had over James we can assume that the relationship was, by modern understanding, homosexual. Of these three men, only Villiers managed to dominate the king in any way, perhaps because youth and vigour were on his side when he became involved with an increasingly enfeebled James. Of course, the term homosexual was not in common parlance in the seventeenth century. For a man to be attracted sexually to other men was not defining in the sense it is now in western culture. An interesting question can be posed, might a male lover have a stronger influence on a king than a female lover? At a time in history when political and monetary power were almost wholly invested in men, is it not reasonable to assume that this would be the case? The historian Charles Carlton proffers this argument in his book, *Royal Mistresses*, and it appears to be sound, particularly in respect to James and Villiers.[24]

James began his loss of mental competence about thirteen years after the beginning of his reign and it is possible to understand the process of his decline when his behaviour is matched against his post-mortem examination. When viewed in light of the autopsy, the severe illness James suffered in 1619 was much more than kidney stones, depression and functional bowel complaints. Fever and ulcers about the mouth and deep into the throat suggest infection with the herpes virus, something considerably beyond fever blisters. The prolonged hiccough connotes involvement of the lower oesophagus, the stomach or, even more likely, a disturbance of the diaphragm or the nerves supplying it (the phrenic nerves) perhaps from a stroke. These symptoms are not specific nor is the fever – they do not combine into a particular disease or syndrome. Apart from these problems, James certainly did suffer another bout with kidney stones, presumably accompanying this acute illness but not the direct cause of it. Surely, the ulcers in his throat made it difficult for him to drink and swallow. Also with fever, he must have been quite dehydrated, concentrating his urine even more than usual, and so promoting the formation of sludge and stones in his bladder and kidneys. This is the first evidence of the heart and blood vessel problem that would bring James down mentally. James's dementia was a consequence of heart and vascular disease, the result of a series of strokes of varying intensity not recognized by James or by those who attended him on a daily basis. In addition to blood vessel disease from hypertension, James had a serious heart rhythm disturbance that is known to cause strokes.

The irregular pulse noted in 1619 was a heart rhythm disturbance, known medically as an arrhythmia, and the most common and striking arrhythmia is atrial fibrillation. This can be intermittent or permanent and is a reflection of underlying heart disease in a middle-aged man. Unfortunately, there is no electrocardiogram of James to show the exact nature of his arrhythmia, but it is certain that his physicians were quite expert and diligent in taking his pulse frequently and noting changes in its strength, regularity and rate. Atrial fibrillation is one of the few abnormal heart rhythms that can be diagnosed by the physician merely taking the patient's pulse, so it is not necessary to listen to the heart or examine an electrocardiogram to make this diagnosis. In atrial fibrillation the pulse is often described as irregularly irregular, that is, the individual beats occur randomly, there is no pattern whatsoever. The fact that his arrhythmia was not immediately life threatening makes atrial fibrillation even more likely. The fact that it would apparently come and go over the eight-day period is especially ominous and important, particularly when we consider his declining mental facilities during the last years of his life.

Atrial fibrillation is a disturbance of the heart rhythm during which the two upper storage chambers of the heart, the right and left atria, stop pumping. Blood collects in these chambers and clots often form there because the blood is relatively still. When blood clots form in the atria they attach to the walls of these chambers. Parts of them may then break loose and travel with the flow of blood to the lower chambers of the heart, the right and left ventricles, from which they are sent on to the two major arterial systems of the body, the right going to the lungs exclusively and the left to the rest of the body. Blood clots that occur in flowing blood are called emboli and this process is called embolization. A clot leaving the right ventricle lodges in a branch of the pulmonary artery in the lung and most often would not even cause symptoms for the patient. Very large clots or even many small ones being sieved out by the lungs can cause acute shortness of breath and even sudden death but such clots usually come from veins feeding into the right atrium, not from the right atrium itself.

Left atrial clots are another matter entirely. Pieces of left atrial clots flow to the left ventricle of the heart and then to all parts of the body through the aorta. Because of flow characteristics, at least a quarter of them will go to the brain. Even a small clot lodging in a brain artery may cause an acute stroke. Atrial fibrillation is a major risk factor for stroke. In modern medicine, patients who have chronic atrial fibrillation are usually put on aspirin or anticoagulants to impede the formation of left atrial clots and thereby reduce the chance of one entering the brain. Patients who have intermittent atrial fibrillation, the problem James had, are at even greater risk of embolization and stroke than those with chronic atrial fibrillation. During the contraction of the walls of the atria, when the heart rhythm reverts temporarily to normal, an attached clot is very likely to sheer off and become an embolus. Thus, presumably 'going in and out of atrial fibrillation' over eight days put James at even greater risk of having a stroke, or perhaps several small ones. James's stroke, or small strokes, damaged the parts of his brain concerned with language. This damage was subtle and not the gross damage we term aphasia. In addition to this, numbers of small strokes are known to cause compromise of intellect. Once a patient has had atrial fibrillation, it is likely to recur or to become the patient's permanent heart rhythm, thereby greatly increasing the risk of embolic stroke.

To compound matters for James, the severely damaged small kidney and his large heart, mentioned so definitely in the autopsy report, make it certain that he suffered from hypertension. Patients with hypertension secondary to a damaged kidney, often called renovascular hypertension, may have blood pressures of 250/150 and even higher. Chronic hypertension itself can damage the arteries of the brain and small strokes from ruptured arteries or small clots formed in the brain (thromboses) are ultimately part of this disease as well. Most of the arterial blood going to the head goes to the cerebrum, the part of the brain responsible for thinking and intellect. In modern terms it can be said that James certainly had cerebrovascular disease. This was probably both the result of emboli from his heart and thrombi (small haemorrhages from his hypertension) and the resultant strokes caused his vascular dementia.

Cerebrovascular disease is the second leading cause of dementia today and is distinct from Alzheimer's disease; it occurs in middle-aged people with severe hypertension and those with atrial fibrillation, as well as the elderly. The change in James's letters and the subsequent decay in the quality of his writing and speaking make this diagnosis all the more certain. Typically, the person with vascular dementia becomes a caricature of himself, personality is usually preserved but there is emotional lability and loss of inhibition. Not only is memory compromised but judgement, too. The Scottish surgeon, Archibald Goodall, was on the right track when he ascribed James's decline in function to hardening of the arteries of his brain. We now know that it is not hardening of brain arteries per se that causes dementia but thrombi and emboli that lead to the discrete vascular episodes we label as strokes. Many such strokes go unnoticed by the patient because the arteries involved are not in critically important parts of the brain. However, the cumulative effect of a number of such small insults to brain tissue is usually compromise of intellect, resulting in dementia. In some patients with vascular dementia, a careful medical history will elucidate several or repeated episodes of slight decline, a sort of stair-step deterioration, although this is not always the case. Vascular dementia is often difficult to recognize and diagnose even in modern times. A good case in point is that of Winston

Churchill, who almost certainly had mild vascular dementia by the end of his last term as prime minister.[25]

In the matter of determining the cause of James's childhood delay in walking and lifelong weak legs, this must be divined by clinical reasoning; the autopsy itself is not helpful. The principal objective findings available are the observations of Theodore de Mayerne, who examined James carefully, probably more than once, and then summarized his findings in 1623. He described James's legs as more than lean, rather atrophied, a pathological state. The diagnosis must then turn on what would cause atrophied legs, from childhood onward. As de Mayerne wrote, 'the leanness and so to speak atrophy of his legs were to be noted as due to the intermission of exercise not calling the spirits and nourishment to the lower parts which from childhood were slender and weak'.[26]

With long, dark winters and poor diet, any child living in Scotland in the sixteenth century might have had poor absorption of vitamin D and developed rickets. However, it is difficult to imagine that even rickets would have delayed walking until five years of age in an otherwise normal boy. Moreover, rickets is always associated with bone pain and bone deformity in children, problems which were not reported in James as an infant or child. A wet nurse would have been chosen because she had milk in adequate or generous amounts and the quality of her milk would not have been significantly changed by her consumption of alcohol. In other words, it could not have been tainted. In adult life James did not have obvious skeletal deformities characteristic of healed childhood rickets, so rickets must be a doubtful diagnosis.

James was obviously of above average intelligence, which rules out delayed motor development due to mental retardation. However, cerebral palsy, with a normal or superior intellect, is a plausible explanation for his delay in walking. It must be considered because of Anthony Weldon's description of James as having weak legs, a peculiar gait, a tongue too large for his mouth, altered speech, tongue protrusion when drinking liquids and random movements of his hands. Weldon reported that James did not even stand until he was seven years of age.[27] This suggests athetoid cerebral palsy, but there is nothing to corroborate this diagnosis. Tempting as this explanation of leg weakness and delayed walking is, it is also, therefore, doubtful.

Leg weakness following unrecognized poliomyelitis, so-called infantile paralysis, bears consideration. De Mayerne described bilateral atrophy but did not mention asymmetry of the atrophy. Also he did not mention scoliosis, that is curvature of the spine, a common problem in seventeenth-century Europe. He would not have overlooked it had it been present in James. Asymmetrical leg muscle atrophy and scoliosis would have been likely had James suffered significant residual weakness after recovery from polio. Of course, de Mayerne did not know of polio as a discrete disease entity – it was hundreds of years before it would be identified as such. Polio did occur in Europe in the seventeenth century and probably even earlier. But the apparent symmetry of the leg muscle wasting and weakness, and lack of scoliosis, make previous polio an unlikely cause of James's leg weakness. Thus, polio is also a doubtful diagnosis.

There is a better explanation for the leg weakness and muscle wasting James suffered and the clue to it lies with his second son, Charles, who was also very delayed in walking. An hereditary neuromuscular disease in both James and Charles, one of the rare mild muscular dystrophies, must be considered. Study of portraits of James in his thirties and early forties made by John de Critz and Adrian Vanson show wasting of his temporal muscles, rather sunken eyes, and very spindly legs. A portrait of his father, Lord Darnley, as a teenager, shows him also to have very spindly legs, raising the possibility of a rare hereditary disease called myotonic muscular dystrophy. One of the hereditary diseases of motor nerves, particularly in the legs, is also a possibility. These motor nerve diseases are now grouped together as the scapuloperoneal syndrome, in plain language this can be called the shoulder–lower-leg syndrome, and Charcot-Marie-Tooth disease is one of these. The heredity of all of these neuromuscular diseases is variable, some are dominant and some are recessive. With the data available the diagnosis cannot be further refined, nor can the exact nature of its inheritance in the Stuart family be determined. No Stuart subsequent to Charles had difficulty walking or leg weakness apart from William, Duke of Gloucester, the son of Queen Anne. The nature of his neurological problem was distinctly and obviously different from that which afflicted James and Charles, however.

James could have suffered the late effects of polio in addition to having an hereditary neuromuscular disease and could even have had a mild case of rickets, but there is an old dictum in medicine which asks that a single diagnosis be adduced to explain multiple symptoms and signs of disease when this can be done. Summing this all up, it is certain that James had an hereditary neuromuscular disease, and that his son, Charles, was less severely affected. Unfortunately, there are not enough data to refine this diagnosis any further, though myotonic dystrophy would be less likely than one of the motor nerve diseases.

James had other medical problems that were chronic, and his principal physician, Sir Theodore de Mayerne, described each one carefully and exactly. Some of these contributed to his physical disability and some did not. The recurrent abdominal pain James suffered throughout his adult life, unassociated with kidney stones and bloody urine, and his separate episodes of jaundice, suggest liver, gall bladder, or intestinal disease. However, the autopsy did not show abnormality in any of these organs specifically; there were no stones in his gall bladder that might explain recurrent abdominal pain and associated jaundice. It can be assumed that James's stomach and intestine were examined minutely in a search for poisons. Surgeon Walton found neither poisons nor structural abnormalities of the gut, eliminating chronic inflammatory conditions, such as Crohn's disease or ulcerative colitis. As James's episodes of abdominal pain and diarrhoea were stress induced and his gut structurally normal, it is certain that he had functional bowel disease, occasionally disabling but never life-threatening. Episodes of jaundice throughout life in the face of a normal liver at autopsy suggest a harmless medical curiosity, the Dubin-Johnson syndrome.

James had a chronic progressive inflammatory arthritis which began at about the age of fifty and involved numerous joints in a rather asymmetrical sort of progression. De Mayerne did not diagnose gout, which was the common arthritic disease of men at that time, characterized by recurrent acute episodes, usually in the feet. Because of the prominent presence of swelling and inflammation in James's joints, osteoarthritis, the very common arthritis of ageing, would not explain this picture either. The most common chronic inflammatory arthritis of adults is rheumatoid arthritis. It is likely that this is what afflicted James and what, coupled with the weakening effects of his hereditary neuromuscular disease, led to his severe disability and inability to walk more than very short distances during the last years of his life. Thus, rheumatoid arthritis can be advanced as a possible diagnosis.

By the end of his life King James was severely disabled both physically and mentally. However, in spite of his various problems he is a fascinating man, an author of considerable ability and a theologian of some repute. He will always be remembered for the 1611 translation of the Bible into the English vernacular, a work done at his instigation and with his oversight. He was not cruel, unlike many monarchs of his time, and he kept his country largely at peace and separated from continental strife, despite the fact that the Thirty Years War was waged across Europe during the latter years of his reign. One has to admire his personal motto, *Beati Pacifici*, blessed are the peace makers, for he is remembered as a monarch who sought peace at home and abroad.

The two disease states newly identified and defined in this study of James had quite different effects on his 25-year reign; one had little actual effect and the other was devastating. He certainly suffered from an hereditary neuromuscular disease which he mastered effectively and there is no evidence that his neuromuscular disease compromised his mind in any way. He remained relatively mobile until his final years when an inflammatory arthritis, possibly rheumatoid arthritis, compounded the problems of his leg weakness and he was often not able to walk more than very short distances. It is also likely that the strokes suffered in the last years of his life further impeded his locomotion. His dementing illness is quite another matter, however, and it contributed to the tragic end of a reign well begun.

James died from a major stroke, certainly the last in a series of strokes. It is also certain that he had vascular dementia, and that his diminished mental state allowed George Villiers to subvert his authority and compromise an already strained relationship with Parliament. James continued to reign in the last years of his life but ceased to rule long before his death. Villiers handled the authority he usurped poorly, he was self-serving and generally resented. Ever the opportunist, he managed the transition from paramour of King James to surrogate older brother of Charles, Prince of Wales. James's dementia and Villiers's avarice started the Stuart dynasty on its free fall to the turmoil of the Civil Wars and the sad martyrdom of Charles I in 1649. It was King Henry IV of France, probably through his great minister, Sully, who called James, 'the wisest fool in Christendom'.[28] In many respects this is a very apt description.

FOUR

Henry, Elizabeth, and Charles

THE STUART MONARCHY COLLAPSES

Charles I was to have spent the last full day of his life, Monday, 29 January 1649, in temporary quarters at St James's Palace without family to comfort him. He had been moved from Whitehall Palace so that he would not be disturbed by the sight and noise of the construction of the platform on which he would die. Henrietta Maria, his wife, and four of their six children, Charles, Mary, James and the baby, Minette, were political refugees, taken in by the courts of Holland and France; he had not seen them for years. Charles was alone, but his request that he be allowed to see his other two children, still resident in England, had been granted. That Monday thirteen-year-old Elizabeth and nine-year-old Henry were taken to visit their father, whom they had not seen in over a year.

As the children went from Syon House to St James's Palace, the revolutionary body constituted to deal with Charles, the High Court of Justice, convened in the Painted Chamber in nearby Westminster Palace. Under the presidency of Joseph Bradshawe, a Cheshire barrister, this body of commissioners faced the task of preparing the actual death warrant for Charles, so that his execution could proceed without delay. Other than the opinions of the nations of the world who supported him, Charles had no court of appeal; he was a doomed man.

London was unseasonably cold, the Thames was frozen over and the day was dark and overcast. On entering their father's place of confinement, Elizabeth was tearful when she greeted Charles, and Henry, usually a bright and active boy, was subdued. The visit was brief and the three Stuarts were not allowed to be alone. Charles loved his children, all six of them, and though it might have been comforting to talk about happier times in the past, he took the few minutes available to speak to Elizabeth and Henry personally, giving each advice for the future, advice that might help protect them from those who would do them harm.

In the Painted Chamber the commissioners composed a succinct warrant instructing that Charles, attainted and condemned of High Treason and other High Crimes, should be put to death by the severing of his head from his body. They ordered that the sentence was to be carried out in the street in front of Whitehall the next day, between the hours of ten in the morning and five in the afternoon. All good people of the realm were required to assist in the execution.

As the commissioners efficiently took care of the paperwork arranging the details of his death, just a short distance away in St James's Palace Charles told Elizabeth that she must remain true to her Protestant faith and he recommended religious readings for her. As she later wrote, he also told her that she should forgive his enemies, as he had, but he added, wisely, that she should not trust them. He asked her to tell her mother that he loved her, and sent with her his blessings for her brothers and sisters abroad.

In the long narrow chamber in Westminster Palace, the assembled forty-eight commissioners took their time in affixing their signatures to the death warrant, each also adding his seal, with space left for other commissioners to add their signatures and seals at a later time. Some signature spaces were written-over and some names deleted, not everyone wanted to have his name on the document that would kill their king. Oliver Cromwell and Henry Marten signed quickly, seemingly in a jovial mood, while some other commissioners signed their names and affixed their seals slowly and with reluctance.

While his death warrant was being signed Charles took Henry on his lap and spoke to him softly, calling him sweetheart. Henry looked directly at his father's face when Charles told him that he would have his head cut off; further, he warned Henry that he might then be made a king in his father's stead. Charles continued by saying that Henry should refuse any offer of kingship for, if he did not, his elder brothers, Charles and James would lose their heads and then, finally, Henry would lose his head as well. Henry's reply, with all the resolve and courage a nine-year-old boy could muster, was that he would never accept the crown, he would have to be torn to pieces first. This gladdened his father's heart and he sent Henry to join his weeping sister. At the end of their visit, Charles went to the two of them, spoke easily and lightly, and kissed them both, giving them his blessing as they departed. Then he went to his prayers with his companion, Sir Thomas Herbert and the pious Dr William Juxon, Bishop of London.

When the commissioners had completed their work and the death warrant was finished, they adjourned and the preparations for the next day's execution were hastened, carpenters working through the night to finish the platform, others draping it in black. The next day, a cold, miserable, dark day, King Charles I of England, Scotland, and Ireland, was led through a first-floor window in Whitehall Palace, out onto the black-draped platform. There, wearing two shirts to protect him from the cold, lest shivering cause witnesses to think that he was afraid, he let the anonymous hooded executioner bring down his axe to sever his head from his body and thereby end the Stuart dynasty and monarchy in all of Britain.

In contrast to this violent ending of his reign, Charles's accession to the throne of England was effortless, uncontested and unique in comparison with the other five Stuart monarchs. By way of illustration, his father, James I, was a foreigner and no certain candidate for the throne at all. Charles II came to the throne by the luck of politics largely beyond his influence or control, while James II just barely survived one exclusion bill after another. Mary, with her Dutch husband, William, had to take the crown by conquest, and Anne got it by default after the ultimate succession was ascribed to the Hanoverians. Charles I, of course, could not have known about the manner of his successors coming to the throne but he would have known about the irregular ways by which Edward III, Henry IV, Edward IV, Richard III and Henry VII came to be kings of England. As the historian Howard Nenner has observed, Charles got the best start possible without any action of Parliament necessary to endorse his claim.[1] Had his elder brother, Henry, become king with this mandate, surely the Stuart dynasty would have been maintained without compromise. Henry would have mended the damage done to his family in the last years of his father's reign and the Stuarts would have stood strong alongside the Habsburgs and the Bourbons on the continent.

The vigour of a ruling house rests on the ability of a monarch to leave heirs of sufficient number and quality to guarantee the continuation of the blood-line and capable rule of the nation after he or she is gone. In this undertaking James and Anne did a credible job, between 1594 and 1607 they had seven children, three boys and four girls. Unfortunately, one of the boys and three of the girls did not survive infancy. But the three survivors, two of them sons, should have been sufficient to further the Stuart line with a capable monarch. At the time of James's death the general relationship between the monarchy and Parliament was damaged but not beyond repair. James had ceded none of his powers to Parliament and the second Stuart inherited a secure throne. The challenge for this second Stuart monarch was to begin anew with Parliament and to shed any baggage left over from James's reign – in particular, George Villiers.

This did not happen. By the time James died in 1625 his eldest son, Henry Frederick, was long in his own grave. James's surviving daughter, Elizabeth, variously known as the Queen of Hearts and the Winter Queen, was, in fact, no longer Queen of Bohemia or the Electress Palatine, but the wife of a minor German nobleman who ruled no territory whatsoever. In 1625 the heir to the Stuart throne was a small, shy, awkward young man with a speech impediment. Though twenty-four years old, Charles Stuart was unmarried – unusual for his age and station in life – and totally dependent for counsel and support on George Villiers, the architect of his father's sad end. In retrospect, Henry, Elizabeth and Charles represented the great hope of the Stuart dynasty, its recasting as the House of Hanover in the eighteenth century and the worst tragedy that can befall a ruling house, the execution of a monarch by his subjects. Thus, the three surviving children of James and Anne affected the Stuart dynasty in ways that could not have been imagined at the beginning of the reign of their father in 1603. Perhaps the greatest irony of the history of the Stuart dynasty is that Henry Frederick, had he lived, is likely to have become a strong and great king.

Henry Frederick Stuart was born to James and Anne at Stirling Castle in Scotland in 1594 and was soon created Duke of Rothesay and Prince of Scotland. Much to the distress of his mother, Queen Anne, the infant Henry was sent to the household of the Earl of Mar to be raised, as his father had been. Anne struggled during the early years of Henry's childhood to remain close to him, to make sure that he knew that she was his mother. Henry was an active and intelligent boy and, unlike his father, there is no record of delay in his walking or other physical development. By the age of six, the management of his care was transferred to a principal tutor, Adam Newton, who treated him with considerable kindness. Henry enjoyed sports and was able to run and participate in the ordinary games of boys, and there is good reason to believe that he had a pleasant and secure childhood.

In 1599, in Edinburgh, James I published his famous book on kingship, *Basilikon Doron*, which contains the musings of a proud father making every effort to prepare his eldest son for the monarchy. In later editions this book was titled, *Basilikon Doron, or, King James's Instructions To His Dearest Sonne, Henry The Prince*. The book combines theology, statecraft, and homely advice about personal conduct, even including James's opinion about suitable sports and exercise for Henry when at his leisure, a sample of which follows.

> But from this count I debarre al rough and violent exercises, as the football; meeter for laming, then making able the users thereof: as likewise such tumbling trickes as onely serve for Comedians and Balladines, to winne their bread with. But the exercises that I would have you to use (although but moderatelie, not making a craft of them) are running, leaping, wrastling, fencing, dauncing, and playing at the caitch or tennife, archerie, palle maille, and such like other faire and pleasant field games . . . I cannot omit heere the hunting, namely with running hounds; which is the most honourable and noblest sort thereof . . .[2]

Nothing in James's book on kingship was left out, he covered diet, the moderate use of alcohol, caution in dealing with the Puritans, avoidance of war and foreign entanglements, living the Christian life, behaving like a monarch, and many large and small details about the obligations of a monarch.

In 1596, when Henry was two years old, his sister Elizabeth was born. As they were so near in age, they developed a warm relationship and formed a significant bond, which lasted throughout Henry's short life. For a royal family this was almost certainly rather unusual, because the custom was for royal siblings to be brought up apart. Prince Charles (later Charles I) illustrates this point rather well because although he was born when Henry was merely six years old, he was raised apart from his elder brother and sister and failed to develop a warm relationship with either sibling. He held his older brother in awe, yearning for Henry to recognize and pay attention to him. This early natural support mechanism for Henry, and a closeness to his sister, would have nurtured a greater degree of humanity and provided him with an important education in matters of emotional responsibility. This responsibility was something that many monarchs over the years had lacked, much to their detriment.

In 1603, when the Stuarts moved to London for James to take the throne of England, Henry and Elizabeth were granted their own separate residence, which came with a large number of servants and retainers to attend them both. At an early age, they were treated with a significant degree of respect and admiration – something that their father had lacked as a child – and they continued their close bond as brother and sister. This would almost certainly have given them particularly regal airs and graces and might perhaps have boosted their sense of self-worth. As a mark of respect for Henry's newly increased status as the first heir to the thrones of both Scotland and England, James invested his young son with the Order of the Garter shortly after they were settled in London, an event which would most probably have found favour with the family's new English subjects.

There is every indication that Henry took his new duties and royal obligations seriously. In doing so, he earned the respect of the members of his father's court, which would have stood him in good stead were he to have become a monarch himself. James enrolled Henry at Magdelen College when he was ten and, by all accounts, he was more than capable of holding his own in argument and debate. In fact, everything about Henry, in terms of personality and accomplishments, points to the fact that he was the ideal heir to the thrones of Scotland and England. It is scarcely surprising, therefore, that in June 1610 he was made Prince of Wales and took up residence at St James's Palace with his own personal court in attendance. Although he was happy to be accorded this independence and respect, he was sad to leave the home he had shared with Elizabeth.

By the time he reached the age of eighteen, Henry was physically mature, well educated, independent of thought and ready to assume significant governmental responsibility. Indeed, James had good reason to be jealous of his accomplished son, perhaps even to the extent of feeling threatened by him. The most widely reported public disagreement between the two concerned the unorthodox Sir Walter Raleigh, confined to the Tower by James in 1603 because of his radical views and his hatred of Spain. Henry was openly critical of his father's imprisonment of Raleigh and considered the famous traveller a friend. While Raleigh's motivation for befriending a prince more than forty years his junior may not have been without selfish motives, nonetheless he did count Henry as a real friend and even dedicated several of his many writings to him. Beyond this, and in quite another direction, it has been suggested that Henry was beginning to express sympathies for the Puritan cause, something that annoyed his father considerably.

Until the autumn of 1612 Henry enjoyed excellent health. He had frequent nosebleeds throughout his young life but these were thought by his physicians to be cleansing rather than a sign of disease. In the summer of 1612, the hottest in the recent memory of that time, Henry spent his days playing tennis and hunting, and enjoyed sumptuous meals of raw oysters and fresh fruit in the evenings. After a full meal he would swim in the Thames for an hour or two. In every sense Henry resembled his famous forebear, Henry VIII; he was muscular, athletic, sure of himself and admired by the English people. He was the very epitome of the prince who would one day be a strong king and respected ruler.

On 10 October 1612 Henry began having fevers but these were not continual and he remained physically active, indeed, he is described as making every effort to overcome the fevers by indulging in games and sports. On 12 October he was given a clyster (enema) which was followed by twenty-five stools. By all accounts he felt better, although he had some weariness and headache. Over the next two weeks, however, Henry slept poorly. More worryingly, he continued to have fevers, looked pale and wan, and had fever blisters on his lips. He got up from his bed on 25 October and played tennis, only to become much worse. Nevertheless, he dined with James that evening, although he was later noted to have the sharp pinched facies (first described by Hippocrates) denoting very serious illness. His pulse was fast, he had a fever, his face was red, his belly swollen and tense, and he was very thirsty.

On 26 October Henry tried once again to be physically active. He even played with his younger brother, Charles, for a while, but he was quite weak and tired quickly. Henry spent a restless night and, for the first time, was noted to have rapid, irregular breathing and twitching movements of his extremities. The next day his fever was worse. There was rumbling in his abdomen with notable swelling and increasing discomfort, and he was purged with senna and rhubarb. Henry's fever seemed to wax and wane, but by 29 October it was nearly continuous. On 30 October he was purged again and suffered a nosebleed, his fever seemed to worsen at night and sweating was described. On 31 October he became delirious and 8 oz of blood were taken from him by phlebotomy on the following day. On 2 November he was alternatively somnolent and delirious and he was constantly confused, boasting and shouting. His attendants had difficulty keeping him in bed, he wanted to be up and to leave his sickroom. The following day he was purged yet again and grape skins and grape stones were noted in his stool.

By 4 November the prince was picking at his bedclothes and singing in his sleep, his twitching movements were noted to be increasing, and by the following day he was having violent convulsive movements. Hard masses were noted in his stool, thought by de Mayerne to presage death in one with his sort of illness. At one point he jumped out of bed and, babbling incoherently, moved his bowels several times spontaneously as he stumbled about his room. Sir Walter Raleigh was allowed by James to send a special medicine from the Tower, perhaps a measure of the desperation of the situation. On 6 November, his last day of life, Henry was delirious and his convulsive movements had ceased. He was clammy, cold, and sweaty until finally, his pulse weakened and he died quietly.

There was concern in some quarters that Henry had been poisoned, and the prolonged course of the illness and the prominent gastrointestinal symptoms and signs lent credence to this fear. A post-mortem examination was ordered and performed, with eminent physicians and political figures in attendance. No evidence of poisoning was found and the cause of death was ascribed to 'a fever', as specific as the physicians of that time could be with the information they had at hand from the course of his illness and the post-mortem findings. The grief of the English and Scottish people was profound. James and Anne were deeply and lastingly affected by Henry's untimely death, as was Elizabeth, his beloved sister. Charles believed, to the end of his life, that Henry had been poisoned, though few others shared his conviction.

In his last words on his deathbed, Henry asked only for his sister, Elizabeth, but she was not allowed to see Henry during the week before his death. By this time, Elizabeth had her own court and they lived apart, although prior to Henry's illness they saw each other frequently and exchanged letters on a regular basis. While Elizabeth cared for her younger brother, Charles, she was never as close to him as she had been to Henry. In fact, once she left England for the continent, memories of her life with her elder brother, Henry, would slip into the past and her relationship with her younger brother would also dim, for she would never see Charles again.

The year 1612 was a particularly difficult time for Elizabeth, she was just sixteen years of age and had already been thrust into the adult world. Her father had made an alliance with the leaders of the Protestant Union of Germany in March of that year and by May a marriage had been arranged between Elizabeth and Frederick V. Also just sixteen, Frederick was already the Elector Palatine and head of the union of Protestant princes. Elizabeth lost her favourite brother in death and would lose her home in England, all within less than a year. However, Elizabeth and Frederick had actually fallen in love before Henry's illness, and Frederick was most attentive and supportive to her. The wedding was delayed by Henry's death and it was not until February 1613 that the two were married in a splendid ceremony in London. They left for Heidelberg, their royal home, in June 1613, and would live there for five years. Frederick was to be an important Protestant figure in the Thirty Years' War and Elizabeth was his dedicated royal helpmate. With neither able to speak the other's language, they spoke French, and every source one reads makes clear that they loved and were true to each other. Although very young, they were principal figures in the politics of northern Europe.

Elizabeth had had a sound Protestant upbringing with Lord and Lady Harington at Combe Abbey in Rutland, and was carefully educated as well as being a skilled horsewoman. She enjoyed good health throughout her life, and she is always described as a lively and interesting person. Before her betrothal to Frederick V Elizabeth was considered an ideal match for Gustavus Adolphus of Sweden. But her Danish mother, and the Danish interests at the English court, kept this Swedish initiative from coming even close to fruition. In England and Scotland, Elizabeth and, ultimately, her offspring were always in the public mind as possible occupants of the Stuart throne, because Charles was regarded as puny, frail, and sickly.

With a home established in Heidelberg, Elizabeth got down to the work at which she excelled, producing children.

Frederick Henry was the first, born in January 1614, and he was followed in time by twelve more. Until her brother Charles had his first child in 1630, Elizabeth remained second in line to the English throne and her son, Frederick Henry, was third, followed by his siblings. Elizabeth and Frederick did not think often of England, their life on the continent was initially pleasant and relatively serene. In 1617 they had a second son, Charles Louis, and in 1618 their first daughter, Elizabeth, was born. However, serenity vanished after they moved to Prague to become the King and Queen of Bohemia in 1619. At the Battle of White Mountain in November 1620, Protestant forces were routed by the Catholics, and Frederick and Elizabeth were forced to flee to Holland with their growing family. In the process they lost everything, even Frederick's hereditary landholdings. Frederick and Elizabeth are remembered as the Winter King and Queen because they ruled Bohemia for just one winter. Neither would ever occupy a throne again. Frederick died in 1632, probably preventing Elizabeth from attaining the honour of being the most fertile woman in the Stuart family. They were both thirty-six years old at the time of his death. Elizabeth did not remarry and after her husband's death her fortunes were tied more to events in England than to those on the continent, thanks to the hapless Charles.

The death of Henry in 1612 and Elizabeth's departure for Heidelberg in 1613 left the twelve-year-old Charles as the immediate Stuart heir to the thrones of England and Scotland, his right to rule uncontested. Unfortunately, he was ill prepared to assume this role. Physically he was spindly and small for his age, and, even for a child, he was socially immature. Charles lacked the commanding presence of Henry and to compound all of this, he had a prominent speech impediment. His speech problem has always been assumed to have been stuttering but, in fact, its exact nature is not known.

Charles was the only representative of the Stuart family at his brother's funeral; his parents and Elizabeth did not attend, for reasons that are not at all clear. A sorrier entry to public life cannot be imagined than this sad little boy following the bier of his brother, the Prince of Wales.

Nearly all the images of Charles's childhood are negative and even his beginnings in life were unpromising. Born on 19 November 1600, he was weak and sickly, and lived every minute of his young life in the very large shadow of Henry. A pertinent description of Charles's inauspicious youth is found in Jacob Abbott's biography of the monarch, published in 1850.

Young Charles was very weak and feeble in his infancy. It was feared that he would not live many hours. The rite of baptism was immediately performed. . . . It was a long time before he could walk, on account of some malformation of his limbs. He learned to talk, too, very late and very slowly. Besides the general feebleness of his constitution, which kept him back in all of these things, there was an impediment in his speech, which affected him very much in childhood, and which in fact, never entirely disappeared.[3]

The memoirs of Alexander Seton, Earl of Dunfermline and President of the Court of Sessions for the period of 1593 to 1605, confirm this description. Seton's memoirs are important because he was in a position to know about Charles first hand and probably observed him personally. He wrote: 'In his early years, Prince Charles showed considerable feebleness in his lower extremities; but in the flux of time, and when he began to look man in the face, those tender limbs began so to consolidate and knit together.'[4]

When James I left Scotland for London in 1603, the young Charles remained behind in Scotland, eventually to be cared for by Sir Robert and Lady Carey. Carey, a respected political figure, was the messenger who rode from London to Edinburgh to take the news of the death of Elizabeth I to James in Scotland. His memoirs are most revealing about the early development of the prince and, while the following description of the young Charles might be viewed as somewhat self-serving, nevertheless it is detailed and probably reasonably accurate.

> The Duke was past four years old when he was first delivered to my wife; he was not able to go, nor scant stand alone, he was so weak in his joints, and especially his ankles, insomuch as many feared they were out of joint. Yet God so blessed him, both with health and strength, that he proved daily stronger and stronger. Many a battle my wife had with the King, but she still prevailed. The King was desirous that the string under his tongue should be cut, for he was so long beginning to speak as he thought would never have spoke . . . but my wife protested so much against them both, as she got the victory, and the King was fain to yield. My wife had charge of him from a little past four, till he was almost eleven year old; in all which time he daily grew more and more in health and strength both of body and mind, to the amazement of many that knew his weakness when she first took charge of him.[5]

There is no disagreement among contemporary observers that Charles suffered from leg weakness and was late in learning to speak. However, things may not have been quite as grim at the outset of the guardianship as Robert Carey described them. Dr Henry Atkins examined the young prince and reported to Lord Robert Cecil, James's secretary at that time, on 3 July 1604: 'He [Charles] is recovering and is beginning to walk alone, which he never did before.'[6] Charles was three-and-a-half years old at that time and not yet in the care of Lady Carey. As reported by a scholar of Stuart times, David Bergeron, Atkins also wrote to the queen: 'His highness now walketh many times a day all over the length of the great Chamber at Dumfermeline like a gallant soldier all alone. He often talketh of going to

London and desireth to see his gracious Queen mother.'[7] Timing apart, Charles was very delayed in walking and his early childhood development was slow.

The small, weak boy with the speech impediment often endured ill-treatment within his family. His brother Henry did not hold him in high regard and one can imagine that he teased Charles, as older brothers are wont to do. A further strain was placed on the filial relationship when James used Charles as blackmail leverage against the arrogant Henry. On one occasion, after lecturing Henry for idleness, James told him that he might leave the crown to Charles if Henry's behaviour did not improve. It does not require a degree in child psychology to imagine Henry's revenge on Charles for such parental remarks. Yet, even as he absorbed the disdain and scorn of his older brother, Charles admired Henry and yearned for his notice and approval. On one occasion he wrote to Henry, 'Sweet sweet brother I will give everything I have to you, both horses and my books, and my pieces [guns], and my crossbow, or anything you would have. Good brother love me.'[8] The uneven relationship between the brothers persisted until Henry's untimely death. Indeed, in 1616, more than four years after Henry's death, when Charles was being invested Prince of Wales, the Bishop of Ely mistakenly prayed for Henry and not Charles. Henry's death, treated as a family and national crisis, could only have increased Charles's feelings of inadequacy in the shadow of his brother.

At sixteen years of age, Charles was said to have had the 'green sickness', an unusual kind of illness for an adolescent boy, even in the seventeenth century, because the term was used to describe wan and pale girls, sickly after menarche. Rarely was this term used to describe a pale or sallow teenage boy, and one must wonder at its use in Charles. Little else is known about Charles's health in his teenage years. He grew slowly in every way but did, by about the beginning of his twenties, finally acquire the physical stature of a man. From measurements taken of his armour it can be deduced that he ultimately attained an adult height of about 5 feet 4 inches (162 centimetres), surely short for a grown man even in his time.

On the death of his elder brother, Charles became the heir to the thrones of England and Scotland and like it or not, his father and the government had to prepare him to occupy those two thrones. While, ultimately, Charles may have left some of his early physical disabilities behind him, he was, throughout adolescence, certainly not in possession of the social or intellectual capacity of his age group. In George Villiers, his father's paramour, who was just two years older than Henry and eight years older than Charles, he ultimately found a surrogate older brother. In the matter of Charles's sexual development, Villiers observed that Charles was very slow to show a romantic interest in the female sex. The contrast between Charles and Villiers could not be greater and it was totally different from the relationship between James and Villiers. David Bergeron has analysed the relationship of Charles and Villiers. He observes: 'Given the nature of court life, Charles's virtuous sexual behavior appeared as an anomaly. . . . Charles rightly felt displaced or supplanted by Buckingham. Whatever hatred he may have felt toward Buckingham transformed into a dependent friendship, especially during the 1623 trip to Spain.'[9]

Villiers, by this time the Duke of Buckingham, used his influence with James in an attempt to arrange a marriage for Charles with the Spanish Infanta. It was also Villiers himself who took Charles to Spain incognito in 1623 to press the suit and negotiate a marriage agreement. In the one-sided negotiations with the Spanish court Villiers roiled the waters of politics and religion, giving much and getting nothing in return, failing even to get the Infanta as a bride for Charles. Villiers's hare-brained scheme gone wrong brought James and England's foreign policy into disrepute and ridicule. It increased even further the number of Villiers's enemies in England and bound the naive Charles to him awkwardly, but firmly. Thus, Villiers wormed his way into Charles's fraternal affections while, presumably, was at the same time actively involved in a homosexual relationship with James. This says much for the wiliness of Villiers and little for the sense and intelligence of James and Charles.

Though clueless about much of real life, on the death of his father in March 1625, Charles ascended to the thrones of England and Scotland knowing he needed a queen. He took to wife, finally, Henrietta Maria, daughter of King Henry IV of France, and the young woman who had been his father's second choice for him, after the Infanta of Spain. Henrietta Maria was just fifteen years of age at the time of their marriage and was a staunch Roman Catholic. Her faith led to suspicion among her new English subjects and proved to be a continuing liability both for her and Charles over the succeeding years. On the French side, the prime mover in arranging this marriage was Cardinal Richelieu who was eager to keep England separated from Protestants on the continent, now deeply involved in the Thirty Years War. The couple were married by proxy in Paris in May 1625 just after Charles came to the thrones of England and Scotland. Henrietta quickly saw through Villiers and, like most people living in England at that time, came to detest him. Villiers's death in 1628 did wonders for Henrietta's marriage to Charles. In fact, George Villiers was stabbed to death on 23 August 1628 by John Felton, a young military officer, who was hailed as a hero by most of the English people.

With the unexpected death of Villiers, Charles and Henrietta came to be a devoted couple and the king's dependence on his queen and her support for him never wavered. Henrietta Maria had eight children, her first, a son, was born in 1629 and lived for only a few hours. Subsequently, she gave birth to Charles in 1630, Mary in 1631, James in 1633, Elizabeth in 1636, Anne in 1637 (died 1640), Henry in 1640 and Henrietta (usually remembered as Minette) in 1644. She lived long enough to see her son, Charles, reign after the Restoration but died before his brother James came to the thrones of England and Scotland in 1685.

When Charles read his father's books about monarchy and how to be a king he apparently did not fully understand them. Charles grasped none of the nuance and subtlety he would need to be a successful ruler. Rather, as he grew into the role of king he seized firmly the concept that he was, by heredity, King of England, a right and responsibility conferred on him by God alone, and he was answerable only to God, not to his subjects and certainly not to Parliament. While the concept of the Divine Right of Kings was a commonly held view in his time, nonetheless the English constitution demanded that the King-in-Parliament was the governing institution for the nation. James had four parliaments and though his relations with them were never smooth, he learned to live with them. Charles had five parliaments and his developing delusion that he could rule England without Parliament led to his execution. The Stuart historian John Kenyon contrasts the flexibility of James and the delusion of Charles succinctly: 'He [Charles] was not as vocal as his father [James] about the Divine Right of Kings, but he believed in it more firmly, and was not prepared to compromise as James had been. James's beliefs, in fact, were largely a reaction to Scots conditions, and . . . he was willing to qualify them. Charles took them over unaltered as a blueprint for the English constitution.'[10]

Charles's life as King of England, from 1625 until his execution in 1649, can be juxtaposed with his five parliaments, which are cogently summarized in the *Historical Dictionary of Stuart England*.[11] Unlike his childhood, his physical health throughout this time was excellent. However, his mental health deteriorated slowly and steadily as he became lost, deeper and deeper, in the delusion that he was the sole government of England, needing no help from Parliament.

The Parliament of 1625 sat during the summer months and saw Charles foolishly expending his political capital in trying to get them to support military adventures on the continent, something James would have avoided at all costs. His adviser, Villiers, roiled the waters of government in both foreign and domestic spheres and added to his increasing list of enemies. Charles received revenues from Parliament but much less than he had asked for and less than his father had received from the Parliament of 1624.

The Parliament of 1626 met in the spring and by now the misguided foreign policy of Villiers had involved England in naval wars with both Spain and France. Parliament expended endless days attempting to impeach Villiers for a long list of charges, including the poisoning of James I. Charles lost what little control of events he had and failed to get any revenue at all from Parliament, having then to raise money by forced loans.

The Parliament of 1628–9 met in the spring of the first year and the winter of the second and was convened because Charles needed a great deal of money. He, with help from Villiers, had got his country into a state of real war both with Spain and with France, as well as participating in the seemingly endless warring in the Germanic states. The Petition of Right, the landmark document that gave Parliament the upper hand over the king in respect to taxation, money management and some military matters, was passed unanimously by both the Commons and the Lords with Charles using every means at his disposal to stop it. In June 1628 Charles accepted the will of Parliament and agreed to the provisions of the Petition of Right. It was a bitter pill for him to swallow and, with the arrogance of a man who believed only in himself, in the succeeding months he continued to raise money by the very means Parliament had closed to him in the Petition, against the law of his own kingdom, a law to which he had agreed. The final session of this parliament in 1629 accomplished little, Charles had no leverage whatsoever, no bills were passed and no money was voted for him.

In less than five years Charles managed to lose wars with three European powers, lose powerful royal prerogatives vis-à-vis Parliament, ignore the provisions of acts he had approved and isolate himself from the respect and regard of many of his subjects, all because of his support of George Villiers, Duke of Buckingham. To compound his problems, when Villiers was assassinated in 1628 Charles lost his single pillar of support. By mid-1629 he had abandoned all efforts to deal with Parliament and entered the 11-year period during which he tried to rule without it. His new adviser was his wife, Henrietta Maria, with whom he had a sort of reconciliation after the death of Villiers. Henrietta Maria stood by Charles without flinching to the end of his life, although the quality of her advice was only marginally better than that which he had received from Villiers. Though Henrietta Maria was respected by Parliament and the people as the Queen of England, nonetheless both became increasingly concerned about the propriety of Charles being advised by a staunch Roman Catholic French princess.

Now together in politics, as well as in marriage and family, Charles and Henrietta Maria began fishing in the deep and murky waters of religion. Their meddling led to the imposition of the arch-conservative policies of Bishop William Laud, who set Anglican practice as the only religious expression allowed. The result was unrest in Ireland, stirred up by the tyranny of Thomas Wentworth, Earl of Strafford, who essentially took Laud's doctrine to the Catholic Irish, and finally the riots in Scotland of 1637 over the imposition of the Book of Common Prayer on the national Church there. The Bishops' Wars of 1639 and 1640 brought Charles's long and disastrous experiment with personal rule to an end. He had to call Parliament into session to beg for money to fight the Scots, the subjects of his other kingdom who then invaded England in 1640, routed Charles's army, and occupied Northumberland and Durham, all to preserve their unique religious identity.

The first parliament of 1640, the Short Parliament, met from 17 April until Charles dissolved it on 5 May. In retrospect, it was a rehearsal for the Civil Wars of the 1640s with Charles having little control over the course of events and the members belabouring him for all the perceived injustices of the previous decade. It raised the spectre of Arminianism (essentially the policy of promoting episcopacy and frowning upon predestination) and the threat of Roman Catholic influence, a fear made quite vivid by Henrietta Maria's devout adherence to her faith. Not surprisingly, Charles received no money from this parliament.

The other parliament of 1640, the Long Parliament, lasted in one form or another until 1660 and was Charles's last. He was forced to call it because he had lost the Second Bishops' War and England now found itself with a Scottish army occupying its northern territories. This parliament gutted the crown of many of its prerogatives, went to war against King Charles and finally took his life in January 1649.

The military struggle between Parliament and the Royalist supporters of Charles began at Edgehill in October 1642 with no clear victory or advantage for either side. Charles actually became a general of some ability, although he had only on-the-job training. He focused solely on maintaining his right to rule England and had little trouble keeping his military priorities straight, doing well in the field until 1645. At this point Parliament put the command of its forces into the hands of proven generals Sir Thomas Fairfax and Oliver Cromwell, who led the New Model Army to a stunning victory at Naseby in June 1645. With his cause lost and his loyal supporters wisely looking for a way out, Charles seized his belief in a special relationship between himself and God with an ever stronger grip and threw caution to the winds in a foolhardy attempt to survive on his own terms. By June 1646, Charles's military headquarters at Oxford had surrendered and shortly he was in the hands of the Scots. They finally gave up trying to reach an accommodation with their unpredictable king and returned him to England where he was imprisoned until the end of his life.

During the final two-and-a-half years of his life, Charles lived out his delusion by pitting one of his kingdoms against the other. Finally even his remaining supporters in Scotland were defeated at Preston in August 1648 and for the first time he was without any military support whatsoever. Even at this point Charles could have made a deal with Parliament and survived as King of England, but he was unable to let go of his delusion and, in spite of opportunities for accommodation and even clearer opportunities to escape to France, he finally found himself alone with his life held in the balance by Parliament. While the legality of his trial and sentencing by a special parliamentary court, the High Court of Justice, is questionable, his execution on 30 January 1649, at the instigation of the Rump Parliament, put a definite end to Charles and his reign. His final remarks from the scaffold in Whitehall, before the headsman's axe ended his life, make it clear that his delusion persisted until his last breath. 'For the people, and truly I desire their liberty and freedom as much as anybody whatsoever; but I must tell you that their liberty and freedom consists in having of government those laws by which their life and their goods may be most their own. It is not having share in government, sirs; that is nothing pertaining to them.'[12]

The stories and legends associated with Charles's trial and execution are rich and interesting. A consistent observation is that he was so confident of his position, so dignified, and so sure of himself during his trial that he spoke clearly without any impediment of his speech. With regard to his burial, the following eyewitness account describes a very limited post-mortem examination of his abdomen and perhaps his thorax.

POST-MORTEM EXAMINATION OF CHARLES I

Charles's execution was accomplished in an efficient manner. He cooperated fully and prior preparations meant that his body was quickly and carefully placed in a casket and his remains removed from the platform and the sight of the crowd. As is recorded by a contemporary source:

> His Head and Trunk was instantly put into a Coffin covered with black Velvet, and conveyed into the Lodgings at Whitehall.

There it was imbowelled by Chirurgions of their own [the abdomen opened by incision], but a Physitian privately thrusting himself into the dissection of the body, relates, that Nature had designed him above the most of Mortal men for a long life. . . .

About a fortnight after some of the King's Friends the greatest of Nobility and Honour, the Duke of Lenox, Marquess of Hartford, the Earl of Southampton, and the Bishop of London begged the body to bury it, which they conducted to Windsor Chappel Royal, and interred it there in the Vault of King Henry the eighth: having only this Inscription upon the Coffin, Charls King of England.[13]

At forty-eight years of age, Charles was in the prime of his life and a physically sound and healthy man. The observations of the physicians attending the preparation of his body for burial would suggest that they saw no evidence of abnormality or disease. In view of his good physical health as an adult it is likely that Charles would have lived a long life had Parliament not ended it.

To understand exactly how the Stuarts had come to such a bad end by the year 1649 it is enlightening to examine the medical particulars of the lives of Henry and Charles that account for their eclipse through disease and disability. It is then useful to trace the Stuart lineage onward from their sister, Elizabeth, to see how Stuart descendants filled the vacant British throne in 1714 on the death of the last Stuart, Anne, through the German Hanover family. This analysis begins with another post-mortem examination, that of the eldest Stuart of this generation, Prince Henry, performed in the presence of Theodore de Mayerne in 1612.

POST-MORTEM EXAMINATION OF PRINCE HENRY

Late in the afternoon of 7 November 1612 a careful post-mortem examination of the body of Prince Henry Frederick was conducted by the surgeons of King James. Many members of the court were also present. It is possible that Frederick V, the Elector Palatine and fiancé of Elizabeth, Henry's sister, may also have been present – reports differ on this matter. Norman Moore's translation from the Latin report of de Mayerne reads as follows:

Skin. Pale: no marks of injury. Some patches of redness about the loins, hips, and back of thighs, from his long lying on his back.

Abdomen. Distended; subsiding on a small puncture being made at the umbilicus.

Stomach. Healthy; quite natural.

Intestines. Distended with air, otherwise not abnormal.

Liver. Paler than natural; on its anterior and upper surface marked with dots, and on its inferior surface with black lines.

Gall bladder. Empty.

Spleen. Of a dark colour above and below; much distended with dark blood.

Kidneys. Natural.

Diaphragm. Below the pericardium (which contained less fluid than natural) stained with black.

Lungs. Very dark in colour, and here and there spotted with black. Full of dark blood and blood-stained serum, which flowed out on section.

Heart. Natural.

Brain. The posterior cerebral sinuses distended with blood.

> The. Mayerne, *Reg. Medicus Primarius*
> Hammon, *Medicus Ordinarius Principis*
> Buttler
> Atkins, *Medicus Regius*
> Gifford, ⎫
> Palmer, ⎬ *Medici Londinenses*
>   ⎭

In 1881, the English physician Norman Moore published an account of his examination of the primary source materials describing the final illness of Prince Henry and his autopsy. Moore was cast from the mould of the great seventeenth-century physicians and spent his entire career associated with St Bartholomew's Hospital in London. In addition to his active clinical life, Moore had a fondness for medical puzzles and for writing, and his historical analysis of the illness and death of Henry Frederick Stuart is a classic gem of medical detective work.[14] His source materials were the notes taken by Theodore de Mayerne, who attended Henry in his final illness, the autopsy report and several non-medical writings of the seventeenth century speculating about the cause of Henry's death.

Henry's physicians were correct, he died of a fever, which at that time vaguely implied infection. Neither smallpox nor plague was a diagnostic consideration, and when the facts about his terminal illness and autopsy are viewed from a modern perspective, an exact diagnosis can be made if one uses the post-mortem examination findings to focus the clinical observations of his physicians. Simply put, this healthy young man quite by chance contracted an infectious disease from which, even without specific treatment, he might well have recovered completely. Unfortunately for the Stuarts and for England, this acute illness took his life.

Moore notes, correctly, that many of the autopsy changes, such as the staining of the liver, spleen, and diaphragm, the gas in the intestine and the fullness of the veins in back of the brain, are of post-mortem origin and, thus, not of importance in determining the cause of Henry's illness and death. The engorgement of the lungs with blood was almost certainly a non-specific change associated with dying. The autopsy report is particularly interesting for what it excludes in the way of acute infectious diseases, including pneumonia, tuberculosis, and typhus, a disease often confused with typhoid fever but caused by a different bacterial form. There was no pus or consolidation in the lung, nor any cavities or scarring, essentially ruling out pneumonia and tuberculosis. Typhus, an epidemic disease caused by a small altered bacterial form called a rickettsia, probably did not cross Moore's mind because there were no prominent skin lesions described before death or seen at autopsy. Moore cites the distinctively enlarged spleen and the dry pericardium (sac around the heart) as typical of typhoid fever, although a significant manifestation of typhoid not found at autopsy is ulcers in the bowel. Moore accounts for this by presuming that the surgeons did not open the bowel. This is a questionable assumption because there was concern in some quarters that Henry had been poisoned and the bowel certainly would have been opened and its contents examined minutely to rule this out. The intestinal ulcers of typhoid fever can be shallow, however, and, in a dim light, might have been overlooked by the physicians and surgeons attending the autopsy. Moreover, although Moore could not have known this, in the twentieth century it was discovered that some patients with typhoid fever do not have bowel ulcers.

The four-week duration of the illness and the prominent abdominal symptoms and signs, diarrhoea followed by a swollen and tense abdomen, are typical of typhoid fever. So is the large spleen, although it is difficult to explain the pale liver. There are skin lesions with typhoid, the so-called rose spots, but they occur early in the course of this illness and, in any case, are evanescent and often overlooked. The light in Henry's sick room was probably not very good and a faint skin rash on his upper trunk, its typical location, might easily have come and gone and been missed by his physicians altogether.

Given the clinical picture, other possible diagnoses that must be considered are infectious mononucleosis (glandular fever), brucellosis, leptospirosis and malaria. Death from mononucleosis is very rare and is caused by central nervous system changes or rupture of the spleen. The course of Henry's illness was too short and the disease too severe for brucellosis, the length of his illness and lack of jaundice largely rule out leptospirosis, and the form of malaria that kills, *Plasmodium falciparum*, did not occur in England in the seventeenth century. So, by process of elimination, the diagnosis must be typhoid fever – Norman Moore was correct.

Typhoid fever is now very rare in the western world and few of the world's practising physicians have ever seen a case. It remains a threat to those living in much of Africa, particularly patients with AIDS. The causative bacteria, *Salmonella typhi*, is found in water and food contaminated by sewage. Although it can attack persons of any age, the typical patient is a young male, and autumn is the season for this disease and its epidemics. Some humans become chronic carriers, the bacteria may live in their gall bladders and not cause disease but is released intermittently in their stools. Therefore, all sewage must be presumed to harbour this organism. It was not until the late eighteenth century that typhoid fever was appreciated as a disease separate from other similar fevers that could cause death and not until 1829 that the French finally characterized and named it. The typhoid bacillus itself was first identified by Georg Gaffky and associated with the disease in 1884, interestingly, three years after Norman Moore published his paper on Henry and typhoid fever.

The best speculation is that Henry was infected with the typhoid bacillus from eating raw oysters late in the summer. Oysters grow best in easily polluted tidal areas and when eaten raw, as opposed to cooked, they pose a threat to infection from the so-called enteric diseases, such as typhoid fever and infectious hepatitis. Swimming in the River Thames might also have been the source of the infection as the Thames was heavily polluted with sewage in the seventeenth century. Perforation of the intestine is often the immediate cause of death with typhoid fever, but this was not found in Henry's autopsy, as the bowel was described as distended with air. It is important to note that even as sick as Henry was, he should have recovered. Typhoid has always been the scourge of armies and war but the death rate for young men with typhoid fever in military campaigns conducted before the advent of antibiotics was in the range of just 10 to 20 per cent.

Henry's untimely death left the future of the Stuart dynasty in the hands of his younger brother, Charles, Duke of York. Charles was not yet twelve years old at the time of Henry's death and he was not made Prince of Wales until he was nearly sixteen. Charles's leg weakness and early inability to walk mirrored his father's childhood problems. It is interesting that previous writers, of the seventeenth century and more recently, have not noted the similarity of father and son in this matter, the single exception being Norman Chevers, who mentioned this in passing in his book on the death of Charles II.[15] It is probable that Charles I suffered from the same congenital neuromuscular disorder as his father, in a milder form.

Charles's delay in learning to speak is disturbing and certainly was not due to a band limiting the movement of his tongue as James imagined. Delayed speech in infants and children usually connotes slowed development of higher functions of the central nervous system. Speech development and intelligence are closely correlated in children and so Charles appears to have been both physically and mentally compromised in childhood, with some of these problems carried over into his adult life. Charles's speech impediment has usually been described as stuttering, although this is not known with certainty. The impediment was sufficiently severe that, when king, Charles often had his speeches read aloud by others, and he is remembered as a man of few words. Speech impediments are now often called dysfluency, and during both childhood and adult life they may be recognized as a disability by schools and employers.[16]

As a teenager Charles was pale and thin, and was described as having the green sickness. This is not the sort of descriptor one would want for a teenage son then or now. Another name for this complaint is chlorosis, and it has been known in one form or another since ancient times. The term disappeared from the medical literature in the mid-twentieth century and it is conceded to represent mild to moderate iron deficiency anaemia in young women as the result of excessive menstrual bleeding. It is interesting that Charles should have been described as having a disease common to well-bred teenage girls. Records of Charles's childhood diet show that meat, fish, and fowl were consumed in generous portions and so the possibility of poor nutrition and the attendant dietary deficiency of iron would be extremely remote.[17] In spite of his frailty when young, Charles enjoyed good physical health as an adult. His mental health as an adult bears some examination, however.

There is great irony that George Villiers adroitly transferred his attention from the failing regime of James to the reign of Charles. One need imagine no sexual relationship between the slippery Villiers and the relatively asexual Charles. Charles was lonely and Villiers made himself available as a friend and surrogate older brother. Charles's need fed Villiers's greed. At great personal cost Charles defended Villiers to one and all right up to the time of his stabbing and death in 1628. Indeed, Charles was one of the few mourners Villiers had. A great measure of Charles's insecurity is that once he was deprived of the support and counsel of Villiers he immediately went to the one closest to him for help, Henrietta Maria, his wife. Between the two of them they brought on the Civil Wars that ended Charles's reign and thereby the first ending of the Stuart dynasty. Civil Wars, not Civil War must be used, because as Jane Ohlmeyer and John Kenyon make clear, there were independent conflicts going on in England, Scotland, and Ireland. There is also the possible division of a first Civil War of 1642 to 1646, a second of 1647 to 1648 and a third from 1649 to 1651.[18]

A national leader who starts a war and then loses it can only be reviled by his people. For the king who starts several civil wars and then loses all of them one can imagine no other resolution than his execution. It is reasonable to believe that there would have been no wars in the 1640s if Henry had been king. However one views this brief period in British history, Charles was a failure as a monarch and his weaknesses became Parliament's strengths, his rule directly degraded the Stuart dynasty. Charles's failure was not because he was delayed in speaking as a child and had a severe speech impediment as an adult, nor because he was not as intelligent as his father or his own children. The major cause of his failure must be sought elsewhere.

There were many reasons for Charles's political downfall and his eventual execution. Primarily he was crippled by an unerring knack for acting on bad advice that reinforced his misguided self-delusion. As the great Stuart historian John P. Kenyon stated, he took his father's doctrine in the *Basilikon Doron* literally and to heart and had immense belief in the supreme nature of kingship. He believed himself – and his position – akin to a god. Charles is scarcely a credit to the cause of kingship, although he was probably basically a good man. He is said to have told Bishop Laud, just before he became king, 'I cannot defend a bad, nor yield a good cause'. These are worthy aspirations but he experienced great difficulty in distinguishing between bad and good causes. His crusade against the Scots for their refusal to accept episcopacy and the new English prayer book illustrates his poor judgement. In this he was essentially defending a bad rather than a good cause, at least as far as his subjects in Scotland were concerned. Charles's part in bringing on the Bishops' Wars is generally accepted as the beginning of the end of his reign. His 11-year stint of monarchical rule without Parliament led to the Short Parliament, which took away his money, and the Long Parliament, which took away his life.

Charles's transition from misunderstood saviour to martyr seems not to have been defined in time, perhaps it occurred over a period of many months or even several years. It is possible to argue that he suffered a disabling mental state, for he can be said to have been deluded. In fact delusion was the glass through which Charles saw himself, his country and its dependencies. He was not psychotic, in the sense that he did not hear voices or have hallucinations or function erratically in the sphere of his everyday life, rather he had a fixed delusion about indefeasible kingship that was unshaken by his life events and political realities he seemed not to comprehend. In 1646, when he had lost his armies and his principal kingdom, England, and was in his other kingdom, Scotland, Charles wrote to Queen Henrietta, 'because I am most confident that within a very small time I shall be recalled with much honour, and all my friends will see that I have neither a foolish nor peevish conscience, whereas otherwise I shall now (I know not how long) lye under (excuse me to say) an unjust slander'.[19] This is not a rational statement, particularly to his closest confidante who knew the reality of his situation well and who was stranded on the continent trying to raise money to save his personal government. The words attributed to him at his execution, biblical in form and substance, are often quoted: 'I go from a corruptible to an incorruptible Crown; where no disturbance can be, no disturbance in the World.'[20] Charles gave up not only his own crown and kingship but the Stuart dynasty as well; he had simply run it into the ground and for more than 11 years it was buried with him.

Charles suffered the delusion of indefeasible kingship and an attendant unique relationship with God to the exclusion of reason and common sense. Although his Tudor predecessors and other Stuart monarchs also believed in indefeasible monarchy, they did not allow this to interfere with governing their country. Charles allowed his delusion to dwarf his kingship. Although one might argue that modern psychiatric diagnoses, such as delusional disorder, are not relevant to figures distant in time, it is clear that modern definitions of common psychiatric diseases, such as schizophrenia and depression, can be accurately applied to persons over all time and in all cultures. In the *Diagnostic and Statistical Manual of Mental Disorders* (fourth edition), an international authority for diagnosis of psychiatric diseases, delusional disorder is characterized as a non-bizarre delusion which involves situations that can conceivably occur in real life. The sufferer is further described as normal in behaviour and appearance when the delusion is not being discussed or acted upon, and a grandiose sub-type is identified which may have religious content. This disorder is often chronic and usually occurs in middle or late life.[21] The fact that Charles's delusion was strengthened by his father's ideas as expressed in the *Basilikon Doron* does not diminish the validity of the diagnosis. Indeed, his biographer, Mark Kishlansky, has described him as having become mentally unstable by December 1648: 'But the King's behaviour had become more erratic since his failure to escape from Hurst Castle. His moods swung wildly between a belief that his enemies had no alternative but to restore him and a desire to become a martyr to his church and his monarchy. As late as Christmas [thirty-six days before his death] he rejected a secret overture that would have restored him to the throne.'[22]

Charles's wife and children were first among his mourners and each believed strongly that he had been martyred by subversive men who had captured the government of England through its parliament. Elizabeth grieved deeply for her brother Charles. As a widow she had a hard life, constantly in need of money, and had to rely on the somewhat grudging generosity of the distant English Parliament and her hosts for thirty years, the Dutch court. The loss of the monarchy in England had severe repercussions for the Stuart family, with effects that would persist into the next generation and beyond.

The restoration of the Stuart monarchy in 1660 finally made it possible for Elizabeth to return to England, after an absence of forty-eight years, to enjoy a brief period of public recognition and relief from financial burdens before her death two years later. The nature of her terminal illness is not entirely clear, she declined over a period of months, had a swollen abdomen which was also described as firm or hard, and coughed up blood a few days before she died, aged sixty-six. As far as can be determined her body was not opened and she is buried in Westminster Abbey, identified as the Queen of Bohemia. It is possible that she died of widespread lung or visceral cancer, although she could also have died of tuberculosis as she was described as having chest complaints for most of her latter years. The death of Elizabeth, only thirteen years after Charles's execution, left her children, the continental branch of the Stuart family, scattered and rootless. They were hinged neither to principalities in Britain nor the continent.

The children of Frederick and Elizabeth were an interesting lot and two of them, Rupert and Sophia, figured strongly in the fortunes and misfortunes of the English Stuart monarchs. Rupert learned soldiering on the continent and by the age of twenty-three was Commander of Horse for his uncle, Charles I. Rupert was quickly recognized as a brave and reckless cavalry officer, fighting on the Royalist side in almost all of the major battles of the Civil Wars. Charles made him Duke of Cumberland, although they subsequently had a falling out when Rupert surrendered Bristol to the Commonwealth forces and Charles had to sack him. Ever resilient, Rupert took service with France for a while and then reappeared on the English scene as admiral of the part of the English fleet still loyal to Charles. Immediately after the end of the Civil Wars, Rupert and his brother, Prince Maurice, lived as privateers, or pirates, preying on English shipping in the West Indies. He returned to England to serve with his cousin, James, Duke of York, when James became admiral of the English fleet and was conducting operations against the Dutch. Rupert took part in the formation of the Hudson Bay Company and lived the last years of his life exploring the boundaries of the physical sciences. He was credited with having a part in the development of the mezzotint, improving military explosives and inventing an alloy of copper and zinc still called Prince's metal. He died in 1682.

The second last of Elizabeth's brood and born in 1630, Sophia was a lively person who saw life with a particular clarity. She is reported to have said of her fertile mother that she didn't much like young children, preferring the company of dogs and monkeys. Already barely escaping being sent to a Protestant convent in Herford near Bielefeld, Sophia married the Protestant prince, Ernst Augustus at the advanced age of twenty-eight. Augustus became the Elector of Hanover in 1692. At the time of their marriage her husband was the Duke of Brunswick-Luneburg. A stolid Protestant he gave her seven children, six sons and one daughter, before dying in a senile state in 1698 and leaving her as the dowager Electress of Hanover. Even at seventy-four Sophia was described by her good friend Gottfried Wilhelm Leibniz, the great philosopher and mathematician, as being in excellent health, erect, handsome and given to walking 2 miles a day. Carrying Stuart genes and securely Protestant, Sophia was in the line of succession to the throne.

Sophia lived to be eighty-four. She died suddenly and quietly in her garden in 1714, less than two months before the death of Queen Anne. This left Sophia's 54-year-old son, George of Hanover, to journey west hurriedly in September 1714 and become George I, King of Great Britain and Ireland. Sophia remains important to the story of the Stuarts because after the Act of Settlement of 1701 she was first in line to the throne. She had many friends in England and her claim to the throne remained a consideration in English politics until her death, although she never once visited the country. Sophia's importance to England in 1714 was a direct result of her uncle's execution – the beheading of King Charles in 1649 proved the defining event in the Stuart family fortunes more than sixty years later.

Whatever the deficiencies of his rule, Charles I did provide three male heirs to the thrones he occupied. Two of them, Charles and James, later ruled England. The third, Henry, Duke of Gloucester, died at the age of twenty from smallpox. There was no question of inbreeding as Charles's parents were not even remotely related, and although he probably did inherit a mild form of neuromuscular disease from his father, it failed to limit him in adult life and does not appear to have been passed on to his children.

Charles I could not have been more different from his father: he was shorter in stature, shorter in intellect and definitely shorter in guile. Labelling Charles with the diagnosis of delusional disorder is risky and this diagnosis can only be raised to the level of possible, in the scheme of *certain*, *possible*, *doubtful*, and of *uncertain meaning*. However, it is a useful tool with which to view what must be seen as one of the most flawed of all English reigns.

As during James's mental and physical weakening at the end of his reign, Parliament gained in power as the English monarchy lost it. In this instance, with the beheading of Charles, Parliament actually severed the monarchy from the government of England altogether and assumed the ultimate political power. Charles regarded himself as a martyr. He knew that he was giving up not only his kingship but also the Stuart family claim to the throne. He presumed that, at his death, his sons Charles and James would not be offered the throne and the day before his execution, he specifically told his youngest son, Henry, Duke of Gloucester, that he was not to let anyone make him King of England. With Charles's death came the apparent end of the Stuart dynasty and the first and only end of monarchic rule in England.

FIVE

Charles II and Catherine

THE STUART FORTUNES RECOVERED

Once again his fever broke and sweat poured from the body of the tall muscular king. Four times during the last Monday of August 1679 Charles II had his servants bring him fresh night clothes and sheets to replace those he had soaked. Unaccustomed to illness, the 49-year-old monarch was a demanding patient, calling incessantly for wine and water, often asking for the urinal but producing little urine.

Charles had been having bouts of fever followed by sweating for a week, each episode worse than the last. He was bled by his doctors in the early hours of that Monday morning and thought himself improved, but shortly the fever came upon him again with a vengeance. On Wednesday, one court insider, the Earl of Ranelagh, wrote to another, Viscount Conway. In his letter he described Charles on Monday as being hot and restless, both sweating and purging until he was weak when trying to move from his sickbed. Of Charles's medical attendants Ranelagh wrote: 'Doctors here we have many and on Monday, when the King found himself so ill after his bleeding, he ordered to send for the two Needhams, Drs Middlethwaite and Lower. We have also here Dr Wetherly, Sir Alexander Fraizer and Dr Dickerson.'[1]

Mindful of the abrupt onset of this illness in their usually healthy and vigorous monarch, this assembled medical team discussed the diagnostic possibilities and, because Charles did not have chills preceding the bouts of fever and sweating, decided that he was suffering from a newly recognized form of fever and not an ague (malaria). Their combined experience told them that Charles's illness was serious and they were cautiously optimistic about his recovery.

However, rumours were flying about, London and England were on edge, the seemingly invincible Charles was proved mortal by his severe illness. Since the restoration of the Stuart monarchy in 1660 he had ruled for nearly twenty years in robust health, but without direct heir; his queen, Catherine, was childless. Suddenly, the possibility of Charles's death had to be addressed, and the assumption that he would be succeeded by his Roman Catholic younger brother, James, Duke of York, heightened the fear already resident in the hearts of most members of Parliament. Seeking to lessen their anxiety Charles had sent James to live in Flanders just five months before his illness began, expressly to keep him away from the gaze of Parliament.

In the several weeks following his worst day of illness, Charles's fits of fever and sweating finally fell into a pattern of occurring every other day, diminishing in intensity with each episode. This pattern of a tertian ague [fever every other day] caused his physicians to reformulate their diagnosis and become very optimistic about his complete recovery. Indeed, in the first week of September, the Earl of Sunderland, a member of the Privy Council, wrote to the anxious Lord Mayor of London that Charles was now up and about and able to visit Queen Catherine in her apartment in the palace. All seemed to be back to normal. Sunderland had barely put down his pen when Charles's younger brother James arrived at the palace.

This unwelcome turn of events was very likely to disturb the order just restored. Sunderland took up his pen again to add a few lines to his letter to the Lord Mayor, warning him of James's return.[2]

Charles II was born to a happy royal couple in 1630. He was the first in an unquestioned line of succession to the thrones of England and Scotland. Throughout his childhood Charles enjoyed robust good health and his physical development was normal. He walked early and without difficulty, escaping the mild neuromuscular disease that had afflicted both his father and grandfather. Quite naturally he enjoyed being the eldest in a large and close family of six children, spread in age over a period of fourteen years. Charles was his mother's favourite. When he was quite young she took him to Roman Catholic mass daily in her private chapel until political pressure demanded that she stop. He was seriously ill only once during his childhood, the nature of the illness that he suffered is not known. Charles broke his arm at the age of nine but in spite of a very active life, including participation in the Civil Wars and an invasion of England from Scotland, he suffered no other injuries. One could observe that, in respect to the misfortunes that visit most human beings, Charles led a charmed life. He was a survivor.

Legend has it that at the Battle of Edgehill in October 1642, the physician William Harvey saved the twelve-year-old Charles and his nine-year-old brother, James, from capture by the forces of Parliament. Harvey was entrusted with their care by Charles I, whom he had been attending as physician, and hid with them under a hedge during the first long day of the battle. He is said to have distracted the two boys by reading to them while the battle was raging.[3] Considering Harvey's presence at Edgehill at that time and the regard Charles I had for him, this story may well have some truth in it. If so, Harvey must be credited with saving two future kings of England from an army that might have done them harm, indeed they might well have been killed had they been captured. As few of Harvey's personal papers have survived it has never been possible to confirm this story.

The Civil Wars uprooted and scattered the Stuart family. The children moved frequently and their mother, Henrietta Maria, had difficulty finding money to support them. Charles was forced to mature and assume adult responsibilities far earlier in life than most princes of his time. He was active in military affairs from his early teens, essentially fighting beside his father, and by the age of fourteen he was in nominal command of the West Country forces of the Royalists. Charles last saw his father shortly before his fifteenth birthday. Not long after, with the war going badly, he left England for exile in France, where he worked with his mother in trying to keep Charles I on the throne. On several occasions, Charles, a handsome and physically mature teenager, was sent by his mother to visit wealthy female cousins who might have proved a source of money for the Stuart cause. Henrietta Maria kept Charles on permanent display, as it were, as a candidate for marriage in the various European courts.

In 1648 he moved to Holland where his sister, Mary, had become the wife of William, Prince of Orange. Charles endured smallpox that first year in Holland and recovered without incident. It was a depressing time for him, however, as slowly and steadily the few remaining resources of the Royalists disappeared. He made every effort in Holland and through his contacts in England to save his father's life, but he was not able to reach any sort of compromise with Parliament. He was in The Hague at the time of his father's execution. Within a few months he had been proclaimed king in the Channel Islands and a few scattered places in the west of England and Ireland. But he was king in name only.

Charles's circumstances were somewhat different in Scotland, however, for although he had little direct executive authority there, he was recognized by the Scots as their rightful ruler. Unfortunately for the Scots, Oliver Cromwell deemed Charles a threat to the stability of England and on that basis invaded Scotland and turned out the Scottish government. In October 1651, Charles led an army of about ten thousand men from Scotland south into England. Picking up less support than he had hoped for along the way, he was soundly defeated at Worcester by Cromwell's much larger army. In fact, he barely escaped with his life. Just twenty-one years of age, Charles was a brave commander who did not flinch in the face of battle, but his forces were no match for Cromwell's large, well-trained army. His escape from Worcester through Brighton and on to France in the autumn of 1651 gave him a reputation for bravery and resourcefulness that lasted the rest of his life.

Charles's flight through England is all the more remarkable because he was truly a fish out of water. Tall and swarthy, he did not look like an Englishman and he did not act like one either, having lived abroad for several years. In temperament and appearance he bore no resemblance to his father or Scottish grandfather; his mother, Henrietta Maria, had given him dark good looks through her Bourbon and de Medici lineage. It was not easy for Charles to escape notice as he moved south through the English countryside. In fact, he was occasionally recognized and it is a measure of the residual support for the Royalist cause in England that he was not handed over to the forces of Cromwell. The story of his hiding in an oak tree while soldiers hunted for him is part of that grand adventure.

Charles spent the years from 1651 until 1660 variously in France, Holland and the Germanic states, even living for two years in Cologne. He was sick only once during this time, and that was merely a spell of ague. Although his supporters hatched other plots to regain his throne for him, he wisely avoided taking risks, preferring to bide his time and wait in relatively penurious exile. Even as a king without a throne, he was highly regarded as a potential husband for princesses in the various courts of Europe. His aunt, Elizabeth, Queen of Bohemia, at one time harboured hopes that he would marry her daughter, Princess Sophia, his first cousin and also a grandchild of James I. Sophia would have made Charles an excellent wife, as she was ultimately proven quite fertile and was very lively in character. The fate of the Stuart dynasty might have been quite different had he married her. However, at the time Charles's mind remained firmly focused on his own future as he kept an eye on England and Parliament, watching the government in some disarray without a true executive head following the death of Oliver Cromwell in 1658.

Subsequent to Oliver Cromwell's death, his son Richard took over the government of England. But Richard lacked the force and charisma of his father and failed to govern effectively. This weak leadership led George Monck, a prominent general and political figure in Cromwell's Commonwealth, to engineer the restoration of the monarchy. Charles accepted the subsequent conditions imposed by Parliament in the Declaration of Breda of 4 April 1660. On his thirtieth birthday, 29 May 1660, after years of exile on the continent, Charles returned to London in triumph to reign as King of England. No monarch ever enjoyed a more enthusiastic reception from his subjects than Charles, and the fortunes of the Stuart family began to rise immediately. His brother James, Duke of York and a capable military commander, moved from the continent to England shortly after Charles arrived. They were joined by the youngest Stuart brother, Henry, Duke of Gloucester, who had garnered a strong reputation as a military campaigner with an English regiment in the Spanish army. The Stuart family had returned home with considerable and impressive presence and the Stuart dynasty seemed truly restored. Unfortunately, before the year was out, the youngest of the three brothers would die from smallpox, leaving only James as heir. But given that James was a mature and seasoned soldier, the Stuarts still seemed adequately represented. All Charles needed to guarantee the future of the Stuart dynasty was a queen and a direct heir. In spite of being relatively poor, Charles easily assumed the role of King of England and he left it to his new government to work through the intricacies of choosing a wife who would bring the greatest political and economic benefit to him and to England.

Contrary to endless rumours that he was married to Lucy Walter in his teens, Charles was, in fact, married only once, and that was to a Portuguese princess eight years his junior, Catherine of Braganza. Catherine was born at Vila Vicosa near Lisbon on 25 November 1638, the third child of the Duke of Braganza who later became King John IV of Portugal. If ever a marriage was made for political and economic reasons, the union of Charles and Catherine was such a match. Her dowry included Tangiers, Bombay, full trading privileges for England in the Indies and a very large sum of money for the impoverished Charles. At twenty-one Catherine was neither young nor pretty and apparently was not considered an important candidate for marriage in other European courts. Spain did not favour the match and the Spanish ambassador spread rumours that Catherine would be a sterile queen, hoping that Charles would look further north in Europe for a suitable wife. Notes which passed during Privy Council meetings between Charles and his chancellor, Edward Hyde, Earl of Clarendon, illustrate Charles's somewhat disinterested acceptance of this match. He even implied to Clarendon that he might not be able to consummate the marriage immediately as he would be tired after the long journey from London to Portsmouth, where he was to meet his bride and her entourage.[4] As it happened Catherine had a cold and slight fever when Charles arrived and she was not up to much more than merely greeting Charles at their first meeting. They were married in a Catholic ceremony at Portsmouth and later were married again at a grand ceremony in London in May 1662. They shared the throne of England as king and queen and, ultimately, they also shared her Roman Catholic faith.

Although Catherine was short and had protruding teeth, she also had quite beautiful long black hair and a pleasant voice and demeanour. Charles described her in a letter to Clarendon as not exactly a beauty but he liked her eyes and thought her, on the whole, acceptable as a wife. The marriage began well but soon Catherine was in the difficult position of having to share Charles with his mistresses. To her great credit, she put a brave face on her personal anguish and discomfort in a situation she could not remedy. She reached an understanding with him, tacit or otherwise is not known, so that she remained queen and enjoyed his affection, protection and respect, while he was free to graze in pastures other than hers.

Charles II's lifelong fascination with women has been titillating and of interest to many over the years, but it is distracting as far as understanding him as a ruler of England is concerned. He regarded his dalliances as recreation, not politics. His four favourite mistresses, Lucy Walter, Barbara Villiers, Nell Gwynne and Louise de Keroualle, were quite different in background, and whether or not they exerted important political influence on Charles is open to question. Louise de Keroualle was an agent of Louis XIV of France and Charles did become a client of Louis. But Charles might have embraced Louis for the money he gave him, regardless of Louise's influence. Charles's own estimate of his experience with women is best summed up in his answer to the man who asked him how many women he had; Charles mischievously answered thirty-nine, explaining that the number of the articles of the Anglican faith was a good enough total for the head of the Church of England.

The one dalliance with political consequences was his affair with Lucy Walter when he was living in exile in Holland. In 1649 she gave birth to a son when Charles was just nineteen years of age. This son, who Charles acknowledged, was ultimately known as James Scott, Duke of Monmouth, and he and his mother caused problems for Charles throughout his life. In spite of Charles's many mistresses, sixteen bastard children and the occasional meddling of Henrietta Maria, who visited them for long periods, Charles and Catherine were happy together. Their court was stable and it restored much-needed pomp and splendour to London.

England and the Stuarts were severely tested in 1665/6 when bubonic plague struck, arriving through London and other seaports. Ultimately it took the lives of nearly one in four of the half-million inhabitants of London. The city was brought almost to a standstill by this terrible epidemic disease. The Royal College of Physicians was a major force in organizing the medical resources of London to deal with the challenge of plague, both as to individual sufferers and the public at large. Charles, Catherine and their court remained in London during the early months of the epidemic and were seen as a stabilizing presence. In the summer the royals moved to nearby Hampton Court and continued to serve as a source of stability for their kingdom, besieged by an enemy against which they had little in the way of defences.

With the plague barely gone, fire destroyed most of London in the autumn of 1666. Although only a few lives were lost in this Great Fire of London, it destroyed about 80 per cent of London's buildings. It was a difficult time and Charles faced it well; with his brother, James, he directed the containment of the blaze on horseback, from the edge of the fire. It was Charles's influence that led to the reconstruction of London, and the replacement of its burned wooden structures with stone. Together, Charles and Catherine were largely responsible for bringing back the social and cultural life of London after the Great Fire.

While his court has often been described as dissolute, certainly in comparison to the grim, grey days of Cromwell, the arts and science thrived during Charles II's reign and the king himself was very much the cause of it. For example, in 1662 he granted a charter to the Royal Society, recognizing the alliance already formed by men of science and strengthening it with the blessing of royal patronage. Catherine joined him wholeheartedly in encouraging this blossoming of culture and knowledge, for she remained every inch his, and England's, queen.

Catherine's principal value to England and to Charles lay in her potential to provide heirs to the throne. There is no reason to believe that Charles neglected his marital duties because Catherine is thought to have been pregnant as many as four times. But in September 1663, Catherine and Charles made an official visit to Bristol and on their return to London she was suddenly afflicted with what Samuel Pepys recorded as a spotted fever, an acute febrile illness associated with a prominent skin rash. This would not have been smallpox, but could have been measles, chickenpox, scarlet fever or even typhus or typhoid fever. She was delirious and ill enough to be given the last rites of her Church. Charles is noted by Pepys to have been constantly at her bedside and sincerely concerned about her welfare. It is likely that she was pregnant at this time and miscarried, as it had been rumoured she was pregnant prior to the visit to Bristol. She apparently also had miscarriages in early pregnancy in 1666, 1668, and 1669. With many women around her, the signs of pregnancy, including missed menstrual periods, morning sickness, and breast swelling and tenderness, would immediately have been noticed. It is only reasonable to assume that she did have these additional three pregnancies, all of which ended in miscarriage.

Catherine's reproductive problems rapidly became a pressing concern for court and government and Charles was endlessly given counsel and suffered criticism from well-meaning advisers. There were even times when Charles faced pressure to divorce Catherine because of her inability to provide an heir. A polygamous marriage with Lucy Walter, his first mistress and mother of his bastard son, James Scott, Duke of Monmouth, was seriously considered as a way out at one point, even by Church authorities. But no amount of pressure would convince the king to desert his queen. Charles protected Catherine and she remained by his side throughout his reign as he slowly and steadily consolidated his power. By 1670, the ten-year anniversary of his reign, he was generally regarded as a vigorous and successful monarch, both at home and abroad.

The ever watchful Venetian ambassadors reported to the Doge at Venice that Charles had reached the age of forty-six in perfect health, and that he enjoyed exercise and sport and seemed likely to live a long life.[5] In fact, Charles was quite conscious of his well-being and did enjoy physical activity, particularly walking, fishing and tennis. By all accounts he did not use tobacco and drank alcohol only in moderation. His subjects were accustomed to thinking of him as a healthy and active man, and although there were always concerns about the lack of a direct heir to his throne, these concerns diminished somewhat over time as he seemed likely to reach a grand old age.

However, the matter of who would succeed Charles if he died without a direct heir grew more and more important to Parliament. His younger brother, James, Duke of York, was not an acceptable option, as he had converted to the Roman Catholic Church. James had made his conversion officially known in 1672 when Charles announced his Declaration of Indulgence, which allowed some tolerance in England for Roman Catholics. Many in England favoured James Scott, Duke of Monmouth, as Charles's heir, and consequently Charles was frequently called upon to legitimize his natural son who, conveniently, was Protestant.

During the latter years of his reign Charles spent considerable effort in careful support of his brother's rightful claim to the throne, all the while keeping Parliament and Monmouth at bay. One of his strategies was to keep his brother out of England and distant from the scrutiny of Parliament, while at the same time carefully suppressing the competing claim of the Duke of Monmouth. Charles was shrewd and an accomplished manager of Parliament. For instance, on 3 March 1670, Charles sent his brother to live in Holland and on the same day had declared formally at Council, that he 'never was either married or contracted to any woman whatsoever but to his now Queen, which declaration was immediately entered in the Council books and thereupon the King signed it and it was witnessed by the Archbishop of Canterbury and the Lord Chancellor'. In the next line of the same entry it was recorded that the parting of Charles and James was very sad.[6] There is no question that

Charles was very fond of his brother and James remained first in line to the throne, although he was to be kept away from England. Charles's declaration meant that none of his illegitimate children could claim to be an heir to the throne. This considerably diminished the political aspirations of Monmouth, although many in England believed Lucy Walter in her long-held assertion that she was secretly married to Charles in Jersey during the exile of his younger years, and was mother to the rightful heir to the throne of England.

It was in this setting that Charles suffered the first serious illness of his life, the bout of malaria which made it clear to all of England that he was mortal and could not live forever, and which brought into sharp focus the rivalry between the Catholic James and the Protestant Duke of Monmouth. Sick as he was, Charles played one off against the other and, in a sense, played both of them off against Parliament. By the end of September 1679 Charles was convalescing in Newmarket. Monmouth had been sent to live in Utrecht, to be supervised by Charles's cousin, Prince Rupert, and James had returned to Flanders.[7]

In political terms these events were unsettling for Parliament, which had worked hard, seemingly in vain, to exclude James from the succession to the crown because he was Roman Catholic. In fact, Parliament passed bills excluding James from the succession three times, once by unanimous vote in the Commons, only to see Charles skilfully manoeuvring to keep these bills from becoming law. It was sobering for Parliament to realize that Charles was vulnerable to illness, and James's return to England in September 1679 to offer support to his ailing brother can hardly have been reassuring. Only after James had been dispatched by Charles back to the continent in November 1679 did Parliament breathe more easily.

Charles remained in good health throughout the winter but the fever returned in May 1680 and lasted for several days. It was followed again by a complete recovery and was presumed to have been a recurrence of the illness of the previous year.

Charles, now fifty, appeared to be losing the vigour of his younger years and the likelihood of his death intensified political manoeuvring in Parliament concerning the future of the monarchy. Seeking independence from Parliament, who held the strings of his purse, Charles looked to the continent for assistance and fell straight into the arms of Louis XIV, the powerful King of France. By making himself a client of Louis, giving France considerable influence in English foreign policy, Charles received annual payments from Louis in the 1680s sufficient to allow him to govern England and hold his court without depending on Parliament for support. Charles was able to dismiss his last Parliament on 28 March 1681. For the last years of his reign he ruled alone, without Parliament.

Monmouth was back in England by 1682 and the following year was involved by his supporters in a plan, never executed, to assassinate both Charles and James, his father and his uncle. This aborted attempt at a coup became known as the Rye House Plot and led to the execution of Algernon Sidney, one of the alleged planners, and others of lesser note. Monmouth himself was exiled to Holland; he barely escaped with his life. Charles emerged from all of this stronger still and he no longer found it necessary to battle with Parliament over the possibility of James as his successor. He had won and Parliament was temporarily out of the picture.

In failing to call another Parliament after March 1681, Charles was ignoring the Triennial Act of 1664 mandating that a Parliament be called at least every three years. But he was careful to avoid challenging accepted religious policy, for example the Test Acts of 1673 and 1678, which excluded nonconformers from military and civil service. During these final five years of his 25-year reign Charles was in a strong position as monarch. He was largely in control of English political life, for Parliament had actually ceded power to the Stuart monarchy during his reign. Had Charles reigned longer, he might have been able to groom his brother to make him more acceptable to those who feared the Roman Catholic Church. He might even have arranged for the crown to pass directly to James's son, James Francis Edward, under a regency if necessary. Given his general good health, there was the chance that Charles might even outlive his younger brother, James, as only three years separated their births. The death of Charles II on 6 February 1685 was unexpected and at the zenith of his reign.

Subsequent to a mild attack of gout in 1684 and a bothersome ulcer on his leg, Charles exercised less and spent more time working in his basement laboratory, where he was preoccupied with the smelting and refining of mercury. As an amateur chemist of considerable ability, he was particularly interested in the medicinal properties of mercury, and with his laboratory staff he also conducted experiments in line with the prevailing fascination with alchemy. To those around him in 1684, Charles seemed to have become irritable and somewhat depressed, problems that had not bothered him previously. Clearly, he was not in his usual good health in the last year of his life. The hours he spent in his laboratory occupied his mind and perhaps helped to relieve his depression.

Charles had supervised an active and productive research programme in chemistry for many years, evidenced by the fact that in 1669 he had established an office of Chemical Physician to the King, basically providing a salaried position for the chief of his laboratory and research team. A government document officially records that: 'May 7 [1669] Warrant for erecting an office of Chemical physician to the King, fee 20 marks a year, and appointing Dr Thos. Williams thereto, his Majesty wishing to encourage so important an art, and hearing of the extraordinary learning and skill which he shows in compounding and inventing medicines, some of which have been prepared in the royal presence; with leave to make experiments in all his Majesty's chemical laboratories.'[8]

Charles had a keen personal interest in science generally, beyond chemistry. In addition to granting the charter to the Royal Society he actually knew the scientists of his day and could converse with them as an equal. Robert Boyle, who defined the principle of the relation of pressure to volume in gases and made clear that elements were the basis for chemical analysis, was one such colleague. Robert Hooke, a pioneer in the microscopic study of plants and the man who anticipated the creation of the steam engine, was another. Chemistry in the seventeenth century was truly an eclectic discipline, mixing hoary tradition, exciting new experimentation and the powerful promise of alchemy, with no one aspect being dominant and all good scientists, including Charles, accepting all three.

Alchemy, which had existed in virtually all of the developed cultures of the world since before the time of Christ, was easily accepted by seventeenth-century scientists, including Boyle, Hooke, Isaac Newton and Charles. It addressed, in both general and quite specific terms, transmutation, that is, change, of elemental substances. The simplest example of alchemy might be the change of water to either steam or ice. Charles kept the well-equipped chemical laboratory that now occupied more and more of his time in the basement at Whitehall, just beneath his own living space. Even the diarist Samuel Pepys visited it, describing it as 'the King's Elaboratory underneath his closet. A pretty place, [where I] saw a great many chemical glasses and things, but understood none of them.'[9]

The chemical experiments in Charles's Whitehall basement laboratory were in line with those of the leading chemists of his day, and given that his principal interest was in medicinal chemistry – the discovery and preparation of chemical compounds used to treat disease – he had some knowledge of medicine as well. Charles believed that mercury itself could be used to treat disease, an idea first proposed by Paracelsus, the famous iconoclastic physician of the sixteenth century. Some thought that mercury might be a universal medicine and it was generally held that most or all metals were composed of varying parts of mercury and sulphur, including gold. To obtain adequate quantities of metallic mercury, Charles and his laboratory staff had to extract it from cinnabar ore. This was done by heating the ore to high temperatures in a large vessel so that the mercury could be distilled as a vapour and then cooled and condensed to the familiar liquid metal.

The details of Charles's last brief illness are well documented and clear. On Sunday, the first day of February 1685, he enjoyed a pleasant musical evening with three of his mistresses, listening to love songs and enjoying the food and the company of these courtesans, his intimate friends of many years.[10] He retired to bed alone, slept well, but awoke the next morning feeling quite ill. He had a seizure that Monday morning, 2 February, was intermittently sick during the ensuing week, and then died shortly before noon on Friday 6 February 1685. The most detailed description of the onset of his illness is to be found in the *Calendar of State Papers – Domestic*, in a 'Newsletter to John Squire of Newcastle'.

When his Majesty arose yesterday morning, he complained that he was not well and it was perceived by those in his chamber that he faltered something in his speech, nothwithstanding which he went into his closet, where he stayed a considerable time. When he came out he called for Follier, his barber, but, before he got to the chair, he was taked with a fit of apoplexy and convulsion which drew his mouth on one side (this was about ten minutes past eight), and he remained in the chair whilst he had three fits, which lasted near an hour and a quarter, during which time he was senseless. His physicians blooded him and he bled 12 oz freely. Then they cupped him on the head, at which he started a little, then they gave him a vomit and a glister [enema] and got him to bed by ten. He spoke before one. He called for a China orange and some warm sherry, in which time both the vomit and the glister wrought very kindly, which his physicians say are very good symptoms. He mended from one to ten last night, when they were laying him to rest, his physicians having great hopes that the danger of the fit is over, since which that hand they feared was dead he of his own accord moved and drank with it and complained of soreness, which they say is an extraordinary good symptom. Last night they sat up with him three Privy Councillors, three doctors, three chirurgeons and three apothecaries, and this morning Dr Lower, one of the physicians that sat up, says that he rested very well and that naturally and not forced. This morning he spoke very heartily, so that now they hope the danger of this fit is over.[11]

On Wednesday 4 February Sunderland wrote to the Lord Mayor, 'The King is better this morning than he has been since his illness. The remedies he takes continue to succeed very well and his physicians are confirmed in their opinion of his being in a condition of safety.' A further letter to John Squire of Newcastle, written on Thursday 5 February, confirms this, stating: 'On Tuesday night his Majesty rested very well and yesterday he took a purge which had good operation and about 12 last night and four this morning he took the Jesuits' powder [from bark of the cinchona tree, the source of quinine] and continues in a hopeful way of recovery, so that the physicians are of opinion that he is past danger. . . . His majesty was blooded on Thursday night in both the jugular veins, which, they say, prevented his having another fit.'[12]

In 1909 Raymond Crawfurd combined the accounts of eight eyewitnesses to get the exact sequence of events of the course of Charles's five-day terminal illness, and published his findings. The pattern of acute symptoms and apparent initial recovery is intriguing. On Tuesday, the day after suffering his first seizure, Charles did seem to be improving. He relapsed on Wednesday, his skin becoming cold and clammy, and suffered more convulsions. On Thursday, the convulsions were worse still, to the extent that his brother James, now back in London permanently, and a priest, Father John Huddleston, visited him. That evening he was well enough to take the Eucharist and was received into the Church of Rome. On Friday morning he was able to see the dawn and ask that the eight-day clock be wound, but by seven o'clock he was breathless, by eight-thirty his speech was failing, and by ten he was unconscious and dying.

His physicians believed that he died of apoplexy, a general term they used to describe a sudden major calamity in the central nervous system. Raymond Crawfurd's exhaustive study of the last few days of Charles's life focused on the impressive number and variety of medicines that Charles received. For the modern physician few of these prescriptions, save Jesuits' Bark, would have any meaning or relevance. Most were essentially harmless botanical preparations. However, by noting the changes in prescribing during the five-day illness, and the variety of preparations used, it is possible to conclude that Charles's physicians were increasingly confused as to what was happening to him and that they were covering their tracks by endorsing one another's treatment regimens. Finally, Charles was administered King's Drops, the extract of human skull invented by Dr Jonathan Goddard, commended by Dr Thomas Sydenham and manufactured in Charles's own laboratory, as well as Oriental Bezoar Stone. These last two preparations were obviously administered in desperation, both being medications of last resort in the seventeenth century.[13]

From the clinical picture it can be concluded that Charles died of an acute insult to his brain, clinically manifested by spells of epileptic seizures, with intervening periods of relief. It is not possible to demonstrate that organs other than the brain were initially involved. For example, Charles was not described as having trouble breathing until just before he died. The short period of hand paralysis following the first group of seizures is a common complication of epileptic seizures, now known as the post-ictal state. Its complete resolution within hours is typical of this phenomenon. Of great interest in determining the nature of the mysterious acute illness is the autopsy, performed the day after the king's death. The most accessible source of this report is in the *British Medical Journal*.[14] The original post-mortem examination report was lost in the Whitehall fire of 1697, and probably the most accurate existing copy of this document is to be found in the archives of the College of Physicians of Philadelphia. Below is the text of this particular copy with a short introduction from the *British Medical Journal* version.[15]

POST-MORTEM EXAMINATION OF CHARLES II

> He expired on February the Sixth soon afternoon,
> Towards the end of the fifth-fourth year of his age.
> In the Body of Charles the Second, Most August
> King of the Britains, when opened after death
>
> Were found:–

1. In the outward parts of the Brain the Vessels fuller of Blood than ordinarily they are found.
2. The Ventricles of the Brain full of Water; as in the whole substance of it a greater quantity of the like serous liquor than is usuall.
3. In the Breast the Lungs on the right side every where adhering to the Ribbs; the other side free as naturally it ought to be.
4. The substance of the Lungs perfectly sound, but full of Blood.
5. The Heart large & very firme as it ought to be.
6. In the lower Belly nothing amisse, only the liver of a colour darker than ordinary, & full of Blood, as were alsoe the Kidneys and Spleen.

Ch.: Scarburgh. Tho: Witherley. Walt: Charleton. E: Dickinson. Pe: Barwick. Tho: Millington. Rob: Brady, Ferd: Mendex. Wal: Needham. Ed: Browne. Th. Short. Rd: Lower. Ch: Fraiser. Edm: King. Jos: LeFevre. Christianus Harel. Martin Lister. Ri: Pile. Jo: Pearse. Aime. Tho: Hobbs.

Immediately after Charles's death there was intense speculation about poisoning, with his brother James cast as a prime suspect, but there is no documentary evidence to support this notion. Nevertheless, the completeness of the autopsy, including a careful examination of the brain, connotes a thorough search for evidence of poisoning. The post-mortem examination findings were probably not immediately helpful to Charles's physicians, except to exclude poisoning as a cause of death. The more astute of them would probably have been puzzled by the brain findings. Until the twentieth century, on the basis of the clinical course of the illness, it had generally been assumed that Charles died of apoplexy, or in other words, a stroke, an acute vascular injury to the brain. While it might be expected that a source of bleeding would be seen in or on the brain after apoplexy, a blood clot in a brain artery could produce the same picture but not be found at autopsy in the seventeenth century.

The term 'seizure' was used rather loosely in the seventeenth century and referred to almost any sort of acute illness associated with altered consciousness and unusual movements. In modern times this term is reserved to describe repetitive abnormal movements of an automatic nature as a manifestation of epilepsy, for example. Charles was not known to have epilepsy or to have had episodes of abnormal movements previously in his life. From the descriptions of those who saw him in the last few days of his life, when he was suddenly very sick, it is certain that he had epileptic seizures. The new onset of epileptic seizures in a person of middle age nearly always portends serious disease of the brain, and his physicians clearly understood this.

In 1861, Norman Chevers, of the Bengal Medical Service, became convinced that Charles died of a 'low intermittent fever with convulsions', what is now known as an acute encephalopathy, or malfunction of the entire substance of the brain.[16] Chevers had seen many Indian children die in this way and although he did not know the actual cause of this common problem he was, in fact, describing cerebral malaria.

Chevers should be remembered for his perspicacity because the febrile illness that Charles suffered in 1679 and again in 1680 certainly was a tertian ague from a malarial parasite, and was common in England at that time.[17] However, a tertian ague in seventeenth-century England was quite different from a tertian ague in nineteenth-century India, and Chevers could not have made this distinction. Chevers's reasoning was good, for his time and for India. There tertian agues now known to be caused by *Plasmodium falciparum*, the most dangerous of the several species of malarial parasites, were likely to cause acute encephalopathy and death. However, this cause of encephalopathy cannot be applied to England in the seventeenth century. There a tertian ague was likely to be caused by the less-dangerous malarial parasite, *Plasmodium vivax*, and was understood to be a disease that would run its course and not progress to convulsions and brain damage. Charles did have an encephalopathy, Chevers was correct about that, but it was not due to malaria. Particularly, because the malarial parasite itself was not discovered by Charles Laveran until 1880, so that Chevers could not have known that this parasite plugged up the small blood vessels of the brain and caused death by a syndrome or disease-state in modern terms called encephalopathy, that is malfunction of the entire substance of the brain.

Another cause of encephalopathy, acute diffuse disruption of brain function, must be sought, one that could include epileptic seizures and could have occurred in London in the seventeenth century. For a clue to what really caused the death of Charles II, it is worth referring to Barbara Cartland's book, *The Private Life of Charles II: The Women He Loved*, first published in 1959. The best-selling novelist was herself intrigued by the increasing amount of time Charles had been spending in his laboratory working on a process to fix (smelt and refine) mercury. She implies that he endured chronic mercury poisoning with its attendant kidney damage leading to uraemia which, in turn, causes convulsions and death.[18] A paper published in the *Notes and Records of the Royal*

Society of London in 1961 by Wolbarsht and Sax, American scientists with an interest in toxicology, was the first scientific work to cite chronic mercury poisoning as a plausible cause of the monarch's death. They observed:

> Even Charles was not immune to the general enthusiasm. He had a laboratory at Whitehall and was far more attentive there than at the council board. The King's scientific endeavours increased near the end of his life when he was prevented by an ulcerated and abscessed leg from walking as usual. He now spent his mornings in his laboratory, where he was running a process of the fixing of mercury. Presumably this process involved the heating and distilling of large quantities of mercury.
>
> . . . Charles' use of large amounts of mercury without any safety precautions and his gradual development of erethismia following this are almost enough to justify a diagnosis of chronic mercury poisoning without any further signs. The manner of his death seems to bear out this diagnosis. He appears to have died of the uraemia attendant upon kidney failure, one of the most common sequelae of mercury poisoning.[19]

Charles's laboratory would have been awash with vapourized mercury generated from its smelting, and from the heating of the metal and sulphur in various combinations in the standard alchemy processes of that day. The vapourised sulphur would have had a noxious quality to it and laboratory workers would have been cautious about breathing in too much. But the vapourized mercury in the air of the laboratory would have been inhaled by the workers without their knowing it was present; mercury vapour has no odour. It would be more than a hundred years before mercury and mercury vapour were recognized as dangerous to human health. In the year before his death, Charles was frequently in his laboratory, so it must be assumed that he was regularly exposed to the vapours of elemental mercury.

Nothing is known about the fates of the men who worked with him in his laboratory but there is reason to suspect that several early scientists who experimented with mercury were, indeed, poisoned by it. Well-known examples who were include Blaise Pascal and Michael Faraday.

Mercury is both acutely and chronically toxic to humans. In acute toxic states it usually gains access to the body through the lungs when its vapour is inhaled in mercury-contaminated air. If the dose of inhaled mercury is very high, soon after the exposure the sufferer may have respiratory symptoms including cough, shortness of breath and a tight feeling in the chest. In very heavy exposure the lungs may be physically damaged. A somewhat smaller dose of mercury vapour may cause few or no respiratory symptoms but the mercury will pass from the lungs into the bloodstream and then directly into the nervous system, causing damage to all of its parts, from the brain out to the nerves of the extremities. In fact, the brain is the principal target in cases of acute mercury poisoning and the shield that usually protects the brain substance from toxins, the barrier between the brain tissue itself and the bloodstream, is readily breached by mercury in both acute and sub-acute states of poisoning.

The nervous system manifestations of acute mercury poisoning include seizures, tremors, headache and disturbance of thinking. When the poisoning is less than acute, namely sub-acute to chronic, the damage to the nervous system is somewhat different. In these cases the signs and symptoms are quite varied and the diagnosis is difficult to make. Manifestations of sub-acute to chronic mercury poisoning include tingling of the arms and legs, slurred speech, unsteadiness in moving and walking, reduced fields of vision, insomnia, nervousness, impaired judgement, shyness, memory defects, emotional lability, fatigue, loss of sexual drive, depression, deafness, blindness, stiffness of the limbs, paralysis and even coma. A peculiar condition called erethism has long been known to be related to chronic mercury exposure. It is characterized by irritability and madness – the behaviour of the Mad Hatter in Lewis Carroll's *Alice in Wonderland* provides a classic example of this syndrome. Hatters used mercury compounds in treating felt and in some communities in Europe and North America during the nineteenth century, there were many mad hatters. In the circumstance of chronic mercury exposure all those affected will have measurably increased amounts of mercury in their bodies, but only some will have symptoms and signs of disease from this toxicity.

If large amounts of mercury are ingested by mouth the gut can be damaged, leading to cramping abdominal pain and diarrhoea. In chronic mercury poisoning the kidneys will be damaged, regardless of the portal by which mercury enters the body. This latter manifestation of mercury poisoning is insidious and the patient will probably not exhibit signs and symptoms until years after first exposure. Long-term exposure to mercury can lead to kidney failure and uraemia, the disease state in which the kidneys can no longer rid the body of waste products. Uraemia is a chronic but progressive state that manifests as increasing anaemia, fatigue, breathing difficulties from acidosis, and eventually coma and death. Prior to modern times, death from uraemia was usually sudden, caused by increased potassium in the blood leading to acute disturbance of the heart rhythm and stoppage of the heart. Such a death is now rare because uraemia is efficiently managed with dialysis and kidney transplantation. Given this insight, it is not likely that Charles died from uraemia.

Charles did show some of the vague symptoms of chronic mercury poisoning in the last year of his life, including fatigue, irritability and perhaps depression. He is reported to have been less physically active during this time and it is likely that these manifestations of his chronic mercury poisoning caused him to spend more and more time in his laboratory, where he finally became acutely poisoned at the end of January 1685. In 1967 Lenihan and Smith, physical scientists with a curiosity about medical history, reported their analysis of hair said to have come from the head of Charles II. Using a sophisticated nuclear activation technique they showed that it contained a level of mercury ten times greater than one might expect to find in the hair of a person not exposed to the metal.[20] Presuming the hair examined actually did come from the head of Charles Stuart it can be stated with certainty that he had chronic mercury poisoning, which probably would have become more obvious had he lived longer.

Charles II died of acute poisoning from inhalation of mercury vapour. Modern understanding of medical toxicology makes it clear that elemental mercury damages the central nervous system in unique and unusual ways and this sheds light on the manner of Charles's death. Mercury crosses the barrier between the bloodstream and the cells of the brain, the so-called blood–brain barrier. When this protective barrier is broached by mercury, the protein-containing part of the blood, the serum, leaks into the crystal-clear fluid surrounding the brain, the cerebrospinal fluid. This is exactly what the examining physicians and surgeons identified at Charles's autopsy: 'All the Cerebral ventricles were filled with a kind of serous matter, and the substance of the Brain itself was quite soaked with similar fluid.'[21] The earlier translation puts this in quite similar words: 'The ventricles of the Brain full of water; as in the whole substance of it a greater quantity of the like serous liquor than is usuall.'[22] Beyond this serious insult to Charles's brain as a whole there undoubtedly was mercury damage to the individual brain cells themselves, causing a general brain poisoning – the acutely damaged state known as encephalopathy. This was the cause of Charles's seizures and the direct cause of his death. Bleeding into the cerebrospinal fluid can be excluded because blood was not found. The surface of the brain was inspected carefully at autopsy and the whole brain was dissected. Nothing found within the brain suggested bleeding or a swelling or abscess, tumour or blood clot in any location. Meningitis can be excluded because he did not have a fever and the description of the cerebrospinal fluid does not suggest the presence of pus. Stroke is not likely because it is rarely heralded by seizures. Acute encephalopathy from mercury is the certain cause of Charles's final illness and death. He did not die of uraemia from either acute or chronic kidney damage.

In the matter of whether or not his kidneys could have been damaged sufficiently to cause or contribute to his death, some inference can be made from what was not found by the autopsy surgeon. Charles was a large man and it would have been difficult to dissect all the way back to the kidneys, which are buried in fat at the very rear of the abdominal cavity. Discounting the description of the kidneys as being engorged with blood, they probably would have been abnormal in other more significant ways in the face of either acute or chronic damage from mercury. With acute damage kidneys are swollen and pale while chronic mercury poisoning of the kidneys leaves them small and shrunken. It can be assumed that the autopsy surgeon was skilled and experienced, so in all likelihood he would have recognized abnormal kidneys had they been present. He did not find the kidneys to be abnormal other than their engorgement with blood, a non-specific finding of no importance in understanding the precise cause of Charles's death.

Some of the other post-mortem examination findings are of interest. For instance the adherence of Charles's right lung to the pleura and chest wall connotes a previous lung infection that had healed. This could have been a result of pneumonia or even previous tuberculosis. The fact that the left lung was normal further strengthens this assumption. The description of his heart as large is moot as Charles did not have any symptoms of chronic lung or heart disease prior to his final illness. The engorgement with blood of his lungs, spleen, liver, and kidneys probably represents terminal heart failure in a dying man, and this would be consistent with his symptoms on the morning of his death. Neither his medical history nor his autopsy suggest that

Charles had syphilis, in spite of the presumption of many modern authors that he did.[23]

Charles's unexpected demise left Catherine a Catholic widow in a Protestant country, albeit with a Catholic king, James II. She felt sincere grief at her husband's death and remained in mourning for several months. All in all, Catherine had done her best over the years for her adopted country and for the Stuart dynasty. Medically she can be described as an habitual aborter and no reason for her problem can be adduced from the scant data available. Although she had given England and Charles no direct heir, she was accorded the respect of a dowager queen and stayed in England for several years, wisely avoiding any meddling in religious or political affairs. This was a good strategy, for Catherine had probably played a part in the famous denouement of Charles's personal religious life, the visit of Father Huddleston to his sickbed, and the king's conversion to the Catholic Church the day before he died.

It was not until after the Glorious Revolution in 1688, and the hurried exit of her brother-in-law, King James, to France, that Catherine made plans to leave England for Portugal. Her relations with James's successors, Mary and William, were cordial but it was not a pleasant time for a Catholic dowager queen to be living in a combatively Protestant country. She left England in the spring of 1692, stopping in France and Spain before arriving in Portugal early in 1693. She was received with great acclaim after her absence of more than three decades. In the final years of her life Catherine was a member of her brother's court and she was accorded great respect and love by her subjects. She was more frequently ill during her years in Portugal and may have suffered gall bladder disease and recurrent bouts of erysipelas, a skin infection caused by a streptococcal infection. Early in 1705, at the age of sixty-six, she became the Regent of Portugal when her brother Pedro became too sick to rule and his son, Joao, was too young to assume the crown. To the surprise of the English she ruled very capably, even managing a war with Philip of Anjou, before dying suddenly in December 1705. She is described as having had an attack of colic – severe abdominal pain – and dying within hours of its onset. There is no way to ascertain the cause of her death from the information available, she could even have died of a ruptured aortic aneurysm, considering the very short period from onset to death. A ruptured gall bladder could also lead to death, but not likely in just hours.

In the final analysis, Charles and Catherine did not serve England or the Stuarts well. Catherine did her best but with respect to succession to the crown upon his death, Charles failed to make any accommodation with a Parliament which wanted a Protestant Stuart to follow him. Tall and handsome, Charles was a Stuart who lived life to the full. He was also a mentally and physically sound monarch until his untimely death from acute mercury poisoning in 1685. Clearly he was a fertile man, but he chose to accept the infertility of his wife, Catherine, rather than making any of his bastard children legitimate. Charles certainly knew James well enough to imagine that Parliament might harass him were he to become King of England. But he obviously loved his brother and no action of Charles ever compromised James's chance of succeeding him. It is not possible to know how long Charles would have lived had exposure to mercury not killed him, but it is reasonable to speculate that he might have lived as long as his brother, James, who died in 1701. Had that been the case, the succession might have been very different indeed.

Charles's failure to assist Parliament in excluding his hapless Roman Catholic brother, James, from the succession to the throne was a major mistake. For dynastic reasons Charles should have divorced Catherine and found a wife who could produce heirs, but more practically he could have legitimized one of the many children born to his mistresses – James Scott, Duke of Monmouth, would have been a reasonable choice, but there was no shortage of other candidates. While, generally, historians of the nineteenth century found Charles severely wanting, biographers of the twentieth century saw Charles as a king who neither diminished nor added to England's peace and prosperity. Charles's death was untimely in several respects; he was a vigorous man at the height of his political power and England was generally prosperous and at peace. He left no legitimate direct heir and so the throne went to his brother, James, who became a deeply unpopular monarch, taking the country into religious and civil strife. Had Charles lived another five or ten years, that strife could have been avoided and James's young son, James Francis Edward, might have succeeded Charles under regency. The Jacobite movement that followed James's abandonment of the throne simmered and festered until the middle of the eighteenth century, and might have been avoided completely had a suitable heir been in place. Charles was no Louis XIV, but he had a compelling regal presence and would probably have kept Parliament under his thumb. This might have spared England the rise of the powerful Whig Parliament, fuelled as it was by anti-Jacobitism, and the successive Whig governments that dominated British politics for almost a century.

In retrospect, Charles's illness in 1679 may have been more important than has been previously appreciated. For the political establishment of England this event laid bare the unstable nature of the Stuart succession to the throne and Parliament saw this clearly. Charles greased the gears of government and made it function, but James was only capable of throwing sand into these same gears. A devious figure at this time was Robert Spencer, Earl of Sunderland, and double apostate, whose religious faith shifted conveniently and smoothly with changing politics. Sunderland, of course, ultimately became James's principal adviser as Secretary of State when James ascended to the throne. In his biography of this wily politician, John Kenyon, the eminent Stuart historian, amplifies on the visit of James to his sick brother in September 1679 and makes crystal clear the disruptive effect James had on English politics.

The Triumvirate [Sunderland, the Earl of Essex and the Marquess of Halifax] had prevented James's return after the dissolution of parliament, partly because of the public hostility to him, partly because they feared his reactionary influence on his brother. Even when Charles fell dangerously ill of a fever on 22 August they hesitated and fumbled. On 24 August Sunderland notified James at Brussels, but it was not until the 25th, when the King suffered an alarming relapse, that it was finally decided to send for him.

James reached Windsor on 2 September to find his brother convalescent. He erupted onto the English political scene like some terrifying djinn, ignoring the Triumvirate's pathetic attempts to return him to the bottle from which they had so unluckily released him. With one short interval he remained in England until the end of November, exercising a decisive influence on Charles and all his ministers, Sunderland not least.

For James was the only man in English politics who possessed fixity of purpose and was plagued by no interior doubts whatsoever. He was superbly self-confident, and above all relaxed, with the easy courage of the limited mind.[24]

Clearly, the House of Stuart was in a stronger position in 1685 on the death of Charles II than it had been in 1649 at the death of Charles I. But the second Charles had sown the seeds of a second demise for the Stuart dynasty by not arranging for a successor acceptable to Parliament. Catherine's failure to provide an heir coupled with Charles's untimely death guaranteed that those seeds would flower, to the detriment of the Stuart family specifically and the monarchy in England overall. Charles's death released the 'terrifying djinn' and the stopper to the bottle which had contained him was thereby lost.

SIX

James II and His Wives, Anne Hyde and Mary Beatrice

THE DYNASTY ENDS AGAIN: THE STUARTS IN EXILE

Labour pains awoke Mary Beatrice, Queen of England, at St James's Palace on Trinity Sunday in June 1688. Her husband, James II, discreetly left her newly decorated bedchamber for his own apartment and she was joined by her maids and bedchamber women. Shortly, her midwife, Mrs Judith Wilkes, and her assistant arrived and they quickly busied themselves with preparing their queen for childbirth. Just after eight o'clock a servant brought a warming pan into the room to make the bed in which Mary Beatrice would give birth to the heir to the throne of England more comfortable. Mary Beatrice of Modena was thirty years old and her obstetrical record was more disappointing; eight pregnancies had not given her a single living child. The 55-year-old James took care of his morning ablutions and, sending his prayers heavenward for a good outcome, returned to the royal bedchamber.

James VI of Scotland, later James I of England (1566–1625), as an eight-year-old boy in 1574 in a portrait by Rowland Lockey copied from the original by Arnold van Brounckhorst. As shown, James is a bright little boy, slender, alert, quite pleased with himself. He shows none of the signs of rickets, a diagnosis often wrongly attributed to him. It is not possible to see signs of the hereditary neuromuscular disease that afflicted him even during childhood.
(National Portrait Gallery)

James I (1566–1625) had ruled England for several years when this portrait was painted by John de Critz the Elder, possibly in 1606. There is some wasting of facial muscles, perhaps indicative of the hereditary neuromuscular disease with which he was afflicted from childhood. James had equal disdain for his physicians and his portrait painters, tolerating them at best.
(National Portrait Gallery)

Anne of Denmark (1574–1619), wife of James I, is shown in a black gown, in this portrait by Marcus Gheeraerts the Younger, 1612. She was probably in mourning for her son, Henry, Prince of Wales, who died that year. Anne had her last pregnancy in 1606 and at the time of this portrait she was at the beginning of a seven-year period of arthritis and swollen legs that led to her death in 1619.
(National Portrait Gallery)

Henry, Prince of Wales (1594–1612), eldest son of James I, and heir to the thrones of Scotland and England. This portrait after Isaac Oliver shows a self-assured sixteen-year-old prince, with the long Stuart face. His death from typhoid fever just two years later deprived England and Scotland of a strong ruler, and left in his place his weak younger brother Charles.
(National Portrait Gallery)

Charles I (1600–49) was a connoisseur of art and enjoyed having his portrait painted, as is evident in this full-length study of the young monarch by Daniel Mytens from 1631. Charles had been King of England for six years, was in excellent physical health and had not yet become involved in the interminable civil wars of the 1640s which led to his execution. (National Portrait Gallery)

Henrietta Maria (1609–69) married Charles I in 1625, just months after he came to the throne. She was the daughter of Henry IV of France and a Roman Catholic. Throughout Charles's difficult reign she gave him her unstinting love and support, to the very end of his life. She gave birth to several children, including two sons who would rule England after the Restoration, Charles II and James II. This portrait, by Sir Anthony Van Dyck, shows her in her early twenties. (National Portrait Gallery)

Five of Charles I's children, in a painting by Sir Anthony Van Dyck, 1637. The future King Charles II is in the centre, flanked on his right by siblings who would become Mary, Princess of Orange, and James II. On his left are Princess Elizabeth and Princess Anne, neither of whom survived childhood. Prince Henry and Princess Henrietta were not born at the time of this portrait. (National Portrait Gallery)

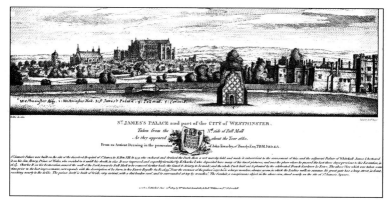

St James's Palace, perhaps the site of more significant Stuart family events than any other royal residence, in a Godfrey print of a Hollar engraving. Mary Beatrice of Modena gave birth to Prince James Francis Edward Stuart here in 1688. Charles I spent the last night of his life here and Charles II, James II, Mary II and Queen Anne were born here. (The Royal Collection, © 2003, Her Majesty Queen Elizabeth II)

The execution of Charles I (1600–49), which ended the Stuart dynasty for the first time, showing the scaffold in front of the old Whitehall Palace, stark on a cold January day surrounded by a crowd of curious Londoners. This engraving was made shortly after Charles was beheaded and has been a popular image of this dread event ever since. (National Portrait Gallery)

Charles II (1630–85) came to the throne in 1660, restoring both the monarchy and the reign of the Stuart family. He was, quite literally, tall, dark and handsome, as portrayed here by an unknown artist, in about 1665. Vigorous, lusty and healthy, he would reign for twenty more years, consolidating the power of the throne. Unfortunately he did not leave any legitimate heirs, and his death from acute mercury poisoning in 1685 was untimely and politically unsettling. (National Portrait Gallery)

Catherine of Braganza (1638–1705), wife of Charles II, was a Portuguese princess who brought a large dowry to England with her marriage. She was generally healthy but was unable to carry a pregnancy to term and therefore provided no heir for the Stuart thrones of England and Scotland. This portrait from the studio of Jacob Huysmans was painted in about 1670, ten years after her marriage to Charles. (National Portrait Gallery)

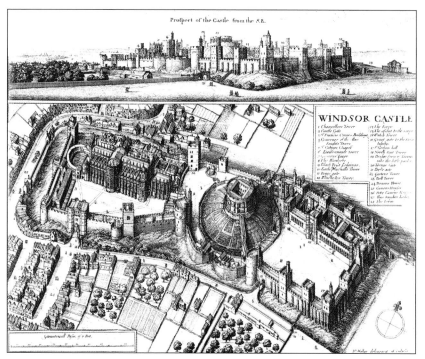

Windsor Castle in the seventeenth century, as seen in a breath-taking aerial view by the great Czech engraver, Vaclav Hollar. (British Museum)

Whitehall Palace in the seventeenth century, in an engraving by Vaclav Hollar, site of much of the drama of Stuart life, not the least the beheading of Charles I and the death from acute mercury poisoning of Charles II. (British Museum)

James II (1633–1701) came to the throne in 1685 on the death of his elder brother, Charles. Openly Roman Catholic and politically inept, James lost his throne to his daughter, Mary, and her husband, William of Orange, in 1688, essentially ending the Stuart dynasty for the second time. James lived in exile in France for thirteen years, finally dying of pneumonia after a stroke. This terracotta bust of James is from the late seventeenth century and is by an unknown sculptor.
(National Portrait Gallery)

Mary of Modena (1658–1718), an Italian princess, was the second wife of James II, marrying him in 1673 when he was still Duke of York, in a painting by William Wissing, from about 1685. After a disastrous obstetric history she gave birth to James Francis Edward Stuart in 1688, providing an heir to the Stuart throne. Unfortunately, he was a Roman Catholic, which brought his father's reign to an abrupt end with the invasion of William of Orange. Mary lived in exile in France for thirty years, finally succumbing to breast cancer. (National Portrait Gallery)

The Bill of Rights was ratified following the Glorious Revolution of 1688, by William III (1650–1702) and Queen Mary II (1662–94), prior to their coronation in 1689. This etching, possibly by J. Carey after Samuel Wale, depicts the moment when the balance of power tipped forever in favour of Parliament.
(National Portrait Gallery)

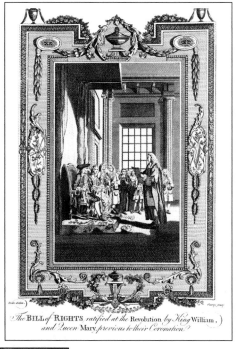

The BILL of RIGHTS ratified at the Revolution by King William, and Queen Mary previous to their Coronation

Prince James Francis Edward Stuart (1688–1766) and Princess Louisa Maria Theresa Stuart (1692–1712), children of James II and his queen, Mary of Modena, are shown at St Germain in France in 1695, at ages seven and three, respectively, in this painting by Nicolas de Largilliere from 1695. Princess Louisa died of smallpox at the age of twenty. Prince James, the Old Pretender, died in old age, long after several bungled attempts to restore the Stuart monarchy.
(National Portrait Gallery)

Prince Charles Edward Stuart (1720–88), the Young Pretender was the son of Prince James Francis Edward Stuart and Princess Maria Clementina Sobieska. The most interesting and exciting of the exiled Stuarts, 'Bonnie Prince Charlie' tried several times to reclaim the Stuart throne. Self-assured, athletic and handsome as a young man, he faded into an old age of alcoholism and abuse, dying in Italy in his late sixties, a tragic failure.
(National Portrait Gallery)

Henry Benedict Maria Clement Stuart, Cardinal Duke of York (1725–1807), was the last Stuart, grandson of James II and great-great-grandson of James I. Having become a cardinal of the Roman Catholic Church at twenty-two, he was Dean of the College of Cardinals at the time of his death in Rome.
(National Portrait Gallery)

The royal family, as seen by the mezzotint artist Bernard Lens, c. 1702. William III, Prince of Orange (1650–1702), and Queen Mary II (1662–94) are at the top and Mary's sister, Princess Anne (1665–1714), and her husband, Prince George of Denmark (1653–1708), are at the bottom. The four appear to be in rosy-cheeked good health, but Mary's death from smallpox eight years earlier in 1694 brought about the third ending of the Stuart dynasty. (National Portrait Gallery)

Queen Anne (1665–1714) and her young son, William, Duke of Gloucester (1689–1700), by Sir Godfrey Kneller, c. 1694. William's rather large head can be appreciated in this view. Though Anne had seventeen pregnancies, William was her only child to survive infancy, sadly dying of pneumonia aged eleven. Anne died of the complications of systemic lupus erythematosus in her fiftieth year, the fourth and final ending of the Stuart dynasty.
(National Portrait Gallery)

Kensington Palace was bought by William III and remodelled in 1689. Sadly, Queen Mary died of smallpox in this royal residence in 1694, William III died here of pneumonia and Queen Anne died here in 1714, ending the Stuart dynasty. (British Museum)

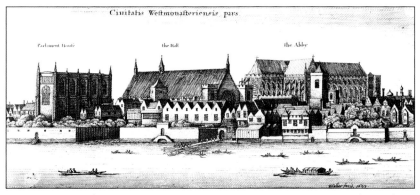

Westminster Palace as it was in Queen Anne's reign, in an engraving by Vaclav Hollar, where she touched thousands of her subjects for the King's Evil or scrofula. It was also the place where the death warrant of Charles I was signed in 1649. (British Museum)

Sir Theodore Turquet de Mayerne (1573–1655) was a Swiss-born physician who became a leader in English medicine in the seventeenth century. He served James I as his primary physician, members of James's family and Charles I and members of his family. Clinical notes written by de Mayerne could be placed in a present-day medical record and read and understood by modern physicians. This portrait by an unknown artist shows him in the prime of his life. (National Portrait Gallery)

Dr William Harvey (1578–1657) is generally acknowledged as the greatest medical scientist of all time, for his description of the human circulation.

He was also a hard-working and accomplished physician and cared for the first three generations of Stuarts. This engraving of the bust of Harvey is a classic image of this very great man. (Clendening Library, University of Kansas Medical Center)

Dr Thomas Sydenham (1624–89) was a soldier in the Civil War and also one of the most accomplished clinicians of all time, often called the English Hippocrates. In addition to putting science into clinical medicine, he was consulted about the illnesses of several of the Stuarts. (Clendening Library, University of Kansas Medical Center)

Dr Richard Lower (1631–91) was a cardiovascular physiologist and a physician of the first rank, being the first person to describe the function of the lungs in oxygenating the blood. Almost an exact contemporary of Charles II, he was his physician as well as his colleague in the Royal Society. This portrait by Jacob Huysmans shows Lower as a young man. (Wellcome Trust Medical Photographic Library)

Dr John Radcliffe (1650–1714) was a physician skilled above his medical peers, an irascible iconoclast, and a generous philanthropist. He attended Queens Mary and Anne, and like him or not, he gave the final medical word in London in his time. Dr Radcliffe was a leading light in London society and served twice in Parliament, though for different constituencies. This engraving of him by G. Vertue was made in 1718 after a Kneller painting. (Wellcome Trust Medical Photographic Library)

Dr Richard Mead
(1673–1754) was one of
eighteenth-century
London's most capable and
accomplished physicians.
He was a practical scientist
and had excellent clinical
skills. According to
Dr Samuel Johnson, 'Dr
Mead lived more in the
sunshine of life than
almost any other man'. He
died aged eighty-one,
having practised medicine
for more than fifty years.
This portrait of him in
1740 is by Allan Ramsay.
(National Portrait Gallery)

Dr John Arbuthnot
(1667–1735) was a
physician and man of letters.
He served Queen Anne and
her family and, in fact, was
her favourite physician.
Dr Arbuthnot was an
intimate of Alexander Pope,
William Congreve and
Jonathan Swift, and, as a
satirist of rare ability,
created John Bull, the
quintessential Englishman.
This pensive portrait shows
him at his best.
(Wellcome Trust Medical
Photographic Library)

Mary Beatrice's labour proceeded smoothly as the large room filled with women. Friends, ladies of the bedchamber and relatives, including the dowager Queen Catherine, widow of King Charles II, were all there to attend the birth. A number of men entered the royal bedroom as well, priests were accompanied by most of the Privy Council and the Lord Chancellor, the latter stationing themselves close to the foot of the bed, partially screened from Mary Beatrice and Mrs Wilkes. This crowd included a good balance of Protestants and Catholics and in all numbered more than sixty people.

James prayed and Mary Beatrice pushed, while the onlookers visited among themselves and offered encouragement to the royal couple. With the labour going quite well, the actual delivery was not long delayed. Just before ten o'clock, Mary Beatrice gave birth to a normal baby whose somewhat delayed cry alerted the distinguished crowd to a new royal presence. James wanted to know the gender of his child immediately. Madame de Labadie, one of Mary Beatrice's bedchamber women, told him that he had a son, and then carried the young prince through the admiring spectators to the adjoining room.

In all of British history no pregnancy was ever more desperately desired than that of Mary Beatrice and no labour and delivery more carefully scrutinized by witnesses. At last there was a new heir to the throne, James Francis Edward Stuart, Prince of Wales. But the political establishment of England was not about to let King James have the satisfaction of a direct male heir who would be Roman Catholic.

The duration of a pregnancy is measured in months, and a period of months allows conspirators more than enough time to do their work. By 1688 James's enemies numbered most of the political establishment in England. And in Holland his eldest daughter Mary and her husband William of Orange, were loath to accept the existence of a Catholic prince, James Stuart, who would eventually become James III of England.

Within a week of the birth Mary had sent her sister Anne a list of eighteen specific questions about the pregnancy and birth. She asked who might have seen her naked before the birth, felt her belly or asked for evidence that her breasts were producing milk. The reason for her letter was the widespread belief that the birth had been a hoax. Anne's answers were honest and straightforward, generally substantiating the fact that Mary Beatrice had been pregnant and given birth to a son.

All can be summed up by the wonderful story of the baby in the warming pan. It was put about in London that Mary Beatrice had not been pregnant at all. In fact, it was said, a male baby was brought into the royal bedchamber in a warming pan by a maid, delivered to Mary Beatrice and Mrs Wilkes from that warming pan into the bed and then, after a feigned labour, shown to the waiting crowd of witnesses. Though he discounts this fascinating story, the eminent obstetrician Professor Sir John Dewhurst has demonstrated to his satisfaction that a baby of nearly 6 lb could easily be placed in one of the large seventeenth-century warming pans.[1] To an ardent English Protestant of 1688, a changeling baby in the warming pan was more than plausible.

The reaction to the warming pan story and other fictions included meetings of bishops, a special commission deposing witnesses (including the royal laundress who was pressed to describe the queen's bed linen, nightclothes and undergarments) and a swell of public opinion that ignored sound evidence so as to make Prince James a nonentity, and his father, King James, a monarch soon to be unemployed. The tenure of the Stuart dynasty was being threatened from within; it was about to be brought down by its own newborn direct heir.

By contrast, fifty-five years earlier, the Stuart succession had been strengthened by his father's birth. James II was also born of a Catholic princess, but was welcomed by Parliament and England. This James joined a happy royal family in London on 14 October 1633, the second son of Charles I and Henrietta Maria. A healthy and active boy who was rarely ill, he went on to live longer than any other reigning Stuart. James II's biographer, F.C. Turner, summarized his health history as including only smallpox at the age of twenty-four, a chest complaint accompanied by fever at twenty-six and several minor hunting accidents from which he recovered without disability.[2] His portraits show him as a handsome man who seems to project self-confidence. Thomas Longueville described him as being slightly above medium height and well formed and muscular. As his portraits attest, his face was long and he was clean-shaven with a prominent jaw. Not unlike his brother, Charles, he was physically active and enjoyed walking, hunting and the other outdoor sports of his time. He was noted to have a slight speech defect, possibly a stammer, but one not as noticeable as that suffered by his father. In summary, James was a copy of his brother, whom he admired, but was not of quite the same quality, physically or mentally.[3]

James grew up in the shadow of his older brother Charles, but their sibling relationship was easier than the one that existed between their uncle and father, Prince Henry and Charles I. James was nine when he and Charles were protected from the forces of Parliament by Dr William Harvey at the Battle of Edgehill. He was the eldest of the three middle Stuarts (James, Elizabeth and Henry) left behind in England during the latter years of the Civil Wars and so he became solicitous of the welfare of Elizabeth and Henry in the absence of their mother. In 1648 at the age of fourteen, with considerable planning and help James slipped away from an evening game of hide-and-seek with Elizabeth and Henry. Eluding his guards, he was then dressed as a girl by his adult conspirators and, continuing to wear this disguise, made his way to Belgium and freedom. James was fifteen years old and living in the Hague with his mother and his sister Mary when his father was executed in 1649. His younger sister, Elizabeth, died at Carisbrooke Castle on the Isle of Wight in 1650 while the youngest Stuart son, Henry, finally managed to leave England and join his mother and older siblings in France in 1652.

After this harrowing and disrupted childhood James took the best course open to a well-bred second son, he joined the army. James identified strongly with the military throughout his life. He even served in the French army under Marshal Turenne in Spain and Holland from 1652 until 1658, by which time he had reached the rank of general. Even in the French Army, his family connections gave him an advantage but he was serious about his military career and many of his best achievements were based on personal merit. He was a brave soldier and a resourceful officer, and would probably have continued this military career on the continent had England not called his brother Charles to the throne in 1660.

Like his elder brother, James enjoyed the company of women, but unlike Charles, he did not have an easy relationship with the opposite sex. Charles once observed of James that his guilt about dalliance made him choose only ugly women as lovers. His first serious flirtation was with Anne Hyde, daughter of Edward Hyde, head of his brother Charles's government in exile. There was little support for their marriage, in fact both Charles and Edward Hyde opposed it. Hyde was horrified that his daughter, a commoner, intended to marry the brother of the man he was trying to get onto the throne of England. James's marriage to Anne Hyde in 1660 seemed ill-starred from its inception and many doubted that it would last.

Anne first met James in Paris in 1656 during a visit to Henrietta Maria, since at that time she was maid-of-honour to Mary, Princess of Orange. The nature of their relationship over the next several years is not clear but in Breda, late in 1659, James contracted an agreement to marry Anne. With Charles II's return to England in May 1660 as king and James's return as the heir to the throne, James could well have escaped from this agreement. To compound matters, Anne's father, now Lord Chancellor to Charles, was so strongly opposed to the marriage that he suggested to Charles that Anne should be put in the Tower and that he would then propose that Parliament have her beheaded. While the opposition of Charles and his Lord Chancellor did cause James to waver in his regard for Anne, nonetheless by the time they reached England Anne was pregnant with his child, and in September 1660 they were married privately, with the blessing of the king. Their first child, Charles, was born in October and before the year was out the marriage was officially made known. The Duke and Duchess of York and their court became a prominent part of London life. Like his elder brother, James was a philanderer and at one time Anne became sufficiently irritated that she even complained to the king about his behaviour. In spite of the awkward beginning of their relationship and James's inconstancy throughout their marriage, Anne won the respect of society and, particularly, of her brother-in-law, Charles, as an intelligent woman who managed everything about her husband but his roving eye.

Between 1660 and 1671 Anne bore eight children, six of whom died in infancy or early childhood and two (Mary and Anne born in 1662 and 1665 respectively) who survived to become queens of England. Considering that their marriage ended with Anne's death in 1671, Anne was pregnant more often than not during her married life. The reasons for the deaths of the four boys and two girls are not known, but Charles and Edgar lived to four years of age so it is likely that infectious or epidemic disease was at least part of the cause.

Both James and Anne were raised as Protestants and their conversion to the Roman Catholic Church was of considerable interest and great importance to the Stuart future. James's mother, Henrietta Maria, was a devout Catholic and her influence on James as a child must have contributed in some part to his conversion, but no particular reason for Anne's conversion can be adduced other than the influence of her husband. It would seem that, apart from their official connection to the Church of England, James and Anne had a private religious life together. They quietly joined the Catholic Church in the late 1660s, an act that would contribute directly to the fall of the Stuart dynasty. James did not publicly announce his conversion nor cease taking communion in the Church of England until 1672, the year of the Declaration of Indulgence, when Charles was able to relax official proscriptions against Roman Catholics. However, with the Test Act of 1673, by which Parliament demanded at least occasional conformance with Anglican communion, James resigned as Lord High Admiral, administrative head of the navy. Whatever one might think of James it must be conceded that he was a man of principle and true to his chosen faith. Devotion to the Roman Catholic Church was a mutually important bond in his marriage to Anne and, subsequently, the root of his problems with Parliament when he became king.

The cause of Anne's early death, at the age of thirty-three, is not entirely clear. The *Dictionary of National Biography* concludes her entry with the statement that she died of breast cancer, but there is no source cited to substantiate this.[4] In the last few years of her life she has been described as grossly obese and given to gluttony, and others have described her final illness as one of slow decline. Queen Catherine was at her deathbed, perhaps one of the reasons why Anne remained true to the Church of Rome, refusing to return to the Church of England. James remained a widower until his marriage to Mary Beatrice of Modena in 1680, but he was not without female companionship during the interim and a number of possible brides came into consideration over these years.

During Charles's reign, James, as the Duke of York and heir to the throne, was never out of political scrutiny. At the death of his younger brother, Henry, in 1660 he had become the sole male heir to the kingdom. Nonetheless James continued his military career and was Lord High Admiral under Charles during the Second and Third Dutch Wars, which finally ended with the Treaty of Westminster in 1674. During the early 1680s James was Charles's representative in Scotland and then briefly returned to the Admiralty. Charles was never sure what should be done with James. While no threat to Charles, he was nevertheless the Roman Catholic heir to the throne of England. This predicament kept Parliament tied in knots, and three bills to exclude James from the succession (1679, 1680 and 1681) were lost not by vote, but by political chicanery on the part of Charles, who was as much James's manager as his brother. James had little influence even on his own daughters, Mary and Anne, whose lives were carefully managed by Charles by keeping them in a sort of sanitized Protestant isolation with the Villiers family until they were old enough to marry. James was not allowed to choose his second wife either. It was Charles's political dealings with Louis XIV and France that led to the choice of a most unlikely candidate, a fourteen-year-old Italian princess, Mary Beatrice of Modena.

Mary Beatrice was born in Modena, in northern Italy between Parma and Bologna. Of the House of Este, her father was Alfonso IV, who became the Duke of Modena shortly after the birth of his only daughter. He died when Mary Beatrice was three years of age and he was succeeded by her younger brother, Francis. The two children were sheltered from the world in this old Roman Catholic family, which was tightly connected to the Vatican and the other ruling houses of Italy. In 1672, barely past puberty and quite innocent in every respect, Mary Beatrice sincerely wanted to be a nun. Suddenly she was a candidate to become the wife of James, Duke of York, a widower next in line to the thrones of England and Scotland, and a recent convert to the Church of Rome. Mary Beatrice was married to James by proxy in Modena and she then journeyed with her mother through France to London. There she was married to James in fact, although he was old enough to be her father. One wonders whether her young mind saw this new life as an opportunity to return the Catholic faith to England, because much of her life was focused to accomplish this end. James fell in love with Mary Beatrice, King Charles thought her charming and her new Protestant step-daughters, Princess Mary and Princess Anne, came to think of her more as an elder sister than a stepmother. Parliament viewed the marriage and Mary Beatrice with suspicion.

Mary Beatrice fulfilled her role as a young brood-mare for the House of Stuart but her fortune in producing children who could survive was even worse than that of her predecessor, Anne Hyde. When Mary Beatrice was sixteen her first child, Catherine Laura, was born, only to die at the age of nine months. Subsequently, she bore Isabel, who died in her fourth year of life, followed by a son and two daughters who died in infancy. After a decade of obstetric disappointment, Mary Beatrice had several bouts of illness and became a less active consort to her husband than she had been before. In addition to her obstetric woes, Mary Beatrice had to compete with Catherine Sedley for the attentions of her husband. Sedley was James's mistress for many years and was the mother of at least two of his seven bastard children. Doubtless much of the illness of the generally healthy young Mary Beatrice was the result of depression due to her succession of losses and the fact that her husband was being urged by some to consider another marriage.

When Charles died unexpectedly and James ascended to the throne of England Mary Beatrice became Queen, and was suddenly given an important mission. As a young queen of known fertility she was called upon to provide an heir for the throne that she and James now occupied. James busied himself ruling his country and Mary Beatrice busied herself trying to get pregnant once again, to ensure the survival of the Stuart dynasty. James called his first and only Parliament and it was quite favourable to him, supporting him and baulking only when he appeared to show tolerance to Roman Catholic subjects. James dealt quite decisively and efficiently with his nephew, James, Duke of Monmouth, when he fomented armed rebellion in July 1685 – the first session of the 1685 Parliament ended with Monmouth's loss of civil rights and then his execution. In the autumn of 1685, Parliament reconvened but James overplayed his hand by criticizing the militia. He also demanded the creation of a standing army for England, under his command, of course, for which he wanted a number of Catholic officers commissioned who would be exempted from the provisions of the Test Acts. After losing his Tory support he turned to the Whigs, a strategy which could not possibly work, finally proroguing Parliament in November. Parliament did not meet again while he was king. So began the downward spiral of James II's reign. His Declarations of Indulgence of 1687 and 1688, lessening official government discrimination against both Roman Catholics and Protestant Dissenters, misfired and brought the whole weight of England's indurate prejudice against Roman Catholicism down upon him. The last straw was his subsequent arrest of the Archbishop of Canterbury, William Sancroft, and six other bishops in June 1688 because of their refusal to have his second Declaration of Indulgence read in their churches.

James was unsuccessful in managing either religion or Parliament, but ironically Mary Beatrice was on the verge of success in her quest to provide an heir to the throne. After extricating James from the tight embrace of Catherine Sedley, Mary Beatrice went to Bath to take the waters in August 1687 in an effort to restore her fertility and shortly after her return to London she conceived. James was no longer a young man and there had been no direct male heir to the throne since the birth of his brother Charles fifty-eight years earlier. In January 1688, the pregnancy was announced and public rejoicing and prayers for the queen were requested.

The pregnancy galvanized opposition to James, even bringing together his daughters, Mary, Princess of Orange, and Anne, Princess of Denmark, who faced demotion on the ladder of succession if Mary Beatrice produced a son. Both strongly Protestant, Mary and Anne had not always got along well as adults but the apparent pregnancy of their stepmother brought them together in the fear that they would be supplanted by a small Roman Catholic interloper. Their own political powers increased during the pregnancy and their father's political capital was nearly spent by the time of Mary Beatrice's confinement. To counter rumours of false pregnancy and deception Mary Beatrice decided to deliver her child at St James's Palace.

The *Calendar of State Papers* documents the controversy over the birth and it is recorded in the summer of 1688 that

A Memorial of the Protestants of the Church of England, presented to their Royal Highnesses the Prince and Princess of Orange. Setting forth their grievances under the abuse of royal authority and the favour shown to Papists, and the reasons for doubting the Prince of Wales to be the Queen's child, and praying their Highness's to insist that the government of England according to law should be restored, the laws against Papists put into execution, the suspending and dispensing power declared null and void and the privileges of corporations restored, and also that the Queen should be desired to prove the real birth of the Prince or, in case of failure therein, the reports of any such birth should be suppressed for time to come.[5]

James and Mary Beatrice were in a tight corner, their earnest prayers for a son and heir had been answered, but those opposing them had crushed the satisfaction and security that a healthy male heir should have brought them. The true identity of the little Prince of Wales was widely debated across the country and on 22 October the report of a meeting of an Extraordinary Council, addressing the birth of the Prince of Wales, was received in the council chamber. It describes the depositions of forty-one people concerned with this event, male and female, aristocracy and commoners, Roman Catholic and Protestant. Mary Beatrice was not deposed but the dowager queen attended the meeting and made a statement. As a final matter it is mentioned that 'It was then ordered that the declarations of the King and the Queen Dowager, together with the depositions, be enrolled in the Court of Chancery; which was accordingly ordered to be done by the Lord Chancellor in the High Court of Chancery on October 27, together with the depositions of the Earls of Huntingdon and Peterborough, who had not been examined at the Council Board'. In this document James also stated that he intended to oppose the Prince of Orange, invasion being imminent.[6]

The medical surprise of a healthy boy being born to a queen with eight previous pregnancies and no living children, and who had been estranged from her husband for several years, was the beginning of the end of James's reign. It is deeply unfortunate for James that those who knew the truth of the birth of James Francis Edward were the ones who brought him down. Moreover, it is surprising that throughout the summer that followed James did not fully grasp that his son-in-law, William of Orange, would seek to depose him in the wake of accusations about his new son's identity. Had he perceived the threat earlier, he would have had ample opportunity to mobilize his army and naval forces against the foreign invader. However, James apparently did not fully realize the danger until William declared his intent in writing in October 1688. Given that James was a seasoned army campaigner himself and had twice commanded the English navy, his actions, or lack of them, are very difficult to understand. His eventual military preparations to face William's invading army were late and modest in scope.

William landed with a large army at Torbay in Devon on 5 November. By 9 November he was at Exeter and ready to move east toward London, not unlike Henry Tudor more than two hundred years before. James had a much larger army and could have attacked William at Torbay. He might well have vanquished him had he done so, but he chose not to attack and instead ordered his army to wait for William at Salisbury. James arrived at Salisbury on 19 November, but already officers were deserting and the following day James had a nosebleed which lasted, albeit intermittently, for three days. This would prove to be the second medical event to speed his downfall. Within four weeks he was in exile in France, never to see England again.

The severity of James's nosebleed has never been clearly established but presumably this was a new medical problem for the ordinarily healthy monarch. Nosebleeds are common and rarely connote actual disease. They are usually regarded more as a nuisance than a disease by a physician or surgeon, and this would surely also have been the case in the seventeenth century. James's bleeding nose has often been accorded military and political importance probably well beyond its actual medical significance. From the *Calendar of State Papers* we know that it occurred on three separate days – 20, 21 and 22 November – and that it was not continuous.

November 21. Salisbury. The Earl of Middleton to Lord Preston. Your [letter] of the 19th I received. His Majesty approves of the directions given concerning Lord Delamer. He can spare no troop from hence but has ordered the Lord Deputy of Ireland to send over what force, both horse and foot, that can be spared. He was yesterday taken three or four times with bleeding at nose, and when he went to bed took *diascordium* [an herbal preparation]. He is this morning very well, blessed be God. It has only put off his going to Warminster, which he designed only to view and so return at night; whence we have the enclosed account from which you'll find that the war is prosperously begun I pray God the end may answer it.

November 22. Salisbury. The Earl of Middleton to Lord Godolphin. I laid both your letters of the 20th before his Majesty. I had already taken the liberty to represent to him the reasons why he ought not to expose his person to any danger, and that the toil he continually puts himself to might prove prejudicial to his health, that the detail might be referred to others, by which the despatch might be quicker and he have the more leisure to consider of the main and important matters. I was much encouraged to perform this duty by her Majesty's commands, which I shall always think myself much honoured to receive and be always very faithful and diligent in obeying them. Last night and this morning his Majesty bled a little at the nose. However, he is very well, God be thanked. The physicians say it is only a ferment in his blood occasioned by too constant and anxious application to business.

November 23. Salisbury. The Earl of Middleton to Lord Preston.

Postscript: The King is very well.

November 24. Salisbury. The Earl of Middleton to Lord Preston. I received yours of the 22nd this morning. Roger Huett brought news from Warminster that Lord Churchill's Grenadiers went last night over to the enemy. Maine was gone in pursuit of them but is suspected to have gone after them. The Duke of Grafton and Lord Churchill are missing, and not doubted but they are gone to the enemy. They went from hence. We have had no advice from Warminster but what Huett brought, which would make one imagine that the whole brigade is gone, commanded by Kirke and Trelawny. It was lucky that the King's bleeding at the nose hindered him from going thither, where they might have seized him. He marches this day to Wallop with all his troops, and so by Andover to London.[7]

A somewhat more dramatic account of the nosebleed is given by Thomas Longueville in his biography of James, showing what time can do to the interpretation of events. As primary sources for his account of the nosebleed he cites *The Diary of Sir Patrick Hume* (Bishop Gilbert), Burnet's *History of My Own Time*, the memoirs of the Earl of Ailsbury and the memoirs of King James himself. All of these accounts were written years after the event and surely represent the selectivity of memory of those present at Salisbury in November 1688.

The King left London on the 17th November, at two o'clock, slept night at Windsor, and reached Salisbury on the 19th. He immediately held an inspection of his troops assembled there. That night he held a council of war. It was scarcely over when his nose began to bleed. Bleeding of the nose was not a discomfort to which he was subject, and the severity of the haemorrhage which set in alarmed those about him. Ordinary remedies having failed, his doctors bled him from the arm, and by degrees the bleeding from the nose ceased. . . .

Instead of keeping quiet on the day succeeding the attack, the King mounted a horse and rode off to see some troops; but presently the bleeding from the nose set in even more profusely than on the previous day. For three more days the haemorrhage came on again, at intervals; and in the course of the week he was bled four times. . . .

Much precious time, from a military point of view, had been lost through James's indisposition. He was too ill to attend to business and important positions were consequently left unfortified and unoccupied, while the enemy was carefully taking positions on points of advantage.[8]

Presumably James was not ill in any other way at the time of the nosebleed and, while it is not possible to determine for certain whether there was bleeding from one or both nostrils, it probably was bleeding from just one nostril. It is unlikely that he had bleeding from any other bodily site otherwise it would have been mentioned. To compound the problem of understanding the nosebleed and James's indecisiveness at Salisbury, there is the additional intrigue of those who were planning to abduct or kill James and whose proposed actions apparently were forestalled by his bleeding nose. James Macpherson wrote of the nosebleed and its effect on the conspiracy to kill the king in his 'secret history' of 1775, implying that it saved James from abduction and perhaps even death.

Two battalions of Dunbarton's, Kirke's, and the Queen's made the other two battalions, and the Queen's regiment of dragoons. But the evening before, his nose fell a bleeding, and doing so next morning a considerable quantity, and continuing to do so several times that day, he was obliged not to go, but to be let blood. It was three days before it could be quite stopped. It is generally believed, had it not been for this accident, that Churchill, Kirke, Trelawny, etc. who deserted soon after, with some in that quarter, had designed to seize the King, in going thither or coming back, and have carried him to the Prince of Orange. It was easy enough to do; the King having no suspicion of them. But, a few days after, he began to doubt some of them; and once intended to secure Churchill and the Duke of Grafton, and have sent them to Portsmouth; but, on further consideration, did not think fit to do so.

Later in his book Macpherson quotes from men who were involved in the activities at Salisbury:

Kirk, Lanier, said Sir George, and many others of our party being there, and most of the guards, and army, that were posted there, right for our purpose; we were resolved to carry him [James] a prisoner to the Prince of Orange: but if Dunbarton, Sarsfield, or any other of the papist officers should endeavour to rescue him, then, said Sir George, little Wood and I, that were on horseback, were to have shot him; and if that had missed, then Lord Churchill, that was provided with a pocket-pistol and a dagger, would have shot or stabbed him in the coach; for there was no other way of saving themselves after attempting the King. But, as it pleased God, saith the informant, his Majesty's nose very happily fell a bleeding, by which his going to Westminster was prevented.[9]

From accounts of this sort, the wonderful idea of divine intervention suggested that God was saving James for the future. Sadly though, he had no future in England, as the events of the succeeding four weeks were to show, for James did not defend his crown, he did not stand up to William, he simply gave up the fight before it could even begin.

The Glorious Revolution was quite inglorious for James; he decamped from Salisbury and headed towards London with what was left of his army. He had faced the desertion of previously dedicated officers and friends, such as John Churchill, his close friend of many years whom he trusted completely and who would one day become the Duke of Marlborough. When James got to London he learned that his daughter, Anne, had abandoned him as well.

Mary Beatrice and her baby, the young James Francis Edward, were dispatched to France and safety while James made a feeble attempt to negotiate with William. Finally, he failed even in an attempt to escape to the continent on 10 December 1688, after throwing the Great Seal of State into the Thames and heading east for the coast. He was detained by fishermen at Faversham, not because they recognized him as the King of England, but because they thought that he was a Catholic priest. James's ignominy was compounded. Just before Christmas Day, William permitted James to leave England for France. Denied even the dignity of escape, James was never to see his native country again. Whether the nosebleed was the cause of his failure to stand up to William or merely a symbol of that failure doesn't matter, rather it represents James's inability to defend his throne and the right of his family to rule England.

James Stuart lived in exile in France for thirteen years, essentially the guest of Louis XIV. His ineffective involvement in political and military affairs there further diminished his reputation. For example, his effort to re-establish his rule in Ireland led to yet another ignominious flight to France after William beat him at the Battle of the Boyne in July 1690. By 1691 James was living in isolation in his estate at St Germain, near Paris. Although he enjoyed the continuing support of Louis XIV and maintained a court in exile, he was a spent political force and never left France again. Mary Beatrice remained his devoted companion and their union produced a daughter in 1692, Louisa Mary. James's eldest daughter, who succeeded him as Queen Mary of England, died at the end of

1694. Her death increased the intensity of the plotting of the Stuart supporters, the Jacobites, but James remained largely remote from Mary's death and was less and less involved in such schemes. Religion began to occupy more of his time and thoughts until, in 1697, the Peace of Ryswick recognized William as King of England and James lost all importance in the political life of England and continental Europe. However, Mary Beatrice, now in her vigorous thirties, did involve herself in Jacobite and other political affairs, and groomed their son, the young James Francis Edward, for the future his ageing father would not see.

THE DEATH OF JAMES II

While attending a Tenebrae service on Good Friday in 1701 James fainted in the chapel and was taken to his lodgings by servants. On Saturday he seemed better and was able to eat, but on Easter Sunday he lost the power of speech and later in the week developed a fever. Shortly thereafter he was dead.[10] No post-mortem examination was performed on his body.

The healthy James succumbed to what was certainly a stroke complicated by pneumonia. His stroke might have been caused by bleeding into the brain, a clot forming in one of the arteries of his brain or a clot going from his heart to his brain. Difficulty in speaking and swallowing are common sequelae of strokes and the latter is associated with aspiration of saliva, fluids, or food into the lung with resulting pneumonia, hence the fever in James a few days after the initial paralysis. James may have had hypertension, thus providing the setting for the stroke, but it cannot be known if this was a contributing factor to his demise.

There is no medical way to account for James's poor judgement, which was the root cause of his failure as a monarch. He was not deluded, as was his father, Charles I, and he cannot be said to have been mentally dull. It is quite possible that he would have continued his reign had Mary Beatrice not given him a Roman Catholic male heir. In the past there have been attempts to attribute his failure as a monarch to disease, but such attempts cannot be substantiated. For example, with no clinical evidence and little more than opinion, his biographer, F.C. Turner, imagined that he suffered from syphilis and that his mental decline from this disease was manifest even before the beginning of his reign: 'There can be little doubt that at the time of his accession [1685] James was suffering from premature mental decline, a decline which had set in some four years earlier when he was in Scotland.'[11]

It is not likely that James had symptomatic central nervous system syphilis. Though this disease is characterized by faulty judgement and compromised intellect, it is usually accompanied by tremors, and within five years of the first manifestations the sufferer is usually dead. James lived for thirteen years after leaving England in 1688 and was never noted to have a tremor.

The cause of James's nosebleed (epistaxis is the correct medical term) has never been properly established. Most historians have assumed that James was suffering from hypertension caused by the stress of facing William and his army at Salisbury, and that this led to the infamous nosebleed, assumed to be severe and unremitting for three days. In the older medical literature it was supposed that a direct relationship existed between hypertension and epistaxis. However, medical studies which supported this relationship were uncontrolled, that is, populations of patients with epistaxis were not compared with populations without epistaxis.[12,13,14] This sort of comparison is necessary if the relationship of epistaxis to hypertension, or any other presumed or imagined cause, is to be determined. More recent controlled studies make it clear that hypertension, per se, is probably not a cause of epistaxis.[15,16] While many people with hypertension do have epistaxis, most do not, and this includes people with severe and uncontrolled hypertension. In fact, most patients with bleeding noses have relatively normal blood pressures, although it is generally conceded that brisk or prolonged epistaxis is likely to cause sufficient anxiety to raise blood pressure temporarily.

Most nosebleeds occur because of the rupture of a small vein on the medial part of the nasal septum, and not of an artery as one might imagine. The blood comes from only one of the nostrils, oozing not spurting, and external pressure will almost always stop the bleeding. In patients with blood-clotting abnormalities there may be continuous bleeding from the nose, often both nostrils. This is usually associated with bleeding from other sites as well, for example the bowel or the urinary tract. Extensive skin bruising or other distinctive skin lesions are also often seen with blood-clotting abnormalities and as these were not described in James, it is very unlikely that he had any sort of blood-clotting problem. Regardless of the initial cause of a nosebleed, once it stops the bleeding may start again if the original clot is displaced. Bleeding then will continue until another clot forms. This would explain the repeated bleeding of James's nose. Moreover, nosebleeds are most common in the winter when the air is cold and dry, causing the interior surfaces of the nose to become dry and crack, allowing small veins to bleed. The typical sufferer is an older male. All of these factors tie in with James's status and situation. He had the nosebleeds at Salisbury because he was an older man exposed to the cold dry air of late autumn and by touching or blowing his nose too vigorously he caused the harmless bleeding to recur repeatedly over a period of several days.

With this background it is reasonable to imagine that James's nosebleed, while inconvenient, was not disabling in and of itself. However, to others it may have appeared to be disabling, and it certainly provided a wonderful excuse for James's failures to rally his forces, attack William and keep William from chasing him out of his country. It may also have prevented him from leaving Salisbury until his return to London and thereby caused him to escape abduction or murder by Churchill and his co-conspirators. There is no reason to believe that James was a coward or that he caused the nosebleed himself. While his physicians and surgeons would not have had the means to identify and cauterize a single oozing vein on his nasal septum, they could have packed his bleeding nostril with a bit of cloth or something similar. But, had they attempted to pack his nose, they might have prolonged or exacerbated the bleeding. Being bled from a vein in his arm, as a treatment for the nosebleed, apparently did him little harm, and it is not even mentioned in the dispatches from the field.

James arrived in France just before Christmas in 1688 in excellent physical and mental health, the turmoil of the preceding weeks and nosebleed notwithstanding. Although James progressively lost interest in affairs in England during his French exile, his wife and his son, James Francis Edward, did not. Louis XIV recognized James Francis Edward as James III of England. This stoked the fires of the Stuart supporters in England and abroad, and kept their political pot boiling well into the eighteenth century, giving birth and long life to the Jacobites and their movement. In some respects the Stuarts in exile were more dangerous to political stability in England than they were when they were on the throne. The continued steady growth in the power of Parliament at the end of the seventeenth century owed much to the perceived threat of the Stuarts abroad.

James, Mary Beatrice, James Francis Edward, and Louisa Mary maintained their court at St Germain, near the court of their benefactor, Louis XIV, in Paris. The French king was unwavering in his recognition of the Stuarts as the rightful monarchs of England and generous in his support of the Stuart court in exile. The lives of Mary Beatrice and the Stuarts in exile who followed her are important in understanding the degradation of the Stuart dynasty and of monarchy in England generally. The story of the fall of James II is not complete without consideration of what became of the continental branch of the Stuart family. For well over a century, from 1688 until 1807, there was a male Stuart living on the continent who had a valid claim to the English, ultimately British, throne, and the Jacobites were strong in their assertion that theirs was the only valid claim. Mary Beatrice became the central figure in

Jacobite affairs in the latter years of the seventeenth century. She had the future of the House of Stuart in her possession and, at the time, Stuart supporters firmly believed that one day the young prince would be able to return to England as its king, as had his uncle Charles. Mary Beatrice lived for nearly thirty years in St Germain as a queen-in-exile and she became ever more active in Jacobite affairs as her ageing husband became less so. Her son James Francis Edward Stuart was her primary concern and her correspondence from St Germain is replete with expressions of her worries about his welfare and his health. The lives of these Stuarts continued to be influenced and changed by a variety of medical events that shaped their destinies, on several occasions directly interfering with their attempts to regain the throne. In 1712, then in their twenties, both of Mary Beatrice's grown children contracted smallpox, probably from the dauphin and dauphine of France, both of whom died of the disease. Louisa Mary also died but James Francis Edward survived. It was, understandably, a very difficult and trying time for Mary Beatrice, who saw herself as the custodian of the future of Stuart monarchs. She had come very close to losing that future.

The final illness and subsequent death of Mary Beatrice is fascinating. In letters cited by her nineteenth-century biographer, Agnes Strickland, the occasions of her finding first one lump and then a second in her breast can be pinpointed to 1700. In 1702 a French surgeon confirmed the diagnosis of cancer originating in her breast. He told her it could not be cured but that it might be controlled by a series of painful operations, assuring her that with the operations she could live for years. Presumably she had an operation or operations at this time. In 1705 another French surgeon performed an operation for recurrence of the cancer. Though often sick, Mary Beatrice lived on for another thirteen years, having one long spell of illness in 1714 that brought even Louis XIV to her bedside. Finally, in April 1718 it was noted that the cancer had recurred and she went into a decline and died quietly on 7 May at the age of fifty-nine years.[17]

It is certain that Mary Beatrice was a rare woman. For seventeen years she survived what was, by modern reckoning, breast cancer never treated with curative intent. From letters and descriptions it is obvious that she had an indolent cancer that spread to the skin of her breast and was managed by surgical excision of individual growths. During this time she passed through menopause and that probably altered the hormonal milieu of her body, a sudden decrease in oestrogen helping in the extension of her life. In 1962 Bloom, Richardson and Harries, in a classic paper in the *British Medical Journal*, described survival in essentially untreated breast cancer in 250 women seen at the Middlesex Hospital in London, most of them diagnosed during the nineteenth century. They determined that with a certain diagnosis of breast cancer and no treatment with curative intent, 18 per cent of patients lived five years, 4 per cent lived ten years and several patients lived beyond fifteen years. Their longest survivor lived eighteen years and three months from the time of diagnosis.[18] Other such series were published fairly early in the twentieth century and other very long survivors have been described; one woman lived for thirty-five years after diagnosis. Despite never being cured of her tumour, she was still alive at the age of eighty. Cancer arising in the breast is one of the few kinds of malignancy in which patient and tumour may achieve a sort of symbiosis, with years of survival for the patient who may even die with the breast cancer and not of it.

At the time of the death of Mary Beatrice in 1718, James Francis Edward was just short of his thirtieth birthday. Although acknowledged by Louis XIV as James III of England, he was styled the Chevalier de St George in France. Several attempts to return James to Scotland had come to nothing, the first was aborted in part because he was said by the French admiral to have the measles. Following the Treaty of Utrecht in 1714, in which France recognized the Hanoverian succession to the British throne, and the death of Louis XIV in 1715, which removed the Stuarts' most loyal supporter, James Francis Edward had no place in France.

James Francis Edward is described as having the occasional quartan ague and in his late twenties had an anal fistula excised by a French surgeon. These medical problems were not disabling but were probably at least partly responsible for his less than aggressive furthering of his, and the Jacobite, cause.

By 1719, James was living in Rome much of the time and while working alongside the King of Spain in planning an invasion of Britain, he was married, by proxy, to Princess Maria Clementina Sobieska, granddaughter of the King of Poland. The military expedition came to nothing but the marriage, and the large dowry that came with it, did buy some time for the Stuarts in exile. The two were later married properly in a grand ceremony in Rome and the Princess Sobieska eventually gave James Francis Edward two sons, Charles Edward born in 1720 and Henry Benedict born in 1725. Theirs was a marriage with many ups and downs, the princess was often depressed, particularly after her two deliveries, and James Francis Edward found solace in other women. In spite of his two sons, the importance of James Francis Edward as the focus of the Jacobite cause, slowly eroded away. The princess became obsessively religious, spending time in a convent and leaving her sons largely in the care of their father. Slowly she declined and eventually died in Rome in 1735 at the age of just thirty-three. Given to stringent fasting and closeting herself for long hours away from others, it is quite likely that Princess Maria Clementina was severely depressed. It is not common to die of depression but there is no question that severe depression, associated with anorexia and weight loss, may pave the way for a relatively minor physical illness to take the life of the patient.

James Francis Edward lived on, slowly fading into the background as his son, Charles Edward, the dashing Bonnie Prince Charlie, moved to prominence in the Jacobite cause. James Francis Edward had stomach problems throughout his middle age and was given to sumptuous late dinners but not, apparently, to abuse of alcohol. In his fifties he developed visual problems but did not have a specific disease that would explain his steady disengagement from the rapidly changing political affairs of Europe and Great Britain. In his seventies James Francis Edward had a hernia and repeated attacks of quartan ague, probably malaria. At the age of seventy-three he had his first epileptic seizure and subsequently had further such seizures. His religious needs were met by his son, Henry Benedict, and Pope Clement XIII, and although he declined physically during the last year of life his mind remained clear. He died on 1 January 1766 in Rome and was buried in the church of St Peter's. Had he actually ruled England, he would have been monarch for sixty-four years, longer than either George III or Queen Victoria. Epilepsy occurring de novo in old age is not common and often connotes a tumour in the brain, a distinct possibility in consideration of his earlier visual difficulties. However, there is no evidence to support this diagnosis, it is only conjecture, and the actual cause of James Francis Edward's death is not known.

James's passing left the fortunes of the Stuarts in the hands of his son, Charles Edward. Charles Edward was a Stuart with charisma, he was self-assured, athletic, not much interested in books or learning, and immensely popular. He enjoyed excellent health until his tragically failed attempt to regain the family thrones in 1745, the last and probably strongest effort by the Stuarts and the Jacobites to win back the monarchy. During his invasion of Scotland and England Charles won the Battle of Prestonpans and got his army as far south as Derby. Nonetheless by January 1746 he was back in Bannockburn and the might of England was gathering to destroy him. His inability to rally his forces was, in part, due to successive illnesses early in 1746, which his biographer, Frank McLynn, has put into perspective. In January Charles had influenza, took to his bed, and soon was being nursed by Clementina Walkinshaw, who became his mistress. His vaunted self-confidence changed into flamboyance and he began to lose control of his troops. In February Charles was sick again with what was thought at the time to be pneumonia. He was unable to control his troops and desertions became common. In March he was taken with a severe febrile illness associated with a prominent red skin rash, thought to be scarlet fever. By April he was near Inverness, and at the Battle of Culloden his army was destroyed by the Duke of Cumberland. Charles Edward escaped to the Hebrides where he was hunted for months, before eventually reaching France in September 1746.[19] He visited London secretly at least once in the 1750s and may actually have become a member of the Church of England, at least temporarily, but was never able to establish a power base in England.

Charles Edward never married Clementina but in 1753 they had a daughter, Charlotte, known as the Duchess of Albany. Clementina and Charles did not have a stable relationship and she left him for good in 1760 taking the six-year-old Charlotte with her. Much of Charles Edward's life after 1745 was given to alcoholism. He had been physically abusive to Clementina and possibly also to Charlotte. He was interested in other women, particularly those with whom a dynastic marriage could be made, but little came of these hopes until he married Princess Louise of Stolberg-Gedern in 1772. No children were produced from this union and the two were finally divorced in 1784 after long and complicated political manoeuvrings. Estranged from everyone who mattered, because of his drinking and violent behaviour, Charles Edward was in steep physical and mental decline during the last several years of his life. He is described as having severe oedema of his legs and probably had several strokes in his early sixties. Finally he suffered a major stroke in January 1788 not long after his sixty-seventh birthday and did not recover from the paralysis; he died at the end of that month, first having been reunited with his daughter, Charlotte, and having received the last rites from his brother, Henry Benedict. Charlotte died the next year of widespread cancer at the age of thirty-five.

Henry Benedict was the last of the Stuart line and, on Charles Edward's death in 1788, became the final Stuart claimant for the throne of England. He had been made a cardinal of the Church of Rome in 1747 at the age of twenty-two and lived a quiet and pious life, in direct contrast to his older brother. He was known as the Cardinal Duke of York and regarded himself as the heir to the Stuart thrones, although he was little involved with the scheming of the Jacobites and cannot be described as a serious aspirant to the throne of England. Ultimately, he was impoverished by the French Revolution and lived out his life at Padua, where he died on 13 July 1807 at the age of eighty-two. A cardinal for fifty-five years, he died Dean of the College of Cardinals, a remarkable office for the last Stuart.

These Stuarts in exile, James Francis Edward, Charles Edward and Henry Benedict, never ceased to believe that they were the rightful occupants of the thrones of England and Scotland. History remembers James Francis Edward as the Old Pretender and Charles Edward as the Young Pretender. Henry was so far in time and distance from the throne that he could barely be called a pretender at all. All three are buried together in Italy. The later Hanoverians took pity on these three men, even helping with the costs of their burials, but for almost 120 years they provided a perceived external threat that gave Parliament an ever firmer hand on the tiller of government in Britain.

Medical misfortune caused terrible disruption in the House of Stuart in the generation of Charles II and James II. The greatest misfortune was perhaps the death from smallpox of the youngest Stuart brother, Henry, Duke of Gloucester, in 1660. Henry was firmly Protestant and, had he lived, he might well have supplanted James as heir to the throne. As with his namesake who died of typhoid fever in the previous generation, it can never be known what sort of king Henry might have become. As a strongly Protestant ruler, however, he would surely have avoided the religious problems and controversy that ensnared James so tightly. The early death of the fertile Anne Hyde, possibly of breast cancer, left James without a queen who could have given him male heirs that might have been raised as Protestants, as were his daughters Mary and Anne.

Mary Beatrice gave more to the Stuart cause than even those of the Stuart blood-line, but her most important contribution was too late to matter. After losing all of her children in early deaths she produced a much needed male heir at a critical juncture. She took him to safety when enemies threatened him and then nurtured the Stuart claimants to the thrones of England and Scotland until the end of her life, a remarkable accomplishment for an Italian woman living in France. Her long struggle with breast cancer is of great medical interest and apparently has not been given much attention before.

James II's place in British history is not large and his reign was very short. Nevertheless he significantly diminished the power of the monarchy and, thereby, strengthened Parliament. His misrule and flight from England led to the Jacobite movement, which remained an important force in British affairs throughout much of the eighteenth century. James compromised his stewardship of the Stuart throne in just three years. He began as a monarch with an overwhelming Tory majority in a Parliament that even had some sympathy for his Roman Catholic sensitivities and concluded as a monarch completely at odds with Parliament, attempting to rule without them. His failure to bring off this show of executive force turned Parliament against him and, had republicans been waiting in the wings, as they were at the time of his father's execution, the English monarchy might have disappeared altogether in 1688. The last Stuarts, Mary and Anne, and the half-Stuart (through his mother) William of Orange, were given the throne of England by a powerful Parliament, now dominated by the Whigs. The Exclusion Bills brought the Whigs into being and ironically they were the agency that ran James II out of England.

SEVEN

Mary and William

THE HOUSE OF ORANGE RULES ENGLAND

Kensington Palace was cold and dark in December 1694 and Mary was depressed and lonely. Her husband, William, weighed down by political and military problems in Britain and on the continent, had taken his camp bed to Whitehall where he slept most nights, constantly being awakened, he told Mary, by messages and dispatch boxes. Feeling run down and further weakened by a cold, at thirty-two the childless Mary had lost the bloom of youth. To increase her isolation even more, London was in the grip of a particularly severe smallpox epidemic and at a standstill. Mary, who had never had smallpox, was fully aware of her risk of acquiring this dreaded disease.

Just a week before Christmas Day Mary awoke feeling worse. Convinced that she must now, finally, be having the first manifestations of smallpox, she ordered that younger members of the palace staff who had not had the disease were to leave immediately. She then took a strong dose of her favourite cordial and, refusing medical attention, set about going through her private papers. It was exhausting, emotionally draining work that continued through the day and well into the night. She burned journals and diaries, and then dealt with letters from her family, spending a long time with those from her father, James II. Finally she looked through the letters from William, her often-absent husband, written to her over the better part of two decades, most of them while he was campaigning against the armies of France. Virtually all of these letters went into the fire. Composing herself, she then wrote a long letter to William, a letter about her love for him, her devotion to him, but also her perceptions of his interest in another woman, whom she did not name. Upon finishing the letter she took to her sickbed, had the letter placed in a box beside the bed and summoned her doctors. Shortly, William abandoned Whitehall for his wife and he was at her side, where he would remain throughout her illness.

Mary knew she had smallpox but her doctors were not at all certain of it. By Sunday 23 December, Mary had a rash on her torso and a cough. On Monday the rash had spread to her face, arms and legs, and she felt much worse. On Christmas Day, she awoke with many red spots on her skin. Her cough was more severe, her face was very swollen and she could barely open her eyes. Measles, though rare in adults, became a strong diagnostic possibility and, miraculously, she felt much better on Wednesday, further strengthening the likelihood that she had measles. The redoubtable Dr John Radcliffe still favoured the diagnosis of smallpox at this juncture, even though the majority of his medical colleagues now favoured measles.

Dr Walter Harris sat up with Mary all night on Wednesday because her breathing was becoming increasingly difficult and she was spitting up large amounts of blood. On Thursday blood was noted in her urine and the blisters, originally thought to be typical of smallpox, became red. A surgeon was called in to lance one of the larger blisters and it was found to contain blood.

Given hope by the diagnosis of measles, William was now drawn back to despair. The physicians finally agreed that his wife had smallpox in its most lethal form. William never left Mary's side, in spite of the work piling up at Whitehall, sleeping on his camp bed in her bedchamber or in the adjoining room. He himself was sapped by worry and fatigue. On Thursday afternoon Mary weakened further and her mind began wandering. She was attended by the new Archbishop of Canterbury, Thomas Tenison, and when she was mentally clear they discussed her death and she received communion. When alert she asked for cordials and also that the archbishop read to her from the scriptures. At one o'clock on the morning of Friday 28 December, Mary died quietly, and so died any pretence that the House of Stuart still ruled England.

Mary had reigned as Queen of England for six years with William as co-monarch. Her death marked the third ending of the Stuart dynasty. Although his mother was a Stuart, William was of the House of Orange through his father, and he would now rule England, Scotland, and Ireland alone. William would remain king because, six years before, Parliament had considered all possibilities before deciding to put him on the throne. Exercising its full power to make and unmake monarchs, Parliament had decided that the line of succession for the throne of England would go to William and Mary and their issue, who would be half Stuart. If they had no issue, then the heirs to the throne would be Anne and her children, who might be considered Stuarts even though their father was a Danish prince. In the event that there was no issue of either sister, then any children from the marriage of William with a new wife would be in line for the throne and the monarchy would pass once and for all to the House of Orange.

So, in February 1689, Parliament was deciding whether and when a Stuart would ever again sit on the throne of England and the immediate challenge for the 38-year-old William and the 26-year-old Mary was to produce heirs. At this point, Anne, next in line to the throne, had just passed her twenty-fourth birthday, and was known to be remarkably fertile. She had borne two babies, suffered a stillbirth and three miscarriages, and was pregnant yet again. All of this had been accomplished within the space of six years. There was a strong possibility that the Stuarts might regain the throne once more even though England was now ruled by an English queen and a Dutch king.

William's claim to the throne of England can easily be traced through his mother, Mary, Princess Royal of England and Princess of Orange. She was born in 1631, the second child of Charles I and Henrietta Maria. Charles I had initially wanted to marry this daughter to the son of Philip IV of Spain but reality and need dictated that an alliance with Holland would be desirable. So, at the age of nine years, Mary was married by proxy at Whitehall to the fifteen-year-old William of Orange. The vicissitudes of the Civil Wars meant she was taken by her mother to the Netherlands in 1642, and in 1644, at the age of twelve, took up her duties as the wife of the young prince. In spite of her youth she functioned effectively in her social role. Her husband rose to become the stadtholder, or head of government, of the United Provinces of the Netherlands, a national entity recognized by the Peace of Westphalia in 1648, which ended the Thirty Years War. Shortly thereafter Mary welcomed her brothers, Charles and James, to the Dutch court, because the political turmoil in Britain had left them homeless. The young William of Orange was involved in trying to eject Spain from the rest of the Netherlands but also provided a home for increasing numbers of his in-laws. Soon Mary was pregnant and the future looked bright for the young Prince and Princess of Orange. They ruled a Netherlands that seemingly was finally gaining an identity as an independent European state, all the while sheltering the Stuart heirs whom they expected one day would be back in London ruling England. In the autumn of 1650 things began to go wrong. William died of smallpox on 6 November, eight days before his son and heir, also named William, was born.

By guile and force of will Mary fought to remain close to her young son and to guide his future. At the age of nineteen she was fighting for her own future, as well as her son's, in the intricate politics of the not-always-United Provinces. To complicate matters further she had to look after her larger family, struggling to survive in an environment that was becoming less and less welcoming, as the government of Holland initially found real affinity with the new Cromwell government in England. Not only was she sheltering her three brothers and mother, but also her aunt, Elizabeth, Queen of Bohemia, and her many offspring who were living in Holland as refugees themselves.

Not long after William's death England and Holland fought each other in a maritime war, precipitated by England's attempt to monopolize colonial trade. Oddly, this war, which lasted from 1652 to 1654, favoured the exiled Stuarts. William was made stadtholder of Zealand when he was two years of age. In the face of diminishing resources, Mary managed to house and feed her large refugee family while simultaneously bargaining with Dutch magnates to assure her son's future in the Netherlands. Mary's staying power was considerable and the fortunes of European politics favoured her cause. By mid-1660 she was strongly entrenched as the sole regent of the young William of Orange, and her brother Charles had returned to England in triumph as its new king, taking with him his two younger brothers, James and Henry. Mary returned to England for a visit but found things not to her liking and was soon back in Holland. However, her influence was curtailed for on Christmas Eve of 1660 she died of smallpox, not yet thirty years of age. She died having left her ten-year-old son, William of Orange, a clear path to assume his father's position as head of the government of the United Provinces of the Netherlands.

William of Orange was a thin, sickly, asthmatic boy, but an exceptionally good student. He spoke Dutch, English, French and German fluently and had a good understanding of Spanish, Italian and Latin as well. Even as a child he was wary, kept his own counsel and was particularly self-reliant.

Considering that he had never known his father, lost his mother when only ten years of age and had no siblings, his was a rather lonely childhood, not dissimilar to that of his great-grandfather, James I of England. William's future was always in the hands of key Dutch political players, including his paternal grandmother, the Dowager-Princess Amalia, who had not enjoyed a warm relationship with his mother. As a child William learned to survive in a cold and hostile environment, acquiring early the ability to chart his own course in life. His relationship with the English branch of his family, his English uncles, Charles and James, and eventually his two younger English cousins, Mary and Anne, was probably not close. He was eleven years old when Mary, the elder of his two cousins and his future wife, was born in London on 30 April 1662.

Mary Stuart was the first daughter and second child born to the Duke and Duchess of York. She was also the first of only two of their eight children who would survive to adult life; her older brother was born in 1660 and died in 1661. At the time of her birth, her parents, James and Anne, had been married two years and her uncle, King Charles II, was about to marry Princess Catherine of Braganza. The following year a brother, James, was born and then in 1665 her sister Anne. James died a year after Anne was born and, of the four subsequent children born to the duke and duchess, only Edgar would live beyond infancy, dying before his fifth birthday. The nursery of the Yorks was busy but had only two graduates.

Mary's entry into the world was inauspicious and apparently without event. Her childhood was secure and happy, she was a very pretty little girl, with dark curly hair and pink cheeks, and she enjoyed the resultant attention. The death of her mother when she was just eight caused some dislocation in her life but, with her younger sister, Anne, she was accorded considerable respect and attention as a Stuart in the line of succession to the throne. The sisters were placed by Charles II at Richmond House as 'children of the State' under the care of Lady Frances Villiers and two Anglican chaplains.

This gave them security while also putting them beyond any religious problems which their father's conversion to the Church of Rome might have engendered, as Charles specifically directed that they should be raised as Protestants. Their idyllic childhood was described by Mary's biographer, Elizabeth Hamilton:

> Well away from the wickedness of the court and breathing the clean country air, the girls lived an uneventful life, wandering in the deer park, playing cards and indulging in a 'bellyful of discourse' with the other young ladies who had been picked as suitable companions. The six Villiers daughters formed the nucleus of the establishment and other girls, such as Frances Apsley, Sarah Jennings and Anne Trelawny, were added to their number. In this girls' school atmosphere . . . the Lady Mary and her friends poured out their hearts on quires of paper with crows' quill pens; they danced, sang and drew, and succumbed to occasional bouts of illness with all the attendant remedies – blistering, bleeding, leeching, taking physic, followed by possett drink 'to make it work'.[1]

In this innocent world Mary began a correspondence with Frances Apsley that would continue into their adult lives, the girls were all close, their relationships somewhere between sisters and schoolmates. At Richmond House the letters between the girls were conveyed back and forth by their drawing master, the dwarf, Mr Gipson. Mary signed her letters as Mary, Marie, Mary Clorine or even Clorine Mary and she addressed Frances Apsley as Aurelia. Some extant letters were published in 1924 by Benjamin Bathurst as *Letters of Two Queens* and they reveal both Mary and her sister, Anne, as highly imaginative phonetic spellers, and not quite as innocent as Hamilton would have us believe. In 1676, at the age of thirteen, Mary wrote to Frances: 'Who can imagine that my dear husband can be so love sike for fear I do not love her but I have more reason to think that she is sike of being wery of me for in tow or three years men are alwais wery of thier wifes and look for Mrs. As sone as they can gett them but I think I am pretty wel asured of the love of my dear but if I had al that is to be had in the world I shold never have anufe if my dearest oh!'[2] While some have seen homosexual innuendo in these letters, it is likely that they were only the product of girls living in a make-believe environment, probably without much exposure to the world.

Although the girls had tutors at Richmond House it is clear that Mary was not much of a scholar. She enjoyed dancing and art, and spoke French fluently, but had little interest in either Latin or Greek. Writing shortly after her death, Gilbert Burnet, Bishop of Sarum, observed: 'Next to the best subjects, She bestowed most of Her time on Books of History, chiefly of the later Ages, particularly those of her own Kingdoms, as being the most proper to give Her useful Instruction. . . . When her eyes were endangered by Reading too much, She found out the amusement of Work.'[3]

Older than her sister by just under three years, Mary was protective of Anne and judging from observations made by each of them later in life, they were very close as children. James was not an important presence in the lives of his young daughters after the death of their mother, his first wife, and it is likely that King Charles was more of a surrogate, though distant, father to them. However, eventually their stepmother, Mary Beatrice, took a sincere interest in Mary and Anne, and they were fond of her, perhaps in part because she was only a few years older than Mary and in that sense more of an older sister. Every effort was made to ground Mary and Anne in Protestant theology, with multiple tutors, including bishops, seeing to their religious education under the aegis of their uncle. In the Villiers household, far from the cares of English and European affairs, Mary grew up to become an attractive and rather frivolous young woman who had neither interest in nor understanding of politics or government – quite a different person from her husband-to-be, William of Orange, who was steeped in politics and international intrigue from his earliest years.

As Mary was breathing the clean cool air of the English countryside without a care in the world, William was already making his own way in the tough and uncompromising world of continental realpolitik. He visited his uncles in England in 1670 and impressed all who met him with his seriousness and strong Protestant religious beliefs. Early in 1672 he led Dutch forces against the vastly superior French army in the defence of his country and although he lost his first battle, nonetheless he impressed his countrymen as a tough and resourceful general. In June 1672, at the age of twenty-one, William was proclaimed stadtholder, essentially first among the equals of the heads of the Dutch provinces, and head of all the Dutch military. Over the next few years he was constantly involved with his military forces in facing superior French armies and he began to acquire an intense dislike for his uncle, Charles II, King of England, whose growing dependence on Louis XIV of France made him a foolish meddler in continental affairs, in William's eyes.

In the throes of governing his small country and leading its army against foreign invaders, the young William remained thin to the point of being gaunt, suffered frequent attacks of asthma and, in 1675, survived a severe attack of smallpox. Although not the figure one would pick for a leader of men, nevertheless William was an excellent field general and led his men in person, pushing himself to the very limits of physical endurance. He never sought to avoid danger or combat and was wounded in the arm by a musket ball at the siege of Maestricht in 1676. With his mind attuned to political and military realities he knew that England must always be accounted for in his plans for Holland. Marriage to an English princess would undoubtedly help to strengthen ties between Holland and England, aiding his long quest to keep France from controlling his country. Negotiations for the hand of Mary were relatively simple and straightforward.

In 1677, when she was fifteen years of age, Mary was

married to the 27-year-old William of Orange and left London for Holland shortly after the wedding. A smallpox epidemic was raging in London and its victims included Mary's sister the Princess Anne and their childhood playmate, Frances Villiers. By leaving London when she did, Mary escaped being infected with smallpox. Anne's illness kept her from attending the wedding but she recovered not long after, although Frances Villiers died.

Mary was well received by the Dutch people and she was initially happy in the court of the United Provinces, despite the fact that William was endlessly fighting with the French. During the twelve years she lived in Holland, Mary matured both physically and emotionally. Her match with William seemed to be a good one and they were a compatible couple, although Mary was often lonely and suffered her share of emotional disappointments. Within the space of a single year, she lost her only two pregnancies, both of which terminated spontaneously and early. Unfortunately, Mary did not become pregnant again, though she was proven fertile and in her best years for childbearing. It cannot be known if William and Mary maintained a constant intimacy, for William was often away, campaigning with his army in the field. At this time, compounding loneliness and disappointment from pregnancy loss, Mary started having attacks of fever.

It is certain that at least some of these fevers were from malaria, then prevalent in the lowlands that constituted most of Holland. The particular form of malaria then common in Holland was *Plasmodium vivax*, found also in the lowlands of coastal England, and usually not severe in its manifestations. However, even malaria of this relatively benign variety may compromise fertility, because it leads to anaemia and general debility, and it may also directly cause miscarriage when malarial parasites affect the function of the placenta. Although *Plasmodium vivax* malaria is virtually never fatal it can exact considerable disability in the sufferer and it may be complicated by other illnesses. Surviving records show that Mary also had 'gravel' in her urine associated with episodes of fever, surely representing significant urinary tract infection. While urinary bladder infections are very common in otherwise healthy young women, Mary might also have had an infection that spread higher up in her urinary tract, to her kidneys. This, of course, is much more serious and, in concert with recurring attacks of malaria, could have considerably reduced her vitality and the likelihood that she would conceive or be able to carry a pregnancy to term.

While William was away at war Mary missed him, but when he was home his presence brought a new threat to her composure. By late 1678, William was less involved in military matters, the peace treaty at Nijmegen having been concluded, and Mary saw more of her husband than she had previously in their marriage. Unfortunately, he may also have been seeing more of Elizabeth Villiers, her childhood friend and maid-of-honour, and this can only have made his presence at court worse for her than his absence. It must be said that proof of romantic involvement between William and Elizabeth is lacking; Elizabeth is thought to have been very intelligent and it is possible that any interest William had in her was intellectual rather than carnal. However, the court was abuzz with rumours about William and Elizabeth, and Mary was ultimately forced to face these distressing speculations head-on, for this scandal was even part of the gossip of the court of her uncle Charles in England.

In spite of this threat to their relationship, Mary came to love William, as evidenced in her diary entries over the remaining years of her life. In like manner William appears to have loved her in return. Elizabeth Villiers apart, and in sharp distinction to his English uncles, Charles and James, William did not maintain mistresses or father bastards. Rather he appears to have been a husband devoted to his wife, rather like his English grandfather, Charles I, had been to Henrietta Maria. Mary was given to ruminations about William and also about her health. Her diary entries show that she had an obsessive concern about her physical health, perhaps in greater measure than was good for her: 'I also found myself very inconvenienced by pains in the kidneys, which he [Dr Drelincourt] judged came from the gravel, so that he ordered me some remedies for that, besides, I was bled; the lack of sleep and the troubles and vexations through which I have been rendered this very necessary. They took from me then on the 8th 8 ounces of blood: on the 9th I took something for the gravel. . . .'[4]

It would not be unreasonable to conclude that Mary suffered from depression at this time and probably even more intensely later in her short life, a further assault on her general health and vitality and another known impediment to fertility and conception. Depression can certainly be set in motion by external events, but it is also an illness just as certainly as pneumonia or arthritis, and it can afflict a patient recurrently, without any particular external stimulus. Mary had fears of illness and death. Some of these feelings were quite morbid and had little to do with the reality of the rather minor illnesses all humans suffer. For example, in 1690, then as the reigning Queen of England, she wrote in a letter to her cousin Sophia, the Electress of Hanover:

Yet I sinned in one thing which was that all the crosses I met with in this world, made me melancholly and even wish to dye or at last grow very indifferent to life, and this I found by a sore throat I had, so that the 7th of Aprill which was upon a Monday old style, I did really thinck my self in danger. Saturday and Sunday I had found myself ill with it, and had endeavoured as much as I could to get my things in order, and Monday found myself so ill, that I did believe I should dye, and was so well satisfied with it, that I was really rather glad then sorry. . . .

My sore throat increased and with it my satisfaction. I spent my time in prayers and meditations when I could be alone. I had often wished to dye of a consumption, but now I thought this yet better; for I thought I should see my self dye and have my senses, which I imagind to be the happiest death that could be; for I found my self in a good state as to my soul; for my only concern was for my debts, which were unpaid. Next day I was forced to be let blood, which gave me present ease, and so with taking physick the next day I recovered.[5]

If the true mark of a depressed patient is the ability to project a depressed mood in speech or written words, then Mary certainly was depressed when she wrote this letter. It was not only concern about her health that bothered her. Family matters also weighed on her mind, for in spite of their closeness as children, in adult life Mary did not always enjoy good relations with her sister, and being in Holland and away from London accentuated her perceptions of this discord. In a letter written to the Electress Sophia at a later time she shows jealousy for Anne's relationship with Sarah Churchill, Lady Marlborough: 'which was the continuance of the coldness between my sister and I, which, had there been none else concerned, I should not have scrupeld speacking of it; but I saw plainly she was so absolutly governd by Lady Marlborough that it was to no purpose'.[6]

In 1678 and the years immediately following the Treaty of Nijmegen, William had time to observe the domestic politics of England more closely, and he courted a variety of English political figures. In 1680 he visited England, meeting with his uncles, Charles and James, and also his cousin, James, Duke of Monmouth. Unfortunately for William and Holland, the Nijmegen treaty allowed Louis XIV and France to gain in strength. So when Charles II died suddenly in 1685, William had a vested interest in maintaining close relations with England and gaining a political ally against Louis XIV.

In 1685 William was in the prime of life and although he had occasional asthma attacks and the early signs of some other pulmonary problems, he enjoyed relatively good health. As James II began to lose control of political life in England and found himself increasingly at odds with Parliament, William became concerned and was more and more sympathetic to those in England who opposed James. Although James did not have the same dependency on Louis XIV as his brother Charles had, nonetheless he was strongly Roman Catholic and William had good reason to imagine that James and Louis would form a military alliance to the detriment of Holland. In England the fault line of religion opened and soon the strongly Protestant William was allied with his fellow Protestants in England against the Catholic James. Holland as a nation was firmly behind William in its concern about the stability of the English monarchy and planning for an invasion of England began early in 1688. The birth of James Francis Edward Stuart in June widened the fault line still further and hastened the planning. Thus, with direct military support from German Protestant princes, William set sail for England in the autumn of 1688 with a large armada. After having been forced to regroup after a storm scattered his 500 ships, he finally landed on the south coast on 5 November. He did not intend to depose James but James's flight, thereby abandoning the Stuart right to rule England, left a power vacuum which William could not ignore. Early in February 1689, Mary arrived in England from Holland to be with her husband and together, at the invitation of Parliament, they became the joint monarchs of England later that month.

When their reign began in 1689 Mary was a plump 26-year-old woman in good physical health; proven fertile, she was, nevertheless, as yet without children. William was nearing forty and was variously described as thin, asthmatic and sickly. Indeed by this time in his life he had already suffered episodes of haemoptysis – coughing up blood. Although the reigning queen in her native land, Mary was scarcely concerned with affairs of state, whereas William was now king of two countries, with double the responsibility. With Holland again being pressed by France, Ireland especially contentious and Scotland still largely loyal to James, it is possible that William had more pressing concerns on his mind than impregnating his wife. Mary was young and healthy and there seemed to be no hurry in seeing to a family. Unfortunately, Mary's good health would be ended suddenly by an acute fatal illness.

The circumstances of Mary's illness and death are particularly well documented. In October 1694 William returned from the seemingly interminable war on the continent to contain the forces of Louis XIV and France. Charles Talbot, Duke of Shrewsbury, had supported Mary as her Secretary of State during William's absence and political affairs in England were going well. It had been noted that Mary had suffered several colds during the autumn, while William was exhausted and even thinner than usual after his campaigning.

On 20 December Mary began to feel ill. Tradition has it that, before informing anyone of her indisposition she put her affairs in order, burning papers and letters, and wrote a letter to her husband. Elizabeth Hamilton has observed in her book, *William's Mary*, that 'Only when she had put her affairs in order did the Queen tell her husband that she felt ill. She guessed that she had caught smallpox and the doctors immediately assumed the same. William abandoned hope at once. . . . All those who had not already had smallpox were sent away from the Palace. The Queen had been treating herself with the remedies she usually took for a bad cold, but nine doctors were now summoned. On Sunday, December 23 there were signs of a rash.'[7] Five days later she was dead.

Exanthems (acute generalized reddened skin rashes associated with fever) in adults are often confusing and measles was considered a possible diagnosis, as was a combination of smallpox and measles. There was disagreement among Mary's physicians, the chance of recovery from measles in an adult being much greater than recovery from smallpox, of course. Charles Creighton, the great, late nineteenth-century chronicler of epidemic illness in England, has provided a medically complete and accurate description of Mary's illness and death, drawing largely from the account written by one of her physicians, Walter Harris.

On the third day from the initial symptoms the eruption appeared, with a very troublesome cough; the eruption came out in such a manner that the physicians were very doubtful whether it would prove to be smallpox or measles. On the fourth day the smallpox showed itself in the face and the rest of the body 'under its proper and distinct form'. But on the sixth day, in the morning, the variolous pustules were changed all over her breast into large red spots 'of the measles'; and the erysipelas, or rose, swelled her whole face, the former pustules giving place to it. That evening many livid round petechiae [tiny haemorrhages into the skin] appeared on the forehead above the eyebrows, and on the temples, which [Dr Walter] Harris says he had foretold in the morning. One physician said these were not petechiae, but sphacelated [gangrenous] spots; but the next morning a surgeon proved by his lancet that they contained blood. During the night following the sixth day, Dr Harris sat up with the patient and observed that she had great difficulty of breathing, followed soon after by a copious spitting of blood. On the seventh day the spitting of blood was succeeded by blood in the urine. On the eighth day the pustules on the limbs, which had kept the normal variolous character longest, lost their fulness and changed into round spots of deep red or scarlet colour, smooth and level with the skin, like the stigmata of the plague. Harris observed about the region of the heart one large pustule filled with matter, haveing a broad scarlet circle round it like a burning coal, under which a great deal of extravasated blood was found when the body was examined after death. Towards the end, the queen slumbered sometimes, but said she was not refreshed thereby. At last she lay silent for some hours; and some words that came from her shewed, says Burnet, that her thoughts had begun to break. She died on the 28th December, at one in the morning, in the ninth day of her illness.[8]

The Burnet referred to was Bishop Gilbert Burnet, who attended Mary and William in Mary's final illness and whose memoirs contain a record of this. A cleric, among physicians, he was a sharp observer. 'I will not enter into another's province, nor speak of matters so much out of the way of my own profession: but the physician's part was universally condemned, and her death was imputed to the negligence or unskilfulness of Dr Radcliffe. He was called for; and it appeared but too evidently that his opinion was chiefly considered, and was depended on.'[9] He went on to recount the irascible John Radcliffe's encounters with the Stuarts. Persona non grata with Anne for his relations with her branch of the family, he was nonetheless given grudging respect because his diagnostic acumen was usually superior to that of his peers, many of whom resented this fact. To compound the problem of his relations with the Stuarts, Radcliffe was a Jacobite, a supporter of King James II, and not given to dissimulation or concealment of his political beliefs.

There is no question but that Mary's final illness presented itself in an unusual form and that the clinical picture seemed to change over the brief course of the illness. Had she been in a modern teaching hospital, the controversy would likely have been even greater still, with consultants suggesting several other dire diseases not recognized in seventeenth-century London. Thus, with physicians and consultants coming and going through Mary's sickroom, all of them observing the evolution of her illness at distinctly different stages in the dead of winter when ambient light must have been meagre, it was not at all certain what the principal cause of her malady was. The anonymous author of the *British Medical Journal* series entitled *Some Royal Deathbeds* observed: 'Sir Thomas Millington, who was Physician-in-Ordinary to the King, gave it as his opinion that the Queen was suffering from measles, but Radcliffe pronounced her ailment to be small-pox.'[10]

Further clarification of these events, but more confusion as to the exact diagnosis, comes from a principal adviser to both

William and Mary, James Vernon, secretary to Charles Talbot, Duke of Shrewsbury. On 25 December, he wrote to Robert Sutton, 2nd Baron Lexington:

Here has been an universal concern for Her Majesty's indisposition, but none more sensible of it than the King, who would never be persuaded to lie out of the Queen's bedchamber, and there had his field bed brought in thither, to be at hand and ready upon all occasions to assist her. It was not till this morning that we have had any abatement in our apprehensions.

On Sunday, about nine in the morning, the Queen began to break out with spots, from whence the doctors concluded she had the small pox, and continued in that persuasion till last night that the nurse who lives with my Lady Pulteney, and is now appointed to attend Her Majesty, discovered it to be more like the measles, which the physicians being called to advise upon, Dr Ratcliffe came over immediately to the nurses's opinion, but Sir Thomas Millington suspended his judgment, as thinking there were symptoms both of the one and the other. The Queen slept several hours last night, and waked in very good temper, and has continued so ever since, getting some more sleep this afternoon, so that the King is more and more satisfied it is the measles, accompanied with an erysipelas, or rash. She is full of spots in her arms and extreme parts, and her head is a little swelled, and her eyes contracted, that she can scarce see: but we hope all will go off again in a short time.

The doctors do say that there was a puzzling composition in this distemper; but if Her Majesty goes on in this way of recovery, as, we thank God, there is great probability of it, the nurse will clearly have the better of the physicians, for they all along, expecting those spots should have filled, and find they did not, began to think the Queen in danger; and there was a great dejection of people's spirits till this happy alteration.[11]

James Vernon found John Radcliffe on the diagnostic side of measles, at least temporarily, in distinction to the author of the *British Medical Journal* series who found him favouring smallpox. Measles, prior to its near elimination in recent years, has always been uncommon in adults, particularly adults in their thirties, unless it reaches protected non-immune populations where all ages would be stricken. Measles and smallpox are highly contagious and spread quickly in epidemics, and the early phases can be confused. While it is unlikely that Mary would have escaped childhood measles, it was a reasonable diagnostic possibility at the beginning of her final illness given the description of its presentation. Two more letters, both to Lord Lexington, then the ambassador in Vienna, one from the Duke of Shrewsbury and the other from James Vernon, help to unravel the confusion about the manifestations and course of Mary's illness:

London, Dec. 28, 1694

It is my duty more than my inclination that obliges me to trouble you at this time; I should not else be fond of being the first to acquaint you with so ill news as this will bring. About a week since, her Majesty taken with an indisposition which seemed at first but slight, but turned afterwards to the smallpox, and that of so fatal a kind, that as soon as the physicians agreed that to be her disease, their apprehensions for her life grew very great; and ill symptoms increasing upon her, it pleased God this morning, about one of the clock, to take her out of this world.

Whitehall, Dec. 28, 1694

But it has pleased God to frustrate our hopes, so that you will now receive an account far different from my last, the alteration beginning that very night; for the next morning the physicians receded from their former opinion of the Queen's having the measles, and were then satisfied it was the small-pox, though a very unkind sort of them, with a mixture of St Anthony's fire [erysipelas], which is said to have occasioned the swelling about her eyes and mouth. Some few spots that were upon her temples began then to appear discoloured, and there were some other ill symptoms; whereupon more physicians were sent for – viz. Stockham, Coladon, and Gibbons, and the Queen was let blood in the temples, and many blisters drawn. She got a little rest towards the former part of that night, but any glimpse of hopes soon vanished again, and death seemed to advance upon her, she visibly declining, and her pulse growing weaker in spite of Sir Walter Raleigh's cordial [a stimulant] and King Charles's drops [extract of human skull]. The Archbishop of Canterbury made known to her her condition on Wednesday, without any dismay, as one long prepared for all extremities; and yesterday she received the Sacrament with great devotion and resignation. Last night a Council was called at Kensington, and some of the physicians were sent for to give an account how they found the Queen. Sir Thomas Millington told them they had observed the Queen to decline very fast till that noon, insomuch that they expected a speedy issue of it, but that she had not grown worse since; but upon her taking the bezoar cordial she appeared to be a little more lively, and that Dr Ratcliff thought her pulse to rise again, but he could not say he perceived any such thing. He told them the spots appeared all along but like so many flea bites, none of them raising the skin, which continued (as he expressed it) smooth like glass.

My Lord President [the Duke of Leeds] was then sent from the Council to his Majesty, to desire he would have some consideration of his own health; which was very necessary advice, since his Majesty has so much neglected himself since the Queen's first falling ill. It was but two nights since that he has been persuaded to lie out of her bedchamber, and then he would only remove to the next room. He has scarce got any sleep or taken any nourishment, and there is hardly any instance of so passionate a sorrow as the King has been overtaken with, which seemed excessive while life yet lasted, and tis risen to a greater degree since; so that he can hardly bear the sight of those what were more agreeable to him before. He had some fits like fainting yesterday, but to-day they have prevailed on him to bleed. Last night the Queen grew delirious, and continued so till she died.[12]

The indecision about Mary's diagnosis and the devotion and constancy of William, at her bedside throughout this terrible illness, are both important. It was difficult to determine whether Mary had a severe and atypical case of measles and would therefore almost certainly recover, or whether she had severe atypical smallpox and would almost certainly die. Secondly, William did love Mary and he put aside everything else in his life to be with her night and day through this terrible illness. Her death from acute haemorrhagic smallpox left William as the sole monarch of England, no longer with a Stuart on the throne beside him. In fact, Mary's death left England with a 44-year-old, widowed, asthmatic, Dutch monarch who was without an heir.

At the time of Mary's death, William was a strong king in control of the political life of England, having faced down Parliament with several vetos over its power vis-à-vis the power of the monarch. He remained the force to be reckoned with in continental affairs but, in spite of these successes, he is remembered as a man in chronically poor health and often near to exhaustion. However, he recovered quickly from a war wound suffered during a campaign in Ireland in 1690 and, in spite of repeated attacks of asthma and haemoptysis (coughing up blood), he was always up to the challenges of being both a king and a general. Indeed there is a remarkable paradox in his reputed poor health when set against his considerable accomplishments, for these accomplishments largely dwarf those of his seemingly much healthier Stuart predecessors. As far as international affairs are concerned, one might consider his crowning achievement the Peace of Ryswick, signed on 20 September 1697. This ended, albeit temporarily, the military adventuring of Louis XIV and France, thereby taking considerable pressure off both Holland and England, and it also recognized William as King of England.

It may be that the Peace of Ryswick was concluded just in time, for not long after that William began the slow physical decline that ended with his death early in 1702. By this time he had chronically swollen legs and he was sufficiently concerned that he consulted Dr John Radcliffe, who is reputed to have told him, as mentioned previously, 'I would not have your Majesty's two legs for your three kingdoms.' Radcliffe also told him that he could live three or four years if he moderated his lifestyle. William's personal physician, the Dutch Dr Govart Bidloo, was attentive and, though not given much respect by the London medical establishment, seems not to have caused any harm to William. William's leg swelling increased and at one point he developed an acute febrile illness associated with blisters on half of his trunk. This was probably herpes zoster, commonly called shingles. He may also have had recurrent boils. William was concerned about his failing health and consulted a number of Europe's leading physicians and surgeons, none of whom seemed to have solutions for his problems.

In February 1702, while riding at Hampton Court, William fell from his horse and broke his collar bone, under normal circumstances a relatively minor injury. The fracture was set by a competent surgeon but William seemed not to recover fully and by early March he had developed fever and shortness of breath. Over a period of several days his breathing became increasingly laboured and finally he was comfortable only when sitting up. He and his physicians knew that the end was nigh and he died quietly on Sunday, 8 March 1702, at fifty-one years of age. Two days later an autopsy was performed and the report was reprinted more than 200 years later in the *British Medical Journal*.[13]

POST-MORTEM EXAMINATION OF WILLIAM OF ORANGE

[The Report of] the Physicians and Surgeons commanded to assist at the dissecting of the Body of His Late Majesty at Kensington, March 10th, 1702. From the Original delivered to the Right honourable the Privy Council, London. Printed for John Nutt, near Stationers' Hall, 1702.

The Right Honourable and the Lord Chamberlain issued out his summons to such Physicians and Surgeons as his Lordship thought fit, appointing them to meet at Kensington and there to examine by Dissection into the State and condition of the Royal Body. The day after the Dissection, the said Physicians and Surgeons being met together again in order to the forming an account of what they had observed, Sir Thomas Millington, Sir Richard Blackmore and Doctor Hannes were deputed as a Committee to draw up the Report.

1. Upon viewing the Body, before Dissection, the following appearances were remarkable. The Body in general was much emaciated. Both the leggs up to the knees and a little higher, as also the Right Hand and Arm as far as the Elbow were considerably swell'd. There was likewise on the Left Thigh near the Hip, a Bladder full as big as a small Pullet's egg, resembling a Blane.
2. Upon opening the Belly, the Gutts were found of a livid Colour; and the Blood Contain'd in their vessels black. The Gutt called Ileon had in some places the marks of a slight Inflammation. The Stomach, Pancreas, Mesentery, Liver, Gallbladder, Spleen and Kidneys were all found and without fault.
3. The Thorax or Chest we observed that the Right side of the Lungs adher'd to the Pleura; and the Left, much more. From which upon separation, there issued forth a quantity of purulent or frothy serum. The upper lobe on the Left side of the Lungs and the part of the Pleura next to it were Inflamed to a degree

of Mortification. *And this we look upon as the Immediate cause of the King's death.* From the ventricles of the heart and the greater Blood vessels arising out of them were taken several large tough flesh-like substances of the kind call'd Polypus. The Heart itself was of the smaller size; but firm and strong.

4. Upon laying bare the Right Collarbone, we found it had been broken near the shoulder; and well set. Some extravasated Blood was lodged above and below the Fracture.

5. The Brain was perfectly sound and without any sign of distemper.

6. 'Tis very rare to find a Body with so little Blood, as was seen in this; there being more found in the Lungs than in all the Parts besides put together.

Doctors Present	*Surgeons Present*
Sir Richard Blackmore	Mr Bernard
Sir Theod. Colladon	Mr Cowper
Dr Hannes – Dr Laurence	Mr Gardner
Doctor Harrel – Sir Tho. Millington	Mr Roujat etc.
Doctor How – Professor Bidloo	
Doctor Hullen etc.	

Mary and William died prematurely, even by the reckoning of the time, and they left the prospects for continuance of any sort of Stuart rule considerably dimmed. In a sense, Mary's death was an aberration. She should have suffered smallpox at a much younger age, perhaps just before her marriage, and had it occurred then, it might have been in a milder form from which she would probably have survived, as did her sister, Anne.

When the several descriptions of her final illness are pooled it is possible to state with absolute certainty that Mary died of haemorrhagic smallpox, suffering the worst manifestations of smallpox known, even at that time. The diagnostic clues were the relatively flat confluent pustules with widespread haemorrhages in skin and mucous membranes, and an early reddish rash (hence the confusion with measles) with haemorrhages into the bases of the pustules. This is one of the least common forms of smallpox, accounting for less than 3 per cent of all cases, and it is always fatal. Medicine is in the debt of Dr Ramachandra Rao, at one time superintendent of the Infectious Diseases Hospital of Madras, India, for classifying the various types and subtypes of smallpox and delineating its natural history. It is the use of his schema that allows the diagnosis of haemorrhagic smallpox to be made in Mary, the manifestations of particular severity being haemoptysis (bloody sputum) and haematuria (bloody urine). The bleeding occurs because the blood's platelets are depleted from acute damage to the bone marrow by the smallpox virus. Without adequate platelets, blood clots poorly and bleeding at many sites is the rule. Women were more likely to experience this most severe form of smallpox than men, although the reason for this difference in incidence between the sexes is not known.[14]

The initial confusion about her diagnosis, smallpox versus measles, is understandable. Measles is caused by the rubeola virus and is highly contagious. Prior to vaccination for this disease it was uncommon to leave childhood without being infected with the rubeola virus and thus, measles has always been uncommon in adults. However, when it does occur it may be much more severe than in children and the prominent confluent reddish rash and respiratory symptoms Mary suffered are quite typical of it. Only the full course of her disease makes it clear that she did not have measles, but quite certainly acute haemorrhagic smallpox. Nothing could have been done to save her life, probably not even had she been in a modern hospital with every possible treatment and support facility available. In a recently published book on the death of English monarchs, the retired surgeon Clifford Brewer identified Mary's death as from 'malignant smallpox', basically the same as the haemorrhagic variety.[15] Smallpox has been eradicated from the world; the last naturally occurring case was recorded in East Africa in 1977. Ironically, there were two subsequent cases in 1978, following a laboratory accident in an English hospital which resulted in the release of the variola virus and the infection of hospital workers.

William died after a long period of failing health and although the cause of the acute illness which took his life is certain, bacterial pneumonia, the cause or causes of his chronically poor health are less clear. By modern standards, the physicians and surgeons who reviewed the autopsy findings were correct in determining that the cause of death lay in the pus and acute inflammation of the upper lobe of the left lung. This is the picture of acute bacterial pneumonia and is quite consistent with the nature of his terminal illness, characterized by fever and progressive shortness of breath. The fact that the lungs were adherent to the inner aspects of the chest wall, on both the right and the left sides, suggests previous pulmonary infectious or inflammatory disease. The small heart and lack of mention of fluid in the lower lobes of both lungs makes congestive heart failure an unlikely part of his terminal illness, but it cannot be wholly discounted either because pneumonia begets heart failure and the fact that he had to sit to breathe towards the end of his life is quite typical of the latter. The detailed inventory of the organs, particularly in the abdomen, means that the autopsy was quite thoroughly carried out. It is difficult to dissect all the way back to the pancreas and the kidneys from an anterior approach, but it should be recognized that the autopsy was more easily performed because William was quite thin, if not wasted, judging by the description of his body before it was opened.

The dark blood mentioned was probably the result of agonal events and the post-mortem state, and the cyst on his thigh was of no importance. It is difficult to understand exactly what is meant by the paucity of blood found everywhere but the lungs; it might mean that the blood seen was pale, as with anaemia. This is a very tempting possibility. The fleshy 'polyps' in the ventricles of the heart that projected into the great vessels were probably old blood clots that were organized and adherent to either the heart valves or the walls of the heart and blood vessels. These had probably been present for weeks or months, or even longer, and may or may not have had much to do with his terminal illness. There is some chance that they might have interfered with heart valve function but this is not likely. There is also the possibility that they contained bacteria and that William had been suffering from sub-acute bacterial endocarditis (infection of the inner lining of the heart) for a few weeks, even a few months. If this were the case it would explain his slow decline and also his possible anaemia, leading to pneumonia and death.

If one combines the many descriptions of illness during William's life – interestingly few of them from physicians – it is possible to conclude that his main lifelong illness was asthma complicated by episodes of acute bronchitis. He probably also suffered chronic bronchitis, explaining his persistent severe cough and occasional bouts of haemoptysis. During attacks of acute asthma the sufferer is quite sick and not able to do much more than struggle to breathe, but between attacks, breathing and lung function are usually normal or nearly normal. Asthma is common in childhood and often does not persist into adult life, although William's asthma continued to the end of his life. Over the years many have assumed that William had pulmonary tuberculosis, but it cannot be stated with certainty whether he did or not. A chronic cough and haemoptysis suggest this, but the lungs at autopsy were not described as having scarring or cavities, the hallmarks of significant chronic pulmonary tuberculosis. Lung scarring and cavitation would undoubtedly have been described if either or both had been present. It should be assumed that asthma and chronic bronchitis were precursors to the pneumonia which ended William's life.

William's four-year decline after the Peace of Ryswick in 1697 was almost certainly unrelated to either lung or heart disease but could well have been from a slowly progressive anaemia. This possibility has been suggested by his biographer, Nesca Robb, who thought that he may have suffered from pernicious anaemia, a disease common in middle-aged northern Europeans caused by lack of ability to absorb vitamin B-12 from the gut. This can only be conjecture but it would explain the swollen legs, progressive pallor and tiredness in a thin man in the absence of obvious heart, kidney or liver disease.[16] Another possibility, of about equal likelihood, would be hypothyroidism, a decrease in the function of the thyroid gland, also capable of producing much the same clinical picture, including anaemia. Thus, it is known that William died of pneumonia after suffering from asthma and bronchitis throughout his life, but it is not known what other chronic disease or diseases preceded this terminal event; pernicious anaemia, hypothyroidism and sub-acute bacterial endocarditis are all possibilities and he may even have had any two or all three of these conditions.

It is not at all clear why Mary and William did not produce heirs. Mary was certainly pregnant at least once and perhaps twice. Some have speculated that the second pregnancy might have been pseudocyesis, sometimes called false or phantom pregnancy, with Mary, desperately wanting to become pregnant, experiencing many of the symptoms of pregnancy, including amenorrhoea. It is well known that women who yearn for pregnancy often show every manifestation of early pregnancy, including missed menstrual periods, morning nausea and even breast tenderness. She who suffers pseudocyesis truly believes that she is pregnant and, as the early months of pregnancy may be an intensely personal experience for a woman, she may easily convince others that she is pregnant. So when a menstrual period finally occurs it is interpreted as miscarriage. Whether Mary's second episode was truly pregnancy or pseudocyesis is moot, but it is known that she was never again thought to be pregnant. However, there is nothing to suggest that she had any gynaecological disease that would have compromised her fertility. In contrast to his Stuart uncles, Charles and James, William was not known to have mistresses who might have had his children, thereby proving his fertility. William might have been of low fertility and, for that matter, Mary might have been of relatively low fertility as well.

The fact that Mary and William were first cousins may have compromised her ability to carry a pregnancy to term, although probably not her ability to conceive. It is known that a substantial percentage of pregnancies in normal women terminate in early miscarriages, with a large portion of these aborted foetuses demonstrating genetic abnormalities. It is further presumed that these abnormalities are a major reason for the unrecognized early end of such pregnancies. The chance of genetic abnormality is increased in first cousin marriages, so Mary would have had an increased likelihood of miscarriage on this basis alone. It must be concluded that the reason or reasons why Mary and William did not produce heirs cannot be determined from the information available.

Mary and William were given their thrones by a Convention Parliament which was strong and able to assert its power, not directly limiting their personal powers, but making clear its supremacy. The Declaration of Rights which came from Parliament in 1689 tipped the balance of power, for all time, from the English monarchy to the English Parliament. No tax would ever again be levied without the consent of Parliament and the monarch's right to ignore its actions was ended. The erosion of the power of the Stuart dynasty through disease and disability in the four kings who reigned during the years from 1603 until 1688 allowed the English Parliament to grow in power until it finally had the upper hand; this was in stark contrast to monarchy and government in other European states. In 1689, giving the throne of England to Mary and William as equals accomplished several things for Parliament. As a Stuart, Mary continued the dynasty. William, a born executive if there ever was one, had the power to rule England but only through the absolute right of his Stuart wife, so in a sense he could not be said to have conquered England and taken its throne. After Mary and William accepted the crowns offered them by Parliament they accepted the Declaration of Rights and so, beyond ruling England for Parliament, the challenge for Mary and William in 1689 was to produce heirs and there was every reason to imagine they would succeed.

Mary's decision not to participate directly in ruling England but rather to defer to her husband from the House of Orange diminished Stuart power, and her failure to become pregnant and produce heirs during the five years she was Queen of England must be seen as disability, further weakening the Stuart hold on the throne. Her death was premature – she was fertile and might well have had additional pregnancies. Perhaps if William had been more available to her and been in better physical health she would have had more pregnancies, but this is mere speculation. Had she not died of smallpox, she would have been thirty-nine years old at the time of William's death, and had she remarried she might yet have been capable of producing a Stuart heir. Mary has been accorded relatively little attention by historians and biographers, as she was perpetually in the shadow of her energetic husband and her sister, Anne. This is unfortunate because Mary, the first truly Protestant English monarch in nearly forty years, was the principal reason why William of Orange was invited by prominent political figures in England to help depose James II. She seemed to hold the future of the Stuart dynasty in her womb, as it were. It had taken the Stuarts eighty-five years to put a native, born and bred member of the Church of England on the English throne, albeit seated beside a Dutchman, and still she failed to provide for the continuation of the dynasty. Her death left her 44-year-old Dutch husband to rule England alone for a further eight years and so the Stuart dynasty sputtered out yet again, as it had with the death of Charles I in 1649 and the abandonment of the throne by James II in 1688.

In 1701, the year of James's death and a year prior to William's death, the Act of Settlement assured the Hanoverian Protestant succession to the English throne. It is to William's great credit that he had more sense than his Stuart predecessors for, after the death of Anne's son and only heir, the eleven-year-old Duke of Gloucester in July 1700, he summoned Parliament to deal with the succession to the throne. To underscore the Hanoverian place in the succession, he visited Sophia, Electress of Hanover and granddaughter of the first Stuart King of England, James I, at Het Loo in September 1700. William clearly wished to leave nothing to chance – he knew the Stuarts well, and he was perceptive enough to anticipate that, with seventeen pregnancies and no living children, Anne would die without an heir. After his lifelong battles with Louis XIV, William would have wanted to avoid at all costs the accession of James Francis Edward Stuart to the throne of England. Louis XIV had acknowledged the Catholic James Francis Edward as James III in 1701, in spite of the tenor of the Peace of Ryswick. Had he become King of England and beholden to Louis, the small Dutch nation would have been in a vice grip between England and France. One wonders how much William's actions were taken to save the Dutch rather than the English, sacrificing the weak and sickly Stuart dynasty to protect his native country, Holland. Whatever his motives actually were, William administered the coup de grace to the Stuart dynasty.

EIGHT

Anne and William, Duke of Gloucester

THE END OF THE STUART MONARCHY

Sir Hans Sloane, physician, botanist and bibliophile, sat down at a desk in his newly acquired spacious Chelsea home and wrote a summary of Queen Anne's medical problems of the past several days. He knew Anne well as a patient, she was morbidly obese, lame with arthritis and her recent illness had brought her close to death. It was not entirely clear to him why she got sick so quickly and, considering her general level of disability and infirmity, how she managed to recover. After organizing his notes and the letters he had received about Anne from other physicians he wrote:

On Friday morning [December] 25 1713 I found about half an houre after seven a letter from Dr Shadwell upon my table enclosing me one from Dr Arbuthnotte to Dr Lawrence giving an account of her Majesty having a great rigor [shaking chills], palpitations of the heart, strait breathing, quick pulse, and vomiting through the

day. . . . [She complained of] a smarting sensation on the
inside of her right thigh [made worse] with the warmth of
her body. This made her uneasy in making water unless
when up. It was thought by Dr Shadwell her physician
who came an hour after me to give her a clyster [enema]
and to wait for an opportunity of throwing in the bark
[quinine]. . . . The clyster was ten ounces of a common
decoction . . . it gave her one stool and it relieved her. . . .
The quickness of the pulse abated and alleviation of all the
symptoms [caused her] to gradually grow better . . . so
that on Saturday morning at four o'clock and all that day
it was quiet tho the pulse and other symptoms were such
as I concluded there might be no more of this fever or if
there were it would after another paroxysm be cured with
the bark. The water [urine] was of a pale amber colour
with a small whitish settlement as in a former intermitting
fever [like] chicken broath. . . . There appeared a smarting
[on] the inferior [aspect] of her right thigh, which
appeared of a reddish brownish colour, the cuticula having
[illegible] some [illegible] on it. It appeared [that] night
from her sitting up more, red on which the physicians
were sent for and Mr Blondell [surgeon]. He . . . said it was
erysipelas. I did nothing but agreed to a foment of calomel
[mercury] to imbrocate it next morning if it increased. . . .
This morning a decoction of bark was begun again.[1]

The account goes on with detailed descriptions of what
obviously was an extensive bacterial infection of Anne's very
plump right thigh. She was given repeated doses of 'The
Bark' which Sloane understood might have caused her
diarrhoea but she did not have the expected transient tinnitus
or deafness so common with larges doses of this powerful and
useful medicine.

Anne was a cooperative and compliant patient, as
evidenced by the facts that she did not baulk at bitter
medicines and uncomfortable treatments. She even allowed
her male doctors to examine her inner thighs in the middle

of the night, presumably with her bedchamber women present. Modesty apart, such an examination is daunting in a short plump female patient in her own bed, even in modern times with adequate illumination and experienced nursing assistance.

Over the next several months Sloane's journal entries about his queen regularly describe the character of her pulse, usually *dure* (hard, bounding) and her stools, sometimes containing blood. His comments on her appetite are telling as well, for Anne thoroughly enjoyed the pleasures of the table and, when feeling well, ate like a field hand at harvest time. In this regard Sloane wrote: 'Wednesday, Thursday, Friday mending, the last day ate a [whole] roasted chicken.'

A Scot like Anne's favourite physician, John Arbuthnot, Sloane was shrewd, wealthy and well connected, and Anne liked him. A botanist of the highest calibre, he had been secretary of the Royal Society for twenty years and knew everyone in London who was worth knowing. He and the small army of Anne's other active attending physicians (including John Arbuthnot, David Hamilton, Thomas Lawrence, John Shadwell and Edward Southwell) were in daily contact as they observed the queen closely, sharing their findings and constantly modifying treatment regimens. Not welcome in Anne's presence, but nonetheless aware of what his medical colleagues were doing, John Radcliffe fussed over the complexities of their dosing her with 'The Bark'.

During the first two months of 1714 Anne daily grew stronger and the infection in her thigh slowly resolved; she enjoyed her forty-ninth birthday celebration with her ladies early in February. In a cooperative effort with her ladies' artifice and her doctors' help and encouragement, Anne gathered all of her strength, put on a new gown and her regalia, and was present at the opening of Parliament in March 1714. Anne's physicians knew that she was living on borrowed time, however; her death and the death of the Stuart monarchy could not be postponed much longer.

As the eighteenth century dawned, the clock of the Stuarts

and of indefeasible monarchy in Britain was starting to run down. It would chime once more, for Anne, and then would stop forever. Parliament had won the seventeenth-century contest for supremacy with the Stuart dynasty, while on the continent the Bourbons and Habsburgs reigned on. Their power would be uncontested until the end of the eighteenth century when bloody revolution would spread across France. The future for the British monarchy would be less violent but almost as final. Anne came to the throne in 1702 sickly and spent, not unlike the Stuart dynasty she represented.

Anne Stuart was born on 6 February 1665 to James, Duke of York and his wife, Anne. At the time of her birth no one could have imagined that Anne Stuart would one day rule England, that she would unite the thrones of England and Scotland, or that she would be the very last Stuart monarch. Anne, like her older sister Mary, was raised by the Protestant Villiers family. She had an uneventful childhood, although the *Dictionary of National Biography* mentions: 'She appears to have been a sickly child, and when about five years of age was sent over on a visit to France for the benefit of her health.'[2] In all likelihood she was not as sickly as her biographical entry suggests but a normal and quite average child of her time.

Anne had smallpox at the age of twelve and so missed her sister Mary's wedding to William of Orange. Eye problems have been mentioned by several biographers over the years but these do not seem to have been of importance to Anne's overall health. It is possible that she had a mild visual problem, perhaps nearsightedness or a squint.

At the age of eighteen, Anne married Prince George of Denmark, who was then thirty years of age. They enjoyed a happy marriage of twenty-five years, ending when George died in 1708. In contrast to Mary and William before them, George did not share Anne's crown. Rather, George was Anne's consort and as such he had no particular responsibility in the government of England, although from 1702 to 1708 he was the nominal head of the army and navy. George was the second son of King Frederick III of Denmark. At one time he had been a serious contender for the throne of Poland, but his strong Lutheran background and unwillingness to convert to Catholicism kept him from the final consideration. George was a kind and decent man and although not much interested in politics, he did have considerable interest in science and navigation and was an active member of the Royal Society. He suffered from asthma and, during a particularly severe attack, was attended by John Radcliffe, whose medical skills impressed Anne greatly. George's role was to assist Anne in providing an heir to the throne. In consideration of the fact that Anne had seventeen pregnancies in total, he can be judged to have been an able assistant. Anne lived for six years after George's death and by all accounts she truly mourned him and missed him. George has often been regarded as a dull and uninteresting man, but it may be that he was merely a stolid, phlegmatic Scandinavian who was not always at ease in the court circles of cosmopolitan London.

Few physical descriptions of Anne by her contemporaries survive, although a succinct and probably accurate one was recorded by John Heneage Jesse, author of *Memoirs of the Court of England from the Revolution in 1688 to the Death of George the Second*. He combined a number of sources, none identified specifically apart from the remarks of Anne's close friend, Sarah Churchill, Duchess of Marlborough.

In person, Anne was of the middle size, and in her youth is said to have been well made. Even after her accession to the throne, the Duchess of Marborough admits that her 'person and appearance were very graceful'; and adds, that there was 'something of majesty in her look'. Her hands were extremely delicate and well-shaped; her features regular and strongly marked; her complexion ruddy; her hair of a dark brown; and though her countenance usually wore a shade of melancholy, yet the impression which it left was not disagreeable. In the last years of her life, her figure, which in her youth had been delicate, became corpulent, almost to grossness. . . . The great, indeed the only charm, in the conversation of Anne, was the peculiar sweetness of her voice, which, to the last, never failed in captivating her auditors, and leaving them irresistibly impressed in her favour.[3]

From this rather tentative and restrained description, and when viewing Anne's portraits, it is fair to say that she was no beauty, but rather a plain, stout woman whose obesity increased progressively during her adult life. We know from many sources that she enjoyed the pleasures of the table, but was not described as using alcohol to excess. She might best be described as matronly in appearance, yet despite her many pregnancies the actual role of matron eluded her.

Anne's obstetric history is quite remarkable and there has been great speculation over the years as to the cause of her problems in bringing her pregnancies to term. It is generally agreed that she had seventeen pregnancies in a 17-year-period. Thus, she became pregnant for the first time not long after her marriage and her last pregnancy ended in miscarriage just before her thirty-fifth birthday. Of these seventeen pregnancies, there were six actual births of mature infants, five living and one stillborn. The durations of some of the other eleven pregnancies are not certain, but it seems likely that at least some were well beyond miscarriage. The most useful account of the six actual births is recorded in a short biography entitled *The LIFE of Queen ANNE*, which was published in 1714, the year of Anne's death.

Issue of her most Sacred Royal Majesty Queen Anne, by her Royal Consort George Prince of Denmark.

A Daughter, of whom her Royal Highness was deliver'd, on the 12th of May, 1684: and being dead, was privately interr'd.

Lady Mary, Second Daughter of this Royal Pair, born at Whitehall, the 2nd of June, 1685: died February, 1686 (1687).

Lady Anne Sophia, Third Daughter, was born at Windsor, the 12th of May, 1686: died the February following.

William, Duke of Gloucester, was born at the Royal Palace at Hampton-Court, the 24th of July, 1689 . . . but after all the promising Hopes this young Prince gave of a longer Life, and of early Virtues, and good Qualities that appear'd in him, he was snatch'd away at the age of 11 years and five Days. . . .

Lady Mary, another Daughter of her Royal Highness, by Prince George of Denmark was born at St James's, in the Month of October, 1690: but died soon after she was baptiz'd.

George, another Son of this Royal Pair, was born at Sion-House, the 17th Day of April, 1692; but died as soon as born.[4]

The most accessible accurate accounting of Anne's seventeen pregnancies is that of the distinguished gynaecologist and obstetrician, Professor Sir John Dewhurst, in his book, *Royal Confinements*. He cites the list of David Green as being the most accurate and complete and provides the time scale for these pregnancies.

1684 12 May a stillborn daughter
1685 2 June Mary or Marie (died 8 February 1687)
1686 2 June Anne Sophia (died 2 February 1687)
1687 Between 20 January and 4 February a miscarriage
1687 October a miscarriage (male)
1688 16 April a miscarriage

1689 24 July William Duke of Gloucester (died 30 July 1700)

1690 14 October Mary (two months premature, lived two hours)

1692 17 April George (born at Syon, lived a few minutes)

1693 23 March a miscarriage (female)

1694 21 January a miscarriage

1696 18 February a miscarriage (female)

1696 20 September a double miscarriage ('a son of 7 months' growth, the other of 2 or 3 months')

1697 25 March a miscarriage

1697 December a miscarriage

1698 15 September a miscarriage (male)

1700 25 January a miscarriage (male)[5]

In addition to the five live births and one stillbirth, five of the miscarriages were far enough along for the sex of the foetus to be determined, and that surely was at least four to five months after conception. The pregnancy which eventuated in a 'double miscarriage' in 1696 was probably a twin pregnancy of seven months' duration with one foetus growing at the expense of the other. Anne's obstetric record can be summarized as follows: her first three pregnancies went to term, resulting in a stillbirth and then two girls, Mary and Anne Sophia, who lived to twenty months and eight months, respectively. After three miscarriages in just over two years, at least one of them occurring as far along as mid-term, she gave birth to three babies in less than three years. Two of these were born at term and the other was premature by two months. The first of these three was William, Duke of Gloucester, who lived to the age of eleven years. In the following eight years one pregnancy went to seven months, four to at least four to five months, and three may have ended sooner.

Anne's reproductive efforts were completed two years before she came to the throne in 1702. Her last pregnancy ended in the miscarriage or stillbirth of a male foetus on 25

January 1700 and she was never pregnant again. Considering that she was only thirty-four years old at this time and her husband only forty-six, one might wonder why she did not have more pregnancies.

Anne's two daughters, Mary and Anne Sophia, died within days of each other in February 1687. Both were still infants, and as best as can be determined the two girls were normal at birth and developed normally. Each had a febrile illness, the nature of which is not known. It is not even known if they suffered from the same illness, although one might imagine that to be the case. Anne was twenty-two years of age at this time and would not carry another pregnancy to term until she was twenty-four.

Sadly, Anne's one child who survived infancy, William, Duke of Gloucester, died on 29 July 1700, four days after his eleventh birthday. William, the last heir to the Stuart dynasty, suffered from arrested hydrocephalus, a condition of increased fluid surrounding the brain leading to enlargement of the head. He was slow in his physical development and walked late, never walking steadily. He seems otherwise to have matured more or less normally. Not surprisingly, there are no portraits of William as a child that show the disparity between his head and body size, rather the surviving portraits and drawings of William show him as a normally proportioned boy. Though probably of normal intelligence William was not a vigorous or active child. He was the product of Anne's seventh pregnancy and after the deaths in infancy of his two older sisters, his mother doted on him. Detailed descriptions of William's early years are recorded in the writings of his devoted Welsh servant, Jenkin Lewis.

[The Duke's] head was grown very long and was so big round that his hat was big enough for most men [William was four or five years old at this time], which was occasioned by the issue in his pole [probably referring to the circumference of his head], that had been kept running ever since his sickness at Hampton

Court, which made it difficult to fit his head with a peruke. Although he was active and lively yet he could not go up and down stairs without help, nor raise himself when down; and he tottered when he walked. . . .

If he tottered whenever he walked in her presence, it threw her into a violent perspiration, thro' fear; yet did she joy in seeing him often come to her dinners after his own, when he would behave very well and not covet sweetmeats like other children. . . .

His birthday was the 24th of July, and he was then 11 years old; he complained a little the next day, but we imputed that to the fatigues of a birthday, so that he was too much neglected. The day after he grew much worse and it proved to be a malignant fever. He died the fourth day of his illness, to the great grief of all who were concerned in him. . . . The Princess attended on him during his sickness with great tenderness, but with a great composedness that amazed all who saw it; she bore his death with a resignation and a piety that was indeed very singular. His death gave great alarm to the whole nation.[6]

William's fatal illness began just after his eleventh birthday party, it was acute and characterized by fever and upper respiratory symptoms, and Anne attended him herself, despite being helpless to alter the four-day course of the illness which took his life. Though poisoning was not a consideration, a post-mortem examination was ordered to be done by surgeons. It was carried out under the direction of an eminent physician, Dr Edward Hannes, accomplishing more than that which was necessary for embalming the body. As is apparent from their report, a very extensive and careful post-mortem examination was performed and the report is detailed and helpful in understanding both the nature of William's hydrocephalus and his fatal illness.

Anne and William, Duke of Gloucester

POST-MORTEM EXAMINATION OF WILLIAM, DUKE OF GLOUCESTER

Upon the death of His Highness William, Duke of Gloucester, which happened on Monday, 29th of July about midnight, the right honourable the Earl of Marlborough, one of their Excellencies the Lords Justices of England and Governor to his late Highness, was pleased to give order, that the Body should be opened.

Accordingly the surgeons appointed by his Lordship (whose names are subscribed) in the presence of Dr Hannes, who was commanded to assist at the operation, and of several other spectators, made the Dissection; and afterwards jointly with the Dr gave in the following report on it, on [Wednesday] July 31 1700.

1. On the inspection of the outward surface of the body, the Head, Chest, Abdomen and Arms appeared livid and tainted more than usual, the legs and thighs not much altered from their proper colour.
2. The Abdomen was first opened, and these observations were made upon the parts contained: The Omentum was found as is natural. The Gutts from the Rectum inclusively upwards to the Duodenum, had the common appearances: excepting only that a few inflammatory spotts were seen disperse upon the small gutts, and that the plerus glandulares of the same gutts were become florid, and therefore more conspicuous than is usual. The Duodenum and stomack and gullet were highly inflamed, especially the stomack which had in its cavity wind and a small quantity of liquor. In the Pancreas, spleen, liver and bladder of gall was nothing remarkable only the spleen and liver were more livid than usual: the substance of the kidneys carried a colour deeper than ordinary: besides which they were not noted to have anything preternatural: as neither had the glandulae renales or the ureters of the

urinary bladder of the Urine expressed from the bladder.

3. Next after the abdomen, the Thorax or chest was examined. Here the Pleura was inflamed to the most intense degree. The Diaphragm and mediastinum [structures in the centre of the thorax] and pericardium [lining around the heart] were thought not to differ from the constitution given them by nature: excepting that the Diaphragm was some thing inflamed. The Humour of the Pericardium was red: and perhaps not without a mixture of blood: And even the Thorax and abdomen were judged to have more blood in their Cavitys than could well proceed from the mouth of the vessels cut by the knife at the time the respective venters were laid open: In the Larynx, the membranes that join the cartilages, cricoides and Thyreoides were very dark with inflammation. The membrane that links the Epiglottis at the root of the tongue was also inflamed insomuch that the glandulae miliares of it which are scarce visible at other times, were much distended and very conspicuous.

4. In the mouth, we found the palate inflamed, as also the uvula; the membrane of which has swelled. The almonds [lymph nodes] of the ears were swelled and had in them purulent matter, there being prest out of one of them, as much of it as filled a tea spoon.

5. Last of all, the head was opened, and out of the first and second ventricles of the cerebrum was taken about four ounces and a halfe of a lympid humour. The Heart was extremely flaccid and weak in its texture, the right ventricle had very little blood, and the left ventricle was altogether empty. The Lungs in both sides were filled with blood to the height of an inflammation. The neck was swollen and upon dissection the condition of the contained parts appeared such as is observed in bodys strangled. At

the place where the jugulares arise above the claviculae, the inflammation approaches very near to a mortification. The glandula threoidea were almost black with the inclosed blood: and being put into scales were found above five drachms in weight. The gullet was much inflamed, as was said above. The windpipe also was affected in the same kind, especially the upper parts of it called the larynx. In this region nothing besides was found particular or differing from the natural state and disposition of it.

Signed: Edward Hannes, MD
Charles Bernard
Edward Greene
William Cowper[7]

This autopsy report painstakingly describes inflammation and infection in the throat and larynx, with a grossly swollen neck and pus expressed from lymph nodes in this region. The lungs are described as both being full of blood, likely this was pus or fluid stained with blood. Put in context with the clinical course of the illness, this is the picture of an acute bacterial infection of the throat with an associated pneumonia in both lungs. This is not the picture of diphtheria, for example, which was a common bacterial infection of the throat in children, and given its short duration of four days neither typhoid fever nor a manifestation of tuberculosis needs to be considered. Interestingly, the surgeons opened the head and took fluid from the ventricles (the cavities within the brain), and found it to be greatly increased in amount and crystal clear. This confirms the diagnosis of hydrocephalus and also, because the fluid was clear, eliminates the possibility of meningitis. Thus, William died of pneumonia and the future of the Stuart dynasty died with him. It was 1700 and Anne's brother-in-law, William of Orange, was on the throne, her sister Mary long dead. To sustain the dynasty Anne would have to produce another baby, one who was strong and who could survive.

However, Anne was ill at this time and moving into the period of disability that characterized the last years of her life. She was not a good candidate for yet another pregnancy and, indeed, was never pregnant again. Her ability to participate in any sort of exercise slowly decreased but her appetite remained hearty, leading to ever increasing girth and corpulence, which began to compromise her mobility. Prince George was bothered by worsening pulmonary problems and nearing the end of his own life, in fact there was little vigour left in any of this family, now the last remnant of the Stuart dynasty. Anne's decline was so slow, yet so relentless, that neither she nor those around her realized that she had a severe chronic disease. Spells of joint swelling and pain plagued her, and she was often stiff and awkward in her movements.

Anne was thought to have suffered from a particularly severe form of gout during the time of her reign. But in fact her chronic rheumatic illness began well before her son's death and it was not gout after all. In examining her letters it is possible to identify the timing of her illness and, in a general sense, the rate and extent of the development of her disability from the chronic rheumatic disease. This illness was characterized by recurrent acute exacerbations, followed by remissions, over a period of at least fifteen years. It culminated in her death at the age of forty-nine in 1714. Letters documenting the progression of her disease were written by Anne to Sir Benjamin Bathurst, a family friend, Robert Harley, Earl of Oxford, Anne's chancellor of the exchequer and treasurer, and the aforementioned Duchess of Marlborough, Sarah Churchill, her childhood friend. The duchess and Anne used the names Mrs Freeman and Mrs Morley, respectively, in their correspondence over the years.

Windsor, October 15 1698 [to Lady Marlborough]

I have been very uneasy since I writ to my dear Mrs Freeman, but not in the cruel fortune I endured yesterday morning, though the gout is now in my knee as well as my foot, and at this time I am a perfect cripple; however, I still hope I may be in a condition next week to have the satisfaction of seeing you at St James's, which helps to support my spirits that are indeed mightily sunk with this bad pain, and, let people say what they will, it is impossible to help having the spleen when one is in such misery.

Windsor, October 15 1699 [to Sir Benjamin Bathurst]

My not coming yesterday to London was not occasioned by any return of the gout, but it has left so great a weakness in my foot and knee, that I thought if I deferred my journey till the beginning of the next week I should be better able to bear it. But I am not fully resolved on the day, and you may be sure I shall not desire you to come hither till it is easy to you.

Windsor, October 22? 1699 [to the Duchess of Marlborough]

. . . for I should be so too if I were able to stir, but when that will be God knows, for my fever is not quite gone, and I am still so lame I cannot go without limping.

Windsor, October 1703 [to the Duchess of Marlborough]

I am very sorry to find by my dear Mrs Freeman's [letter] of this morning that she is lame, and I hope it is not the gout, knowing by too much experience how painful a complaint that is; though if it were certain that it is a preserver of life, I should wish it you, yours being very dear to your poor, unfortunate, faithful Morley, who is still so lame that she can hardly walk the length of a room, and that with two sticks, which makes me mightily afraid I shall hardly be able to go out alone by the fourth of November.

Hampton Court, November 3 1711 [to the Earl of Oxford]

. . . for though I thank God I am much better than I

was, I am not out of pain and the weakness always continues a good while after.

Windsor, October 11 1712 [to the Earl of Oxford]
  I thank God my pain begins to abate, but I have had a great deal since I writ to you last, and am still far from being easy.

St James's, July 5 1713 [to the Earl of Oxford]
  I am very sorry you continue so much indisposed and therefore concluding I shall not have the satisfaction of seeing you to-day I give you this trouble to inquire after your health and to let you know that I find myself so much tired with the little fatigue of yesterday that it will be impossible for one to undertake that of going to St Paul's [to attend the Thanksgiving Service for the peace].[8]

These personal letters, though few, tell us that Anne was often made invalid by acute joint inflammations and occasional fever; lameness is also mentioned, it was intermittent at first and then probably permanent. A good record of Anne's physical limitations and decline during her reign has been set out by R.O. Bucholz in his book *The Augustan Court: Queen Anne and the Decline of Court Culture*. He has drawn from a variety of primary sources, including the correspondence of Lord Godolphin, newspapers and magazines of the time, court calendars, and a wealth of private papers. All are carefully cited in great detail in this excellent book. Bucholz shows that Anne attended public thanksgiving services annually but cancelled most progresses and trips out of London after about 1703, the second year of her reign.

There seems to have been very little daily monarchical ritual, such as a morning *levee* or dining in state, at Anne's court, even early in the reign, when her physical maladies were not yet so far advanced as to preclude them. . . .

Only a few days before, Godolphin had feared Anne too 'unwieldy and lame' to go to the House because of the gout. Yet she not only went, but was, by all accounts, resplendent. . . .

Unfortunately, the Duke's [Marlborough] military prowess could provide excuse for no more than about one thanksgiving per year, on average, before his fall in January 1712. . . . Nor would the Queen's responsibilities or health allow more than one or two progresses a year through 1707.

(1706) Anne was ill with gout; the next morning Prince George fell seriously ill.

(1708) Anne was ill: 'The Queen lame and Indisposed, and Prince, complimented by a Numerous Court.'

(1712) There was much speculation, most of it Whig, that the Queen would be forced to cancel or postpone the festivities because of a recent attack of the gout; but on the night Wentworth reports, 'there was as much fine cloaths as ever, and I thank God the Queen appear'd both morning and afternoon as usual . . . the Guards were doubled, some people affirm there was no accation for it'.

(1713) 'The Queen is not well enough to see the Lady's in the morning but at Seven A'Clock she dos . . . there will be a great Crowd. Because of her gout, the Queen had to be carried into the Great Presence Chamber in the evening.'

(1714) Celebrated at Windsor, where the Queen had been seriously ill all winter; nevertheless she 'on Her Birthday entertaind Company above three hours'.

The ostensible reason for the subdued tone in 1708 was royal illness. As noted previously, 'the gout' had already rendered Anne periodically lame by 1702. Although she managed to walk at her going to Parliament on 11 March, she had to be carried to the door of Westminster Abbey on 23 April. By mid-reign, she had lost most of the use of her limbs and was often too ill to participate in regular or elaborate public ceremony. Worse, her visible physical decline could not help but undermine, for those with access to her person, the very image of monarchy such ceremony was supposed to promote. As described, for example, by Sir John Clerk of Penicuik, Anne emerges as a pathetic figure. Clerk found her at Kensington 'labouring under a fit of the Gout, and in extrem pain and agony', her face 'red and spotted', her dress 'negligent', her gouty foot 'tied up with a pultis and some nasty bandages', her surroundings 'in the same disorder as about the meanest of her subjects'. The irony that this pitiable creature aspired to be the nursing mother of those subjects was not lost on Clerk: 'I was much affected by this sight, and the more when she had occasion to mention her people of Scotland. . . . What are you, poor mean like Mortal, thought I, who talks in the style of a Soveraign? Nature seems to be inverted when a poor infirm Woman becomes one of the Rulers of the World.'[9]

The picture that emerges from these descriptions is of a woman in her late thirties and forties suffering a progressively crippling rheumatic disease. Acute episodes of inflammatory arthritis seem to have occurred periodically and may have been accompanied by fever and other symptoms, for example facial rash. Anne's physical disability increased steadily throughout the twelve years of her reign, and in her final year she was barely able to leave her palace. By any standard one could apply, Anne was profoundly disabled by the last year of her reign, weak, feeble and able to walk only short distances.

On Christmas Eve in 1713 Anne had a violent attack of fever followed by several hours of stupor or coma. Sir Hans Sloane, one of her primary physicians, recorded a detailed account of this somewhat prolonged illness, as presented at the beginning of this chapter. She largely recovered from this episode. (Sloane's medical notes are now contained among the Sloane Manuscripts in the British Library.) Anne had symptoms and signs of systemic illness – fever, stupor and rapid pulse – so the infected area must have been quite extensive. It is interesting to note Dr Sloane's medical slang (of the time), the physicians waited for the most opportune time to 'throw in the bark'. Erysipelas, a streptococcal infection of the skin, was most probably the correct diagnosis as the streptococcus bacterium produces toxins which may cause the sort of systemic symptoms Anne suffered. She had another, milder, fit of shivering, but then was apparently relatively well by April.

There are several descriptions of Anne's final illness and most are obscured with the presumption that the gout or its 'translation' to other organs was the root cause of her problems. Many physicians were involved in her care and there was disagreement among them about the best course of treatment before her death and then, after her death, about what had really happened to her. The best and most complete account of her final illness is to be found in Abel Boyer's biography published shortly after her death.

Tis certain, that on Thursday Morning the Queen found herself indisposed with a dozing Heaviness, and a shooting Pain in her Head, upon which her Domestick Physician Dr Arbuthnot, having confided with Four others of her Majesty's Physicians in Ordinary, viz. Dr Theo. Lawrence, Sir David Hamilton, Dr Shadwell, and Dr Sloane, it was judged proper that her Majesty should be let Blood, by Cupping; an Operation which her Majesty even liked better than Phlebotomy and which had often given her Ease in the like apparent Symptoms. Mr Ayme, Surgeon, and her Majesty's Cupper in Ordinary, being immediately sent for, perform'd his Office, between Twelve and One in the Afternoon, in the Presence of Dr Arbuthnot, Serjeant Surgeon Dickens, and the Lady Masham; took about Eight Ounces and a Half of Blood, which he observ'd was very thick; and took Notice, and at the same time, that the Queen's Eyes were dim and glassy. Her Majesty found her self somewhat better; went to Bed at the usual Hour; rested pretty well till Three a Clock in the Morning when she waked and finding something lie heavy on her Stomach, and reaching to vomit, she brough up some Matter, and then composed her self to sleep. Towards Seven a Clock, her Majesty waked again, and finding her self pretty well, rose from Bed, and got her Head comb'd. This done, toward Eight, her Majesty went to look on the Clock, and Mrs Danvers, one of the Bed-Chamber Women, taking Notice, that her Majesty fixed her Eyes a long time on it, ask'd her Majesty, What she saw in the Clock more than Ordinary. The Queen answer'd her only with turning of her Head and a dying look; at which Mrs Danvers being frighted, she call'd for help. Dr Arbuthnot, and such other Physicians in Ordinary as were in Waiting, judging that her Majesty was seiz'd with a Fit of Apoplexy, caused her to be let Blood, which Operation Mr Dickens, the Serjeant Surgeon, perform'd and took about Ten Ounces and a Half. Her Majesty came to her self again, and was pretty quiet till a little after Nine, when hearing some Noise, she ask'd What the Matter was? Answer was made, That the Lady Masham, being inform'd of her Majesty's Indisposition, had fainted away, upon which they thought fit to carry her to her Apartment, which occasioned the Noise her Majesty had heard. Towards Ten a Clock, her Majesty was seiz'd with a second Fit of Heaviness and Dozing, which encreased so much upon her, that for above an Hour she was speechless, motionless, and unsensible. Those about her Majesty judging she was either dead, or near expiring, the Dutchess of Ormond, one of the Ladies of the Bed-Chamber then in Waiting, sent with all speed, a Messenger to her Consort, with this melancholy News; which being brought to the Committee of Council, then assembled at the Cockpit near Whitehall, they immediately broke up, and went to Kensington. In the mean time, Dr Arbuthnot, Sir Richard Blackmore, and other Physicians, thought proper to give her Majesty a Vomit, which not having the desired Effect, they administered another Medicine proposed by Dr Mead, upon which she recovered her Speech and was sensible.

The Council in the mean time was constantly sitting, and the desperate State of her Majesty's Health spreading abroad, the Dukes of Somerset and Argyle assumed their Seats in Council, without the usual Form of being summoned; which was done, it was moved that the Queen's Physicians might be examined, and give an Account in Writing of the Queen's Illness. This done, one of the Council represented how necessary it would be, in case it pleased God the Queen should die, that the Place of [Lord] Treasurer should be filled; to which the whole Board assenting, the Duke of Shrewsbury was proposed, and unanimously approved. And the Physicians who had been examined, assuring the Council, that the Queen was sensible, and might be spoke to; the Lord Chancellor, with the Duke of Shrewsbury, and some other Lords, were ordered to attend her, and lay before her the full Opinion of the Council; upon which her Majesty said, They could not have recommended a person the better approved; and giving the Treasurer's Staff into the Duke of Shrewsbury's Hands, bid him Use it for the Good of her People.

About Three a Clock in the Afternoon, the same Day, 30th of July, the Queen relapsed into a kind of Lethargick, or Apoplectic Fit; out of which she was hardly recovered by proper Applications. Her Physicians there fore thought fit to apply Blisters in several Parts, in order to it, to have her Head shaved; and at the same time acquainted the Council, That her Majesty's Life was in the utmost Danger, and entirely depended on the Effect of this last Remedy.

All this Night her Majesty continued in a Lethargick

Dozing, which increased to such a Degree, that about ten on Saturday Morning, July 31, that her Physicians thought it fit to declare to the Council, that no Hopes remained of her Life. All necessary Orders were immediately given for Security of the Kingdom, which occasioned a rumour that the Queen was dead, who still retained so much Spirit, as to be able to take some Spoonfuls of Broth. After which she continued in a dozing condition until about four or five in the Afternoon, when her Pulse beating somewhat faster and higher, some about her began to entertain Hopes; but these lasted not long, for the next Morning (being Sunday the first of August) she expired a little after Seven a Clock in the Morning (without being able to receive The Holy Communion which the Bishop of London was ready to administer to her) in the 50th Year of her Age, and the 13th of her Reign.[10]

John Radcliffe did not attend Anne in her final illness because, ironically, he was himself sick with the 'real gout'. Apparently he was not officially summoned in any event, although he suffered considerable opprobrium from the public and Parliament because he was not present to help Anne when she needed him most. Excerpts from two of his letters are quite illuminating about royal deathbeds generally and Anne's in particular. These were extracted from British Library sources by Dr Charles Green Cumston and published in 1911:

I know the nature of attending crowned heads in their last moments too well to be fond of waiting upon them, without being sent for by a proper authority. You have heard of pardons being signed for physicians before a sovereign's demise; however, ill as I was, I would have gone to the queen in a horse litter, had either her Majesty or those in commission next to her commanded me so to do.

I don't doubt, but you have heard an account of her Majesty's illness; and here we are all in the dark as well as the doctors. At first they said it was an ague, and then they gave the Jesuits' bark. She took but three doses, and that was left off, so that I suppose they found it no ague, or else she would have taken more or none at all. Then it was conjectured to be the gout in her stomach; and now it is thought to be the gout all over excepting the joints. One of the doctors declared, because there was no intermission on the second day, that it was a tertian postponed. Another which was Sir David [Hamilton], declared now, God be thanked, her Majesty would certainly be well; and when he was asked the reason, he told them she had grown deaf, and that was a sign the bark had taken effect; and at that time she had but taken two doses, and never took but one afterward. Shadwell was asked how the queen did, and he said she would do very well, but the *pouls* was *dure*, which puzzled all the maids of honour.[11]

POST-MORTEM EXAMINATION OF QUEEN ANNE

An autopsy was performed and the report of it has been reproduced several times over the years. The following account appeared in the *British Medical Journal* series about royal deaths:

At the Council Chamber, St James's, the 3rd August, 1714.
Present:
Their Excellencys the Lords Justices in Council.
   The Physicians called in and Dr Laurence delivered the following paper, containing [an account of] what was observed at the opening of her late Majesty's Body.
Kensington Palace
2 August, 1714
   Upon opening the Body of her Late Majesty of Blessed Memory, We found a small Umbilical hernia Omentalis without any excoriation, a large Omentum well Coloured.

No water in the Cavity of the Abdomen. The Stomach thin, and its inward coat too smooth. The Liver not Schircous, but very tender and Flaccid, as were all the rest of the Viscera of the lower belly. The Gall, Bladder, Kidneys, and Urinary bladder without any stone. There was a very small Scorbutic Ulcer on the left leg. We can give no further account, being forbid making any other inspection than what was absolutely necessary for Embalming the Body.

The Physicians' Report to their Excellency's deliver'd by Dr Lawrence as Principal Physician.

[Signed]   Jo. Shadwell

          Thos. Lawrence   Hans Sloane

          David Hamilton   Amb. Dickens

          Jno. Arbuthnott   Rd. Blundell

A true copy.

          [Signed] Edward Southwell[12]

The autopsy is of little help in identifying the cause of Anne's chronic rheumatic illness and does not identify a cause of her death. However, it is possible to conclude that her abdominal organs were essentially normal. Her thoracic and cranial cavities were not examined and the ulcer on her left thigh was small and offers no clue to understanding her chronic illness or her death. In the same vein, the autopsy gives us no clue as to the cause of Anne's tragic obstetric history, but in describing a normal urinary bladder we can assume that the autopsy surgeon looked into her pelvis, from the opened abdomen above, and that nothing grossly abnormal was seen in her ovaries, Fallopian tubes or uterus. In conclusion, the post-mortem examination of Anne's body does not provide much information to advance the understanding of her medical and obstetric problems; the denouement must come from studying clinical information.

By contrast, the autopsy of William, Duke of Gloucester, was thorough and the findings settle both the reason for his chronic disability and the reason for his unexpected death, there being no relationship between the two. Apparently the surface of his brain appeared normal but the amount of cerebrospinal fluid aspirated from the cavities within his brain, the cerebral ventricles, was far above what might have been expected in the brain of an eleven-year-old boy. This makes the diagnosis of arrested hydrocephalus certain, and explains his large head size and the mild neurological deficits that were noted during his life, for example tottering when walking. His death was caused by an acute bacterial infection of his throat and lungs, and the bloody fluid in the lungs makes it certain that he died of bacterial pneumonia. Until the age of antibiotics, death from pneumonia (usually from a bacterium called the pneumococcus) was very common, and perfectly healthy young people could contract pneumonia and die of it, as did William.

William's two unrelated medical problems are easily understood, but Anne's problems are quite complex and, when finally explained, are intertwined in interesting ways. Disease and disability compromised Anne's reign more significantly than that of any of the preceding Stuart monarchs and, surprisingly, it is possible to ascribe all of her problems to a single disease. Her medical problems may be divided into three parts: first, she had a tragic reproductive history; second, she suffered a chronic rheumatic disease; and, finally, she had an untimely death. The first manifestations of her illness are found in her early obstetric misadventures.

In understanding recurrent pregnancy loss in modern times, a general schema of the possible diagnoses is constructed. This is often called a differential diagnosis list and it would, for example, apply equally well to Catherine of Braganza on the basis of her own series of miscarriages. The differential diagnosis list for habitual pregnancy loss includes genetic errors in the foetuses, anatomic malformations of the woman's reproductive tract, hormonal abnormalities in the woman, and chronic infections, serious systemic diseases and immunologic factors which might damage the placenta, essential for nourishing the foetus in the uterus. As Anne and George were not related there is no reason to suspect that Anne's foetuses would be consistently genetically flawed. It seems unlikely that she would have had any anatomic abnormality of her reproductive tract, particularly her uterus, because many of her pregnancies went to term and nothing abnormal was described in her pelvis at her autopsy. It is known that she had normal and regular menstrual periods to the very last year of her life, so hormonal abnormality would be unlikely. While a chronic infection would be possible, for example syphilis or brucellosis, she had no other manifestations of chronic infection so this would be only a very remote possibility. However, Anne did have a serious chronic systemic rheumatic disease, and some of these diseases are associated with immunological abnormalities, which in turn may lead to insufficiency of the placenta, the source of nourishment for the foetus.

In carefully reconstructing Anne's obstetric record, Professor Dewhurst concludes that some of Anne's miscarriages were, in fact, deliveries of foetuses fairly far along and probably dead in utero for some time prior to delivery. Laying to rest some older speculations, he discounts pelvic deformity in Anne and syphilis in George as possible causes, and he discounts altogether the possibility of congenital or hereditary factors being operative. Though offering no single explanation to account for all of the queen's obstetric problems, Dewhurst suspected that rhesus incompatibility might have contributed to Anne's consistent loss of foetuses late in pregnancy. However, underlying all of this he favours insufficiency of the placenta as the most likely culprit, intuitively the single factor that could best explain her tragic obstetric record.[13]

Rhesus incompatibility, an immunologic mismatch of maternal and foetal red blood cell antigens, is actually a very plausible explanation, although with rhesus incompatibility the foetuses become increasingly anaemic with succeeding pregnancies and some would surely have displayed hydrops foetalis, a striking gross oedema of the foetus, which would have been noted and mentioned by some observer. The best explanation of Anne's obstetric problems comes from the Canadian pathologist, H.E. Emson, who published his assessment of Anne's situation in 1992, essentially putting an exact diagnosis to Professor Dewhurst's suggestion that placental insufficiency had to be the root cause of the problem.

Emson believes that Anne suffered from disseminated lupus erythematosus, a serious chronic systemic rheumatic disease, found particularly in young women and long known to cause foetal wastage. Further he suggests that Anne had the lupus anticoagulant, an autoantibody (an antibody the patient makes against herself, as it were) common in lupus in young women, and which is closely correlated with obstetric compromise.[14] Given the vicissitudes of modern immunology, the lupus anticoagulant is not really associated with preventing blood coagulation – it is found in diseases other than lupus and is now more accurately identified as an antiphospholipid antibody. The presence of such an autoantibody may constitute a syndrome in its own right, the antiphospholipid antibody syndrome, without the other manifestations of lupus. This is an area of intense research at the present time with a seminal review paper recently published in *The New England Journal of Medicine*.[15]

Pregnancy in disseminated lupus erythematosus, particularly in the presence of the antiphospholipid antibody, is associated with miscarriage, placental damage and insufficiency, and foetal death. In modern times this antibody can be identified easily in some women who have lost more than one pregnancy and among the treatment options to sustain subsequent pregnancies is a single aspirin tablet taken daily. In all likelihood in the early eighteenth century the equivalent was actually available as salicylic acid in herbal preparations containing willow bark, although its efficacy in Anne's condition could not have been known at that time. Clearly Emson was right, Anne had the antiphospholipid antibody and, in consideration of her chronic inflammatory arthritic disease, it would seem that she might have had systemic lupus erythematosus as well.

Anne's suffering from spells of acute arthritis is incontestable. These spells were not the result of gout or, in modern terms, episodic acute inflammatory arthritis caused by crystals of the chemical uric acid forming in joint fluid. Not only did Hippocrates describe gout, but he stated emphatically that it was rare in women and did not occur before menopause. Anne's confidant and physician, Sir David Hamilton, confirms that Anne was not postmenopausal, her menstrual periods continued to the end of her life: 'I mention'd to her what health she had from the keeping off, of disquiets by my Lord Godolphin, and acting for her at the time when occasions of disquiet met her, Yea the Menses happend to her as if she had been but 20 years old, the good effects of which care to ward off Disquiet I mention'd to her, to her death, on purpose to remind her not to be uneasy.'[16]

In Anne's time the combination of the rheumatic symptoms from which she suffered – intermittent pain and swelling in joints – was labelled gout. It was a disease of status, one must be well off and well fed to get 'The Gout', it did not affect the poor. Gout is almost exclusively a disease of men, often considered the disease of affluent men who can afford fine wine and rich food. Thomas Sydenham made it a very popular disease in his time and, as often happens in such circumstances, gout was subsequently over-diagnosed in the seventeenth and eighteenth centuries. It is therefore not difficult to see why Anne, although a woman, was assumed to have gout. As a woman of substance and then a monarch, she could be considered to bear a burden similar to that of a successful man. She was an honorary man doing a man's work and therefore subject to the perks – or otherwise – of that status and role.

So, knowing that Anne did not reach menopause before her death, it is possible to state with certainty that she did not have gout. She certainly did have some form of chronic crippling arthritis with periodic acute exacerbations, however.

Anne was too young to be affected by the common arthritis of ageing, the degenerative joint disease also called osteoarthritis. Apart from several very rare syndromes, there remain just two diagnostic possibilities.

The first is rheumatoid arthritis, the common inflammatory arthritis which leads to joint deformity and disability. This disease can wax and wane over the years, usually leading to increasing joint deformity, particularly in the hands. Anne's friend, Sarah Churchill, who saw the queen frequently over the years, described her hands as extremely delicate and well shaped, virtually impossible in rheumatoid arthritis. If Anne did have normal hands she could not have had rheumatoid arthritis.

The second possibility, systemic lupus erythematosus (lupus), is the more likely candidate. This is a systemic autoimmune disease occurring primarily in young women. Its manifestations are protean with joint deformity being absent or minimal but acute arthritis, that is acute inflammation of the soft tissues of joints, very common. A skin rash, particularly on the face, is found in 75 per cent of patients with this disease.[17] Fertility is not impaired in lupus sufferers, but there is considerable foetal wastage, and women with lupus are very likely to have antiphospholipid antibodies. Today the diagnosis of lupus depends on various highly specific serologic tests. However, it is not many years since a constellation of clinical and laboratory findings was used to validate the diagnosis of lupus. Non-deforming arthritis and facial skin rash were the most prominent clinical manifestations. To this day, it is nearly impossible to make a diagnosis of lupus without both of these being present at one time or another in the course of the patient's illness.

Other common clinical manifestations of lupus include Raynaud's phenomenon (blanching of the fingers with exposure to cold), skin sensitivity to sunlight, oral ulcers and alopecia. There is no evidence that Anne had any of these, but there is little medical information available prior to her final illness, so it is not possible to be sure. Systemic lupus erythematosus remains the best explanation for Anne's ill-starred obstetric history and the disabling rheumatic disease she suffered in the last decade or so of her life. This is in agreement with the opinions expressed by Emson, cited previously, and also serves the principle of adducing one disease to explain all of Anne's medical problems.[18] Clifford Brewer has come to the same conclusion.[19] It is certain that Anne had systemic lupus erythematosus and that the progression of this disease led to her premature death from a cerebrovascular event – a stroke – common among sufferers of this disease.

Anne's terminal illness lasted for three days and was characterized by fluctuations in consciousness, ranging from stupor to alertness, resulting in coma. As described by Boyer, her headache, initial nosebleed, nausea, vomiting and deafness are not specific symptoms and signs, and do not locate the organ or organs principally affected. Although Sydenham was wrong about gout, he was astute to observe that 'The Bark' was not given to Anne in sufficient quantity to cause her deafness, as quinine can cause both deafness and ringing in the ears when given in large doses. The 'hard pulse' noted by her ladies-in-waiting suggests that her blood pressure was very high, a circumstance common both in lupus and when there is acute brain damage. As chills and fever were not prominent, the infection on her leg must have been quiescent at the time and not the problem it was the previous year. A stroke, or similar vascular event, would seem the most likely cause of her stupor and other less specific symptoms and signs.

Stroke can occur without localizing paralysis and often ends with increasing brain swelling that eventually compromises the lower centres of the brain, causing breathing to cease. With a background of lupus and the antiphospholipid antibody (which itself promotes clotting of blood within arteries), and Anne's ever-changing neurological picture during the last several days of her life, the principal pathology may have been a stroke from a blood clot or clots in the arteries of her brain. A diagnosis of equal likelihood is acute inflammation of the arteries of the brain and surrounding tissues, the meninges, which often occurs in lupus. Thus, regardless of the exact mechanism, it is certain that Anne died of acute vascular disease of her brain, a consequence of her systemic lupus erythematosus.

It is worth noting that Anne was obese, perhaps very obese by the time of her death. Although it is not possible to find any estimation of her height or weight, her later portraits show a very stout woman. Anne might have suffered recurrent thrombophlebitis in her leg veins, as pregnancy, obesity and the antiphospholipid antibody all predispose to recurrent thrombophlebitis and eventual insufficiency of the leg veins with severe leg oedema. The possibility that clots in her leg veins may have gone to her lungs needs to be considered, but as breathing difficulty was not described in any of the accounts of her death, that is not likely.

The political drama attendant to Anne's death, and the death of the Stuart dynasty, was intense, and it is reasonable to assume that Anne was actually either stuporous or comatose at the time she 'passed' the rod of office of Lord Treasurer to Charles Talbot, Duke of Shrewsbury, ensuring the Hanoverian succession to the throne. The compelling concern of the Privy Council at the end of July 1714 was, sadly, not mourning for their queen but getting George, Elector of Hanover to London to take her place as soon as possible. For, as the Jacobite rebellion of 1715–16 would prove, James Francis Edward Stuart was poised and waiting to reclaim the English throne his father had abandoned less than thirty years before.

The Hanoverian Succession Collection in the Spencer (Rare Books) Library at the University of Kansas contains preliminary drafts of letters to George from the Privy Council on 31 July (the day before Anne's death) and from the Lords Justices and Regents for George I on 1 August (the day of her death). The scratched-out words and editing on each of these manuscripts sharpen the sense of urgency that was felt in getting George to England to claim his throne. Thus the Privy Council wrote to him on 31 July:

> We make it our humble and [*sincere wish* is crossed out] earnest request to your RH that you would vouchsafe, upon first notice, to favour [*your* is crossed out] this nation with your immediate presence, as what will quiet the minds of these [*nations* is crossed out] Kingdoms, and disappoint the senseless designs [an indecipherable phrase heavily crossed out] of the Enemies to your Highness & our Constitution as by Law Established. A Squadron of Men of War is to be gott ready [*for that purpose only* is crossed out] with all expedition to attend on your Royal H.

Anne's body was not yet cold, early on that first Sunday morning of August, when the Regency Council – essentially the Privy Council with a different title – drafted another letter to George telling him of the death of Queen Anne and urging his immediate departure for England.

> Wee humbly beg leave to assure your Maj'ty of our utmost fidelity, in discharge of that Trust with which [*you have been pleased to Honour us* is crossed out] we are at present Honour'd. And wee make it our most earnest Request to your Maj'ty that you will hasten over to your People, who with great impatience wait your coming. Your Royal Presence being the best and surest support of our Religion, Laws and Liberties.[20]

In reconstructing the medical circumstances of Anne's death and its political meaning it can be stated with certainty that she died of acute vascular disease of her brain from systemic lupus erythematosus. It can also be said that in the last three days of her life she was not mentally sound. Indeed she was almost certainly stuporous much of the time and comatose at the end. In spite of the Act of Settlement of

1701, some have imagined that she really intended the throne to go to her half-brother, James Edward Francis Stuart. However, this would not have been consistent with her lifelong Protestant beliefs and disdain for the Jacobite cause. Anne was physically feeble and mentally drained, even apart from the stroke. The likelihood is that she did not give the rod of office of Lord Treasurer to Charles Talbot, he simply took the rod to ensure that crown and government would go to George, waiting in Hanover, and not to James Francis Edward Stuart, waiting in France.

Thus, from the vascular dementia of Anne's great-grandfather, James I, to her own lupus and acute brain injury and death, the Stuart dynasty was steadily worn down by disease and disability. Thereby Parliament won power in England, and monarchy lost it.

The best epitaph for Anne, and indeed for the Stuart dynasty, was delivered by the Scottish physician John Arbuthnot, who was present at the end. John Arbuthnot was Anne's favourite physician, faithful and attentive to her very last breath, always considering her comfort and welfare through the long years of physical infirmity that characterized her reign. What he wrote to his dear friend, Jonathan Swift, after Queen Anne's death, reflects the feelings of a physician for his patient who has suffered a long debilitating illness, and his words, soft and sweet, are fitting both for the end of the life of a queen and the end of a dynasty. 'My dear mistress's days were numbered even in my imagination, and could not exceed certain limits . . . I believe sleep was never more welcome to a weary traveller than death was to her.'[21]

NINE

Post-mortem Examination of the Stuart Family

Nowadays at the end of an autopsy report the pathologist often adds a brief summary of the life of the patient and the disease or diseases which took that life. In examining the steady decline in the health and well-being of the English Stuart monarchy such a statement would seem to be appropriate here.

Vascular dementia in James I and then disabling delusion in Charles I brought the Stuart dynasty to its first, sudden end in 1649, with the surgical death of Charles I by beheading. The mild hereditary neuromuscular disease that afflicted James and Charles proved to be of little importance to them and did not affect subsequent Stuarts. Prince Henry Frederick, who would have made a strong Stuart monarch, died of typhoid fever in 1612 without ever seeing the throne of England. Charles II's untimely death from acute mercury poisoning left James II with a throne he was incapable of holding. His inability to manage events as simple as the birth and acceptance of his Roman Catholic male heir led to his abandonment of the throne and the second ending of the Stuart dynasty in 1688. The death of Mary II from acute haemorrhagic smallpox gave the Stuart throne to her husband, William of Orange, in 1694, ending the dynasty for a third time. Mary II's sister, Queen Anne, succeeded William as monarch upon his death. She had seventeen pregnancies but the only child to survive infancy, William, Duke of Gloucester, died of pneumonia at eleven years of age. Lupus erythematosus and the antiphospholipid antibody syndrome physically weakened Queen Anne, the last English Stuart. Having severely compromised her ability to produce an heir, lupus erythematosus took her life in 1714, ending the Stuart dynasty for a fourth and final time.

If one refers to Appendix IV, a complete accounting of the forty-five members of the English Stuart family shows that more than half of the children born were dead by early childhood, a high mortality rate even for the seventeenth century. There was no important limiting hereditary disease in this family nor was there any single disease that exacted significant mortality, except for smallpox, which killed one reigning monarch, a princess royal and one prince second in line to the throne. The Stuart dynasty was brought down by disease and disability, decimating each generation from King James I to Queen Anne.

APPENDIX I

Review of the Stuart, Bourbon and Habsburg Dynasties

While the eras of the Stuarts, Bourbons and Habsburgs were not concurrent they match in time fairly closely. The English Stuarts began with James I who was born in 1566, became King of England in 1603 and died in 1625. He was followed by his son Charles I, born in 1600, crowned in 1625 and executed in 1649. After the interregnum of the Cromwells, the throne was restored with the son of the late Charles I, Charles II, who was born in 1630, crowned in 1660 and died suddenly in 1685. Charles II's brother, James II followed. He was born in 1633, crowned in 1685, absconded in 1688 and died in exile in France in 1701. James II was succeeded by his daughter, Mary II, who reigned jointly with her husband, William III. Mary was born in 1662, ascended to the throne in 1688 and died in 1694. Her husband reigned alone until his death in 1702. Mary's sister, Anne, followed William as monarch. She was born in 1665, crowned in 1702 and died unexpectedly in 1714. This ended the English Stuarts.

The House of Bourbon came to power in France with Henry IV. Henry was born in 1553 and ascended to the throne of France in 1589 on the extinction of the male line of the Valois family. He was assassinated in 1610. Henry's son, Louis XIII, born in 1601, attained the throne on his father's death. He died in 1643 to be followed by his son, Louis XIV. Born in 1638, Louis XIV became king in 1643 and left a regency behind him in 1651. He reigned until his death in 1715 and was succeeded by his great-grandson, Louis XV. Louis XV died in 1774 and was succeeded by his grandson, Louis XVI, who died in the French Revolution in 1793.

The Habsburg genealogy is more complex and has two branches. For our purposes we can begin with Charles V, Holy Roman Emperor from 1519 to 1556 and King of Spain as Charles I from 1516 to 1556. Charles was born in 1500 and died in 1558. He gave the imperial crown to his brother, Ferdinand I, in 1553 and the crown of Spain to his son, Philip II, in 1556. The Austrian branch of the Habsburgs went through Ferdinand I, who was born in 1503 and crowned as the King of Austria in 1521. Ferdinand became emperor as well in 1564 and died in the same year. He was followed by his son Maximilian II who was born in 1527, crowned emperor in 1564 and died in 1576. Maximilian was succeeded by his son, Rudolph II. Rudolph was born in 1552, crowned emperor in 1576 and reigned until 1612. Rudolph II was the first Austrian Habsburg to reign at the time of the English Stuarts. He was followed by his brother, Matthias. Born in 1557, Matthias was elected emperor in 1612 and reigned for just seven years until his death in 1619. He was followed by his cousin, Ferdinand II, who was born in 1578 and served as emperor from 1619 until his death in 1637. Ferdinand II was followed by his son, Ferdinand III. Born in 1608, he was Holy Roman Emperor from 1637 until his death in 1657. Leopold I was the son of Ferdinand III. Born in 1640 he became emperor in 1658 and reigned until his death in 1705. Two of his sons succeeded him, Joseph I and Charles VI. Joseph was born in 1678, became emperor in 1705, and died in 1711 to be followed by his brother, Charles. Charles VI was born in 1685, became emperor in 1711 and died in 1740. The Austrian branch of the Habsburgs remained on the throne until 1918.

The Spanish Habsburg branch proceeded from the emperor Charles V (also Charles I, King of Spain), to his son Philip II. Philip was born in 1527 and was king from 1556 until his death in 1598. The next king was his son, Philip III, whose mother was Anne of Austria. Philip III was born in 1578, became king in 1598 and reigned until his death in 1621. He was the first Spanish Habsburg to reign during the time of the English Stuarts. His son, Philip IV, succeeded him. Born in 1605, Philip IV became king in 1621 and died in 1665. He was followed by his four-year-old son, Charles II, born in 1661. Charles II reigned from 1665 until his death in 1700. Mentally feeble, he died without heir, despite having been married twice. So ended the Spanish Habsburgs. Charles II's death precipitated the War of the Spanish Succession and he was followed by a Bourbon, the French prince Philip V, born in 1683. Philip was King of Spain from 1700 until his death in 1746, although his son, Louis I, reigned for a single year of that time, in 1724.

APPENDIX II

Chronology of the Stuart, Bourbon and Habsburg Monarchs

Year	Stuart	Bourbon	Spanish Habsburg	Austrian Habsburg
1600		[Henry IV]	[Philip III]	[Rudolph]
	James I/VI			
1610		Louis XIII		
				Matthias
				Ferdinand II
1620				
			Philip IV	
	Charles I			
1630				
				Ferdinand III
1640				
		Louis XIV		
	[execution]			
1650	*			
	*			
	*			Leopold I
1660	Charles II			
			Charles II	
1670				
1680				
	James II			
	Mary II			
1690				
	[death]			
	*			
1700	*		Philip V	
	*			
	Anne			Joseph I
1710				
				Charles VI
	[death]			
1720				

```
*
* = No Stuart on the throne
*
```

245

APPENDIX III

Physicians of the Stuart Monarchs

It was always an honour to be appointed physician to a monarch. Some court physicians saw their royal patient frequently, some rarely and some not at all. In time of severe illness, an 'unappointed' consultant physician might be called to see the monarch. Physicians were almost always associated with the Royal College of Physicians. Beyond this select group of qualified and certified medical doctors, the royal medical household included surgeons, apothecaries, midwives and the occasional eclectic medical practitioner. The annotated list of physicians herewith appended is by no means complete. It is focused on those who actually attended a Stuart monarch for medical advice and assistance. The best and most complete compendium of physicians to the Stuarts is that of Professor E.L. Furdell, *The Royal Doctors, 1485–1714: Medical Personnel at the Tudor and Stuart Courts*, published in 2001 by the University of Rochester Press. Short biographical notes can be found for almost all of the royal physicians in *The Roll of the Royal College of Physicians of London*, written by Dr George Munk and published by that college in 1878. Some of the royal physicians can be found in the *Dictionary of National Biography (DNB)*, some cannot. Records of personal papers are found for some of these men in the *National Register of Archives (NRA)*. Only a few of these physicians left written materials pertaining to their famous patients, and these writings may be found only in case notes,

246

letters and diaries, not biographies. As a general rule it has always been thought unethical and unseemly for a physician to write about his or her patient for public consumption, and there have been few exceptions throughout history, the most notable being Lord Moran's medical biography of Winston Churchill, published in 1966, just a year after Churchill's death.

The annotated list identifies only physicians, not surgeons and other medical practitioners. Many of these men attended more than one of the Stuarts but their names are listed only once, with the monarch with whom they are principally associated.

JAMES I OF ENGLAND AND VI OF SCOTLAND

James had a medical staff in Scotland but few of them accompanied him to London, save David Beaton, about whom little is known, and John Craig, who attained recognition in London, as indicated below.

Henry Atkins, MD (1558–1635). He frequently saw James as a patient but nothing has been listed among his papers pertaining to James. Correspondence relative to his attendance on Prince Charles can be found in Hertfordshire Record Office and he is listed in both the *DNB* and *NRA*.

Henry Blackwood, MD (died 1614). Though an academic physician in Paris and widely published, Blackwood left no written record of James. His biography may be found in the *DNB*.

John Craig, MD (died 1620). Craig was interested in mathematics and may have given John Napier his first hint about logarithms. He apparently left no papers and wrote nothing about James, although he is mentioned by others as believing that James had been poisoned. His son attended Charles I (see below). An interesting biographical record may be found in the *DNB*.

George Eglisham, MD (fl. 1612–42). A Scottish physician, he surely did attend James. Eglisham is famous for the polemic he wrote against Buckingham and published after James's death, *The Fore-Runner of Revenge*. It is cited in the text and described, in detail, how he believed that Buckingham and his mother poisoned James. Other mentions of James in his writings apparently did not address medical matters. He is recognized by the *DNB*.

William Harvey, MD (1578–1657). Harvey, responsible for the discovery of the movement of the heart and circulation of blood, is probably the most famous physician of all time. He kept case notes on his patients but most of these are said to have been destroyed when his London house was ransacked during the Civil War and the remainder destroyed during the Great Fire of London in 1666. Harvey saw James as a patient and also attended his son, Charles. Some of his papers are in the Sloane Archives of the British Library. Harvey is represented in the *DNB* and *NRA*.

de Mayerne, Sir Theodore Turquet, MD (1573–1655). This physicians' physician is extensively quoted in the text. Many of his case notes are in the Sloane MSS of the British Library. It is not clear to this author that they have ever been catalogued. Others of his papers are at the Bodleian Library, the Public Record Office and the Cambridge University Library. His extensive biography may be found in the *DNB* and he is listed in the *NRA*.

Sir William Paddy, MD (1554–1634). Paddy saw James as a patient but apparently left no notes of this. He published some poetry but nothing else. The *DNB* has a complete biography of this man.

A number of other physicians' names are associated with James. These include: William Butler, James Chambers, John Durel, Jonathan Goddard, Thomas Grent, John Hammond,

Sir Matthew Lister, John Macelo (from Scotland), Michael Malescotius, Joseph Mead, Duncan Primrose and Thomas Ridgely.

CHARLES I

It should be noted that Charles enjoyed excellent health during his short life and rarely had the need of a physician's services.

John Craig, MD (died 1644). He was physician to Charles I but left no notes or records. He has a biographical entry in the *DNB*.

Additional physicians to Charles include: David Beaton, Samuel Bispham, William Denton, Sir Edward Greaves (who wrote the seminal account of typhus fever), Arthur Johnston (from Scotland) and others of lesser note.

CHARLES II

When Charles II put the monarchy back together at the Restoration he expanded the medical staff, appointing a number of physicians who saw members of the Stuart family and the court but probably not Charles himself.

Sir Edmund King, MD (1629–1709). A prominent physician who began his career as a surgeon, King attended Charles frequently including during his final illness. He is not cited by others as having written about Charles. His papers are in the Sloane MSS in the British Library and at the Royal Society, and he appears in the *DNB* and the *NRA*.

Richard Lower, MD (1631–91). Lower was a pioneer in experimental physiology and wrote extensively, although nothing he might have written about his patients has been preserved. He was a pioneer in attempting the transfusion of blood. His personal papers are not identified in the *NRA* but his biography appears in the *DNB*.

Sir Charles Scarburgh, MD (1616–94). Of a medical family, Scarburgh attended Charles before and at the time of his death. Charles Crawfurd used his account of Charles's death to write his own detailed description, finding Scarburgh's writings in the library of the Society of Antiquaries. Scarburgh's name is prominent in both the *DNB* and the *NRA*.

Thomas Willis, MD (1621–73). Willis was the man who first studied the anatomy of the brain and came to the conclusion that thought originated in the cerebrum. He was Sedleian Professor of Natural Philosophy at Oxford and was often consulted by members of the Stuart family. He left no notes on any of these consultations. As would be expected he appears in the *DNB* and the *NRA*.

Other physicians to Charles II include: Sir John Baber, Samuel Barrow, Peter Barwick, George Bate (known as an anatomist), John Bateman, Robert Brady, Peter and Hugh Chamberlen (of the famous family of obstetricians), Timothy Clarke, Edmund Dickinson (sometimes written Dickerson – a chemist of repute), Albertus Otto Faber, Sir Alexander Frazer (a Scot and a court intimate), John Hinton, Thomas Hobbs, Caspar and Walter Needham, James Pears, William Quartermaine, Thomas Waldron, Edward Warren, Tobias Whitaker (an early writer on medical topics for the general public) and Thomas Witherley.

JAMES II

James enjoyed exceptional health during his lifetime and his reign was short. For these reasons, it is difficult to find any records of physicians who may have attended him, even during his famous nosebleed or in France at the end of his life. There are three men, however, who were considered by James to have been royal physicians. These are: Francis Bernard, Robert Brady (who attended Mary Beatrice at the birth of Prince James Francis Edward) and David Bruce.

MARY II

Although her life and reign were short Mary had excellent physicians, probably including those in Holland. By and large she shared physicians with her husband.

Walter Harris, MD (1647–1732). Harris was Mary's personal physician and attended her before and during her final illness. A letter of his about Mary is cited in Strickland's *Lives of the Queens of England*. A useful biography may be found in the *DNB*.

Sir Thomas Millington, MD (1628–1704). Millington may have attended Mary during her final illness; it is not clear. He was one of William's physicians. Millington had definite opinions about Mary's death, and thought she suffered measles and not smallpox. He has a biography in the *DNB* and has papers cited by the *NRA*.

John Radcliffe, MD (1650–1714). Clearly the brightest physician of London in his time, Radcliffe criticized the management of Anne during her final illness but did not see her. An avowed Jacobite, his reputation for brilliance is balanced by his reputation for irrascibility. His papers are distributed among the Radcliffe Science Library at Oxford, the Badminton Estate Office and the Hertfordshire Record Office. An excellent biography may be found in the *DNB*.

Additional physicians to Mary II include: Richard Blackmore, John Hutton (who knew Mary and William in Holland and moved with them to England), Thomas Lawrence (or Laurence) and William Stokeham.

ANNE

Considering her lifetime burden of illness and her extensive obstetric history, Anne had relatively few physicians.

John Arbuthnot, MD (1667–1735). A Scot and the favourite physician of Anne. His few observations on Anne are cited in the text. Arbuthnot wrote widely on many topics, medical and non-medical. Letters to Hans Sloane are among the Sloane MSS and letters to Jonathan Swift among the Add. MSS in the British Library. He has an excellent biography in the *DNB* and, because he has identifiable papers, is listed in the *NRA*.

Sir David Hamilton, MD (1663–1721). Hamilton's important diary and medical observations of Anne are cited in this book. He was the most prominent gynaecologist in London at the time, and the confidant of many prominent women. The *DNB* contains a useful biography of Sir David.

Sir Edward Hannes, MD (died 1710). Hannes probably did attend Anne but died long before her final illnesses. He left no papers that would contain references to Anne. However, he has a biography in the *DNB* and his name is listed in the *NRA*.

Martin Lister, MD (1638?–1712). Although appointed a physician to Anne in about 1710, Lister may have never attended her. He died before her final years of illness. His private papers are in the Bodleian Library at Oxford and letters to Hans Sloane are in the Sloane MSS at the British Library. He appears in the *DNB* and the *NRA*.

Richard Mead, MD (1673–1754). Although relatively young, Mead attended Anne during her final illness. He was a friend of John Radcliffe and is not known to have written anything about Anne. No relevant collection of clinical papers has been identified, although he wrote on a variety of topics. He has a fine biography in the *DNB* and is listed in the *NRA*.

Sir Thomas Millington, MD (1628–1704). Millington probably attended Anne before she became queen, and died long before her final illnesses. He has listings in both the *DNB* and the *NRA*.

Sir John Shadwell, MD (1671–1714). Shadwell's observations are cited in the text. He was a physician of some note. Letters to Hans Sloane are in the Sloane MSS in the British Library. He is listed in both the *DNB* and the *NRA*.

Sir Hans Sloane, MD (1660–1753). The most prolific medical writer of his age: cited in the text is his original description of Anne's medical problems from his manuscripts in the British Library. Sloane's manuscripts are vast and this author has reviewed only a very small part of them. He has a long biography in the *DNB* and is listed in the *NRA*.

Other physicians known to have attended Anne are: Richard Blundell, James Chase, Ambrose Dickins, Thomas Lawrence and Edward Southwell.

APPENDIX IV

Stuart Family Members and Their Deaths

Causes of death are listed only when certain, and otherwise are denoted as uncertain; no causes of death are listed for infants or young children. Additional important confirmed medical diagnoses are listed in parentheses, whether or not they contributed to death. Finally, the term 'acute abdomen' is applied when sudden abdominal pain led to death within hours, probably a surgical condition which could not be addressed during Stuart times.

Monarchs are listed in bold type with their consorts directly below. Beneath and indented from both are their children.

Mary Queen of Scots	1542–87	beheaded
Stuart, Henry, Lord Darnley	1545–67	murdered
James (I) *see below*	1566–1625	stroke (vascular dementia)
James I		
Anne of Denmark	1574–1619	uncertain (chronic oedema)
Henry Frederick	1594–1612	typhoid fever
Elizabeth, Queen of Bohemia	1596–1662	uncertain
Margaret	1598–1600	–
Charles (I) *see below*	1600–49	beheaded
Robert	1602–?	–

| Mary | 1605–7 | – |
| Sophia | 1606–? | – |

Charles I

Henrietta Maria	1609–69	uncertain
Charles (II) *see below*	1630–85	acute mercury poisoning
Mary	1631–60	smallpox
James (II) *see below*	1633–1701	stroke
Elizabeth	1636–50	fever, exact cause unknown
Anne	1637–40	uncertain
Henry	1640–60	smallpox
Henrietta (Minette)	1644–70	acute abdomen

Charles II

| Catherine of Braganza | 1638–1703 | acute abdomen |

James II

Anne Hyde	1637–71	uncertain
Charles	1660–4	–
Mary (II) *see below*	1662–94	smallpox
James	1663–6	–
Anne *see below*	1665–1714	systemic lupus erythematosus
Charles	1666–7	–
Edgar	1667–71	–
Henrietta	1668–9	–
Catherine	1670–1	–
Mary Beatrice of Modena	1658–1718	breast cancer
Catherine Laura	1675	–
Isabel	1676–81	–
Charles	1677	–
Elizabeth	1678	–
Charlotte Margaret	1682	–
James Francis Edward *see below*	1688–1766	uncertain (seizure disorder)
Louisa Mary	1692–1712	smallpox

Mary II
William III of Orange   1650–1702   pneumonia

Anne
George of Denmark   1653–1708   uncertain
                                          (asthma)
   Mary   1685–7   –
   Sophia   1686–7   –
   William Henry 1689–1700   pneumonia
                                          (arrested
                                             hydrocephalus)
   Mary   1690   –
   George   1692   –

The Stuart Family in Exile

James Francis Edward
Maria Clementina Sobieska,   1702–35   depression
   Princess
   Charles Edward *see below*   1720–88   stroke
                                          (alcoholism)
   Henry Benedict, Cardinal   1725–1807   uncertain

Charles Edward
Louise, Princess of   1753–1824   uncertain (chronic
   Stolberg-Gedern   oedema)

Notes

CHAPTER ONE

1. Personal communication, Professor R. Neil Schimke, University of Kansas Medical Center, Kansas City, Kansas, USA.
2. Hill, C., *The World Turned Upside Down*. London: Penguin Books, 1991, 348.

CHAPTER TWO

1. Holmes, F.F., 'Anne Boleyn, the Sweating Sickness and the Hantavirus: a review of an old disease with a new interpretation'. *Journal of Medical Biography*, 6 (1998), 43–8.
2. Major, R.H., *Classic Descriptions of Disease*. Springfield: Charles C. Thomas, 1945, 241.
3. Furdell, E.L., *The Royal Doctors, 1485–1714: Medical Personnel at the Tudor and Stuart Courts*. Rochester: University of Rochester Press, 2001.
4. Lamont-Brown, R., *Royal Poxes and Potions: The Lives of Court Physicians, Surgeons, and Apothecaries*. Stroud: Sutton Publishing, 2001.
5. Harvey, W., *Excercitatio Anatomica de Motu Cordis et Sanguinis in Animali*. Frankfurt: Wilhelm Fitzer, 1628.
6. Klippel, J.H., ed. *Primer on the Rheumatic Diseases*, eleventh edition. Atlanta: Arthritis Foundation, 1997, 234–5.
7. Post, J. and Robins, R.S., *When Illness Strikes the Leader: The Dilemma of the Captive King*. New Haven: Yale University Press, 1993, xiv.

CHAPTER THREE

1. Weldon, A., *Court and Character of King James the First*. London: John Wright, 1650.

2. Maxwell, John (Baron Herries), *Historical Memoirs of the Reign of Mary Queen of Scots*. Abbotsford Club, no. 6, ed. R. Pitcairn, Edinburgh, 1836, 79.

3. Willson, D.H., *King James VI and I*. London: Jonathan Cape, 1956, 17.

4. Akrigg, G.P.V., *Letters of King James VI and I*. Berkeley: University of California Press, 1984, 41.

5. James VI/I, 'A Counterblaste to Tobacco' in *The Works of the Most High and Mightie Prince James*. London: James Bishop, 1616. James's most remarkable diatribe against tobacco use, which resonates even in modern times with respect to health consequences of smoking.

6. Keynes, Geoffrey, *The Life of William Harvey*. Oxford: Clarendon Press, 1966, 138–9.

7. McClure, N.E., *The Letters of John Chamberlain, vol. II*. Philadelphia: The American Philosophical Society, 1939, 219–20.

8. Ibid., 232.

9. Carleton, C., *Royal Mistresses*. London: Routledge, 1990, 44.

10. Eglisham, G. (also written Elsingham), *The Forerunner of Revenge*. London: 1626 and reprinted in 1642.

11. Keynes, *Life of Harvey*, 144.

12. Macalpine, A. and Hunter, R., 'The "Insanity" of King George III: A Classic Case of Porphyria.' *British Medical Journal*, I (8 January 1966), 65–71.

13. Macalpine, I., Hunter, R. and Rimington, C., 'Porphyria in the Royal Houses of Stuart, Hanover and Prussia: A Follow-up Study of George III's Illness'. *British Medical Journal*, I (6 January 1968), 7–18.

14. Macalpine, I. and Hunter R., *George III and the Mad-Business*. London: Allen Lane, Penguin Press, 1969.

15. Dean, G., *The Porphyrias: A Story of Inheritance and Environment*, second edition. London: Pitman Medical, 1971, 138 ff.

16. Kenyon, J.P., *Stuart England*. London: Allen Lane (Penguin Books Ltd), 1978, 75.

17. Goodall, A.J., 'The Health of James the Sixth of Scotland and First of England'. *Medical History*, 1 (January 1957) 17–27.

18. Akrigg, G.P.V., *Jacobean Pageant in the Court of King James I*. London: Hamish Hamilton, 1962, 271.

19. Public Record Office, 'Alvise Valaresso, Venetian Ambassador in England, to the Doge and Senate', *Calendar of State Papers, Venetian Series, of the Reign of James I*. London: HMSO, 1900, 567.

20. McClure, *Chamberlain Letters*, 548.

21. Akrigg, *Letters of King James*.

22. Williams, K., Holmes, F., Kemper, S. and Marquis, J., 'Written language clues to cognitive changes of ageing: an analysis of the letters of King James VI/I'. *The Journal of Gerontology: Psychological Sciences*, 58B, 2003, 42–4. These findings were first presented by the authors at a meeting of the American Gerontology Society in San Francisco, November 1999.

23. Akrigg, *Letters of King James*.

24. Carlton, C., *Royal Mistresses*. London: Routledge, 1990, 44.

25. Indeed, vascular dementia is often overlooked by physicians, and a classic case in point is that of Winston Churchill. His personal physician, Lord Moran, wrote a controversial medical biography of his famous patient, publishing it in 1966, the year after Churchill's death. While many in the medical establishment criticized Lord Moran for this apparently self-serving act, nonetheless this biography is very readable, especially for physicians. Lord Moran documents emotional incontinence, an early symptom of vascular dementia, in Churchill as early as 1953, and also documents a stroke in 1954, one year before Churchill left 10 Downing Street. Not once in his book does he mention dementia or even senility, the code word of the time for dementia. Winston Churchill certainly had vascular dementia during his last year as Prime Minister and he was profoundly demented by the end of his life, as described by Lord Moran, but Moran never offers anything approaching this diagnosis. Lord Moran (Wilson, C.), *Churchill, Taken From the Diaries of Lord Moran*. Boston: Houghton Mifflin Company, 1966.

26. Keynes, *Life of Harvey*, 138 ff.

27. Weldon, *Court and Character*.

28. *The Oxford Dictionary of Quotations*, second edition. London: Oxford University Press, 1955, 242.

CHAPTER FOUR

1. Nenner, H., *The Right to be King: The Succession to the Crown of England, 1603–1714*. Chapel Hill: University of North Carolina Press, 1995, 4.

2. James VI/I, *Basilikon Doron, or King James's Instructions to His Dearest Sonne, Henry the Prince*. London: M. Flesher for Samuel Meare, 1682.

3. Abbott, J., *History of King Charles The First*. London: Thomas Allman, 1850, 5–10.

4. Seton, A., *Memoirs of Alexander Seton*. London: William Blackwood and Sons, 1882, 56.

5. Mares, F.H., ed., *The Memoirs of Robert Carey*. Oxford: Clarendon Press, 1972, 68–9.

6. Public Record Office, 'Dr. Hen. Atkins to Lord Cecil', 3 July 1604, *Calendar of State Papers, Domestic Series of the Reign of James I* (1603–1610). London: HMSO, 1857, 128.

7. Bergeron, D.M., *Royal Family: Royal Lovers*. Columbia: University of Missouri Press, 1991, 117.

8. Carlton, C., *Royal Childhoods*. London: Routledge, 1986, 80.

9. Bergeron, *Royal Family*, 159.

10. Kenyon, J.P., *Stuart England*, second edition. London: Penguin Books, 1985, 102.

11. Fritze, R.H. and Robison, W.B., eds, *Historical Dictionary of Stuart England, 1603–1689*. London: Greenwood Press, 1996.

12. Stephen, L., ed., 'Charles I', *Dictionary of National Biography, vol. IV*. Oxford: Oxford University Press, 1968, 67–84.

13. Sanderson, W., *The Compleat History of the Life and Raigne of King Charles From His Cradle to His Grave*. London: Humphrey Moseley, Richard Tomlins, and George Sawbridge, 1658, 1138.

14. Moore, N., 'An Historical Case of Typhoid Fever', in, *St. Barts Hospital Reports*, XVII, 1881, 131–50.

15. Chevers, N., *An Enquiry Into the Circumstances of the Death of King Charles the Second of England*. London: R.C. Lepage & Co., 1861, 10 ff.

16. Personal communication, Dr Mary Carpenter, University of Kansas Medical Center, Kansas City, Kansas, USA. It may be that the importance of Charles's dysfluency has been underestimated, certainly in the twenty-first century he would be treated for this disability.

Notes

17. Turner, E. in a letter to Brand, J., *A Declaration of the Diet and Particular Fare of K. Charles the First, When Duke of York*. London: Society of Antiquaries of London, 1802.

18. Kenyon, J. and Ohlmeyer, J., *The Civil Wars: A Military History of England, Scotland and Ireland, 1638–1660*. Oxford: Oxford University Press, 1998.

19. Bruce, J., ed., 'Charles I', in *1646, Letters of King Charles The First to Queen Henrietta Maria*. London: Camden Society, 1856, viii and xxvi.

20. Charles I, *King Charles His Speech Made Upon the Scaffold at Whitehall-Gate, Immediately Before His Execution on Tuesday the 30th Jan. 1648, With a Relation of the maner of his going to Execution (Published by Special Authority)*. London: Peter Cole, 1649.

21. American Psychiatric Association, *Diagnostic and Statistical Manual of Mental Disorders*, fourth edition. Washington, DC: American Psychiatric Association, 1994, 296–301.

22. Kishlansky, M., *A Monarchy Transformed: Britain 1603–1714*. London: Allen Lane, Penguin Press, 1996, 185.

CHAPTER FIVE

1. Public Record Office, 'The Earl of Ranelagh to Viscount Conway, *Calendar of State Papers, Domestic Series*. London: HMSO, 1909, 95–6.

2. Ibid., 234.

3. Munk, William, *The Roll of the Royal College of Physicians of London, Vol. I*. London: Harrison and Sons, 1878, 130.

4. Macray, W.D., *Notes Which Passed at Meetings of the Privy Council Between Charles II and the Earl of Clarendon, 1660–1667, Together With a Few Letters*. London: Nichols and Sons, 1896.

5. Public Record Office, 'Pietro Mocensio, Venetian Ambassador in England, to the Doge and Senate', *Calendar of State Papers, Venetian Series*. London: HMSO, 1937, 66.

6. Public Record Office, 'The Earl of Ranleigh to Viscount Conway', 4 March 1679, *Calendar of State Papers, Domestic Series*. London: HMSO, 1909, 95–6.

7. Ibid., this series of letters may be found between pages 226 and 234.

8. Public Record Office, 'Warrant for erecting an office of chemical physician to the King', 7 May 1669, *Calendar of State Papers, Domestic Series, of the Reign of Charles II (October 1668–December 1669)*. London: HMSO, 1894, 315.

9. Pepys, S. (Latham, R. and Matthews, W., eds), *The Diary of Samuel Pepys*, vol. 9. London: G. Bell and Sons, Ltd, 1983, 416–7.

10. Fraser, A., *King Charles II*. London: Weidenfeld and Nicholson, 1979, 443–5.

11. Public Record Office, 'Newsletter to John Squire, Newcastle', 3 February 1685, *Calendar of State Papers, Domestic Series, of the Reign of Charles II. (May 1684–February 1685)*. London: HMSO 1938, 309–10.

12. Ibid., 310–1.

13. Crawfurd, R., *The Last Days of Charles II*. Oxford: Clarendon Press, 1909, 7.

14. Nova et Vetera, 'Some Royal Death Beds: Charles II', *British Medical Journal*, vol. 1 (25 June 1910), 1557–60.

15. This particular copy may well be the oldest one in existence. The differences between this manuscript, the one published in the *British Medical Journal* in 1911 and a Latin copy of Scarburgh's long account of Charles's death now in the library of the Society of Antiquaries, are minimal, as noted by E.B. Krumbhaar, 'Two contemporary manuscripts Bearing on the death of Charles II of England', *Transactions and Studies of the College of Physicians of Philadelphia*, 6 (1938), 51–9. So the consistency and accuracy of the observations recorded is sound.

16. Chevers, *Death of King Charles the Second*, 10 ff.

17. Bruce-Chwatt, L.J., *The Rise and Fall of Malaria in Europe: A Historico-epidemiological Study*. Oxford: Oxford University Press, 1980, 131–45.

18. Cartland, B., *The Private Life of Charles II: The Women He Loved*. London: Frederick Muller, Ltd., 1958, 210–1.

19. Wolbarsht, M.L. and Sax, D.S., 'Charles II, a Royal Martyr', *Notes and Records of the Royal Society of London*, vol. 16 (November 1961), 154–7.

20. Lenihan, J.M.A. and Smith, H., 'Activation Analysis and Public Health', *Nuclear Activation Techniques in the Life Sciences*. Vienna: International Atomic Energy Agency, 1967, 601–14.

21. Nova et Vetera, 'Some Royal Deathbeds: Charles II', *British Medical Journal*, (25 June 1910), 1557–60.
22. Archives of the College of Physicians of Philadelphia, Report of the post-mortem examination of the body of Charles II. Also found in: Krumbhaar, E.B., 'Two contemporary manuscripts bearing on the death of Charles II of England', *Transactions & Studies of the College of Physicians of Philadelphia*, 6 (1938), 51–9.
23. Lamont-Brown, *Royal Poxes and Potions*, 269.
24. Kenyon, J.P., *Robert Spencer Earl of Sunderland, 1641–1702*. Aldershot: Gregg Revivals, 1992, 30.

CHAPTER SIX

1. Dewhurst, J., *Royal Confinements: A Gynaecological History of Britain's Royal Family*. New York: St Martin's Press, 1980, 16–26.
2. Turner, F.C., *James II*. London: Eyre & Spottiswoode, 1948, 17–19.
3. Longueville, T., *The Adventures of King James II of England*. London: Longmans, Green and Co., 1904, 135.
4. Stephen, L. and Lee, S., eds, 'Anne Hyde, Duchess of York', in *Dictionary of National Biography*, vol. X. London: Oxford University Press, 1968, 366–9.
5. Public Record Office, 'A Memorial of the Protestants of the Church of England' (June or July), *Calendar of State Papers, Domestic Series, (June 1687– February 1689)*. London: HMSO, 1972, 226.
6. Ibid., 327.
7. Public Record Office (several dispatches from the front at Salisbury), *Calendar of State Papers, Domestic Series (June 1687–February 1689)*. London: HMSO, 1972, 358–61.
8. Longueville, *Adventures of King James II*, 393.
9. Macpherson, J., *Original Papers; Containing the Secret History of Great Britain From the Restoration to the Accession of the House of Hannover, To Which Are Affixed Extracts From the Life of James II, As Written By Himself*, vol. 1. London: W. Strahan and T. Cadell, 1775, 22 ff.
10. Scott, W., ed., 'An Exact Account of the Sickness and Death of

the late King James II. As also of the Proceedings at St. Germains thereupon, 1701. In a Letter from an English Gentleman in France, to his Friend in London', in *A Collection of Scarce and Valuable Tracts (The Somers Collection of Tracts, in Sion Library), vol. XI*. London: T. Cadell and W. Davies, 1814, 339–42.

11. Turner, *James II*, 234.

12. Mitchell, J.R.A., 'Nose-Bleeding and High Blood Pressure', *British Medical Journal*, I (3 January 1959), 25–7.

13. Charles, R. and Corrigan, E., 'Epistaxis and Hypertension', *Postgraduate Medical Journal*, 53 (May 1977), 260–1.

14. Holger, J., 'Epistaxis: a Clinical Study of 1724 Patients', *Journal of Laryngology and Otology*, 88 (1974), 317–27.

15. Weiss, N., 'Relation of High Blood Pressure to Headache, Epistaxis and Selected Other Symptoms', *New England Journal of Medicine*, 287 (28 September 1972), 631–3.

16. Petruson, B., 'Epistaxis: a Clinical Study with Special Reference to Fibrinolysis', *ACTA Oto-Laryngologica, supplementum 317* (1974), 1–72.

17. Strickland, A., 'Mary of Modena', *Lives of the Queens of England, vol. XII*. Philadelphia: George Barrie and Sons, 1902, 331–3.

18. Bloom, H.J.G., Richardson, W.W. and Harries, E.J., 'Natural History of Untreated Breast Cancer (1805–1933)', *British Medical Journal*, II (28 July 1962), 213–21.

19. McLynn, F., *Charles Edward Stuart: A Tragedy in Many Acts*. London: Routledge, 1988, 201–17.

CHAPTER SEVEN

1. Hamilton, E., *William's Mary: A Biography of Mary II*. London: Hamish Hamilton, 1972, 19.

2. Bathurst, B., *Letters of Two Queens*. London: Robert Holden & Co., Ltd, 1924.

3. Burnet, G. (Bishop of Sarum), *An Essay on the Memory of the Late Queen*. London: Richard Chiswell, 1695, 79 and 82.

4. Bowen, M., *The Third Mary Stuart, Mary of York, Orange and England. Being a Character Study With Memoirs and Letters of Queen Mary II of England, 1662–1694*. London: John Lane, Bodley Head Ltd, 1929, 132.

5. Doebner, R., ed., *Memoirs of Mary, Queen of England, 1689–1693. Together With Her Letters and Those of James II and*

William III. To the Electress Sophia of Hanover. Leipzig: Veit and Comp., 1886, 25.

6. Ibid., 24.

7. Hamilton, *William's Mary*, 327–8.

8. Creighton, C., *A History of Epidemics in Britain, vol. 2.* London: Frank Cass, 1965, 459.

9. Burnet, G. (ed. Martin Joseph Routh), *History of His Own Time.* Hildesheim: Georg Olms Verlagsbuchhandlung, 1969, 5–6.

10. Nova et Vetera, 'Some Royal Deathbeds: Mary II', *British Medical Journal*, II (16 July 1910), 148.

11. Sutton, H.M., ed., *The Lexington Papers or, Some Account of the Courts of London and Vienna; at the Conclusion of the Seventeenth Century.* London: John Murray, 1851, 31–2.

12. Ibid.

13. Nova et Vetera, 'Some Royal Death-Beds: William III', *British Medical Journal*, II (20 August 1910), 461–2.

14. Fenner, F., Henderson, D.A., Arita, I., Jezek, Z. and Ladnyi, I.D., *Smallpox and its Eradication.* Geneva: World Health Organization, 1988, 5–39.

15. Brewer, C., *The Death of Kings: a Medical History of the Kings and Queens of England.* London: Abson, 2000, 190–4.

16. Robb, N., *William of Orange: A Personal Portrait. Vol. 2: 1674–1702.* New York: St Martin's Press, 1966, 565–6.

CHAPTER EIGHT

1. Sloane, H., Account of Queen Anne's Illness. December 1713–January 1714. Sloane MSS, 4034 ff, 46–50, British Library.

2. Stephan, L., ed., 'Queen Anne', in *Dictionary of National Biography, vol. 1.* Oxford: Oxford University Press, 1968, 441–73.

3. Jesse, J.H., *Memoirs of the Court of England from the Revolution in 1688 to the Death of George the Second.* London: Richard Bentley, 1843, 292–3.

4. [Boyer, A., probably], *The LIFE of Queen ANNE.* London: printed for A. Bell at the Bible and Cross-Keys in Cornhill; W. Taylor at the Ship and J. Baker at the Blackboy, in Pater-Noster Row, 1714, 414–16.

5. Dewhurst, *Royal Confinements*, 31–2.

6. Lewis, J., *Memoirs of Prince William Henry, Duke of Gloucester.*

London: Messrs Payne, Mews Gate; J. Murray, Fleet Street; Messrs Robson and Clarke, New Bond Street; Messrs Prince and Cooke, and J. Fletcher. Oxford: 1789, 9 ff.

7. Dewhurst, *Royal Confinements*, 189–91.
8. Brown, B.C., *The Letters and Diplomatic Instructions of Queen Anne*. London: Cassell and Company Ltd, 1935, 66 ff.
9. Bucholz, R.O., *The Augustan Court: Queen Anne and the Decline of Court Culture*. Stanford: Stanford University Press, 1993, 202 ff.
10. Boyer, A., *The Life of Queen Anne*. London: A. Bell, W. Taylor and J. Baker, 1714, 406 ff.
11. Cumston, C.G., 'Some Medical Gossip Pertaining to the Last Illness of Queen Anne of England, *New York Medical Journal*, 94 (22 July 1911), 179–81.
12. Nova et Vetera, 'Some Royal Death-Beds: Queen Anne', *British Medical Journal*, II (12 November 1910), 1530–2.
13. Dewhurst, *Royal Confinements*, 31–2.
14. Emson. H.E., 'For the Want of an Heir: the Obstetric History of Queen Anne', *British Medical Journal*, vol. 304 (23 May 1992), 1365–6.
15. Levine, J.S., Branch, D.W. and Rauch, J., 'The Antiphospholipid Antibody Syndrome', *New England Journal of Medicine*, 346 (2002), 752–63.
16. Hamilton. D. *The Diary of Sir David Hamilton (edited by Philip Roberts)*. Oxford: Clarendon Press, 1975, 6.
17. Klippel, ed., *Primer on Rheumatic Diseases*, 106.
18. Emson, 'For the Want of an Heir', 1366.
19. Brewer, *Death of Kings*, 202–8.
20. Hanoverian Succession Collection. Draft copies of letters to George I, in the Manuscripts Department of the Spencer Library, University of Kansas, Lawrence, Kansas, USA: Pryce MS P5:1 and Pryce MS P:2. The author is in the debt of Ms Anne Hyde, retired manuscript librarian, for making these two draft letters available.
21. Trevelyan, G., *England Under Queen Anne: the Peace and the Protestant Succession, vol. 3*. London: Longmans, Green and Co., 1934, 309.

Bibliography

Research for this study spanned more than a decade and a variety of sources were reviewed. Following is a list of most of these, only part of which is actually identified in the text and the Notes. This bibliography is divided into Primary and Secondary source materials.

PRIMARY SOURCE MATERIAL

Akrigg, G.P.V., *Letters of King James I & VI*. Berkeley: University of California Press, 1984.

Archives of the American College of Physicians (Philadelphia). Report of the post-mortem examination of the body of Charles II. Also found in: Krumbhaar, E.B., 'Two contemporary manuscripts bearing on the death of Charles II of England', *Transactions & Studies of the College of Physicians of Philadelphia*, 6 (1938), 51–9.

Bathurst, Benjamin, *Letters of Two Queens*. London: Robert Holden & Co., Ltd, 1924.

Bill of Rights, *An Act Declaring the Rights and Liberties of the Subject and Settling the Succession of the Crown*. Obtained from the Internet.
http://wiretap.spies.com/Gopher/Gov/World/england.bil.

Boyer, A., *The LIFE of Queen ANNE*. London: Printed for A. Bell at the Bible and Cross-Keys in Cornhill; W. Taylor at the Ship and J. Baker at the Black-Boy, in Pater-Noster Row, 1714.

Brown, Beatrice Curtis, *The Letters and Diplomatic Instructions of Queen Anne*. London: Cassell and Co. Ltd, 1935.

Buchanan, George, *A Detection of the Actions of Mary Queen of Scots, Concerning the Murther of Her HUSBAND, and Conspiracy, Adultery, and pretended Marriage with the Earl of BOTHWELL*. London: Richard Janeway, 1689.

Burnet, Bishop Gilbert, *History of His Own Time*, vol. III, second edition. Oxford: at the University Press, 1833.

——, *An Essay of the Memory Of the Late Queen*. London: Richard Chiswell, 1695.

Carey, Robert (ed. Mares, F.H.), *The Memoirs of Robert Carey*. Oxford: Clarendon Press, 1972.

Charles I. (ed. Bruce, John), *1646. Letters of King Charles The First to Queen Henrietta Maria*. London: Camden Society, 1856.

——, *King Charles His Speech Made Upon the Scaffold at Whitehall-Gate, Immediately Before His Execution on Tuesday the 30th Jan. 1648, With a Relation of the manner of his going to Execution (Published by Special Authority)*. London: Peter Cole, 1649.

Charles II (ed. Macray, W.D.), *Notes Which Passed at Meetings of the Privy Council Between Charles II and the Earl of Clarendon, 1660–1667, Together With a Few Letters* (reproduced in facsimile from the originals in the Bodleian Library). London: Nichols and Sons, 1896.

Clark, J.S., *The Life of James the Second, King of England, etc. Collected out of the memoirs writ by his own hand together with the King's advice to his son and his majesty's will*. London: Longman, Hurst, Rees, Orwe, and Brown, 1816.

de Mayerne, Theodore, *Theo. Turquet Marernii, Equitis Aurati Baronis Auboniae Medici & Philosophi Suo Aero Celeberrimi Opera Medica. In Quibus Continentur Consilia, Epistolae, Observationes, Pharmacopeia, Variaeque Medicamentorum Formulae*, 1703.

——, 'Autopsy of Prince Henry', Egerton MSS 2877, f. 160b, British Library, London.

Doebner, R., ed., *Memoirs of Mary, Queen of England, 1689–1693. Together With Her Letters and Those of James II and William III. To the Electress Sophia of Hanover*. Leipzig: Veit and Comp., 1886.

Edmonds, Thomas, 'Letters of Introduction of Dr Theodore de Mayerne to King James I', Stowe MSS, 172, f. 39 and 175, f. 174, British Library, London.

Eglisham, George, *The Fore-Runner of Revenge*. London, 1642.

Ellis, John, *Letters Written During the Years 1686, 1687, 1688 and Addressed to John Ellis, Esq*. London: Henry Colburn and Richard Bentley, 1831.

Fraser, J., *A Brief Account of the Nullity of King James's Title and the*

Obligation of the Present Oaths of Allegiance. London: Richard Criswell, 1689.

Fyfe, James Gabriel, *Scottish Diaries and Memoirs 1550–1746*. Stirling: Eveas Mackay, 1927.

Hamilton, David (ed. Roberts, Philip), *The Diary of Sir David Hamilton*. Oxford: Clarendon Press, 1975.

Hanoverian Succession Collection. Draft copies of letters to George I. Manuscripts Department of the Spencer Library, University of Kansas, Lawrence, Kansas, USA: Pryce MS P5:1 and Pryce MS P:2. The author is indebted to Ms Anne Hyde, retired manuscript librarian, for making these two draft letters available.

Harrison, G.B., *A Second Jacobean Journal*. London: Routledge and Kegan Paul, 1958.

Harvey, W., *Excercitatio Anatomica de Motu Cordis et Sanguinis in Animali*. Frankfurt: William Fitzer, 1628.

James I/VI, 'A Counterblaste to Tobacco', in *The Works of the Most High and Mightie Prince James*. London: James Bishop, 1616.

——, *Basilikon Doron*. Menston, England: Scolar Press, 1969.

——, *Basilikon Doron, or King James's Instruction to His Dearest Sonne, Henry the Prince*. London: M. Flescher for Samuel Mearne, 1682.

Lewis, J., *Memoirs of Prince William Henry, Duke of Gloucester*. London: Messrs Payne, Mews Gate; J. Murray, Fleet Street; Messrs. Robson and Clark, New Bond Street; Messrs Prince and Cooke, and J. Fletcher. Oxford: 1789.

Macray, W.D., *Notes Which Passed at Meetings of the Privy Council Between Charles II And the Earl of Clarendon, 1660–1667, Together With a Few Letters*. London: Nichols and Sons, 1896.

Mares, F.H., ed., *The Memoirs of Robert Carey*. Oxford: Clarendon Press, 1972.

Mary, Queen of England (ed. Doebner, R.), *Memoirs of Mary, Queen of England, 1689–1693. Together With Her Letters and Those of King James II and William III. To the Electress Sophia of Hanover*. Leipzig: Veit and Comp., 1886.

McClure, N.E., *The Letters of John Chamberlain, vol. II*. Philadelphia: American Philosophical Society, 1939.

Pepys, S. (eds Latham, R. and Matthews, W.), *The Diary of Samuel Pepys, vol. 9*. London: G. Bell and Sons, Ltd, 1983.

Price, J., *An Account of Some Experiments on Mercury Made at*

Guildford in May, 1783 in the Laboratory of J. Price MD, FRS, second edition. Oxford: Clarendon Press, 1783.

Public Record Office, 'Giovanni Carlo Scaramelli to the Doge and Senate', 28 May 1603, *Calendar of State Papers, Foreign Series, of the Reign of James I/VI (March 1603–May 1607)*. London: HMSO, 1900.

——, 'Dr Hen. Akins to Lord Cecil', 3 July 1604, *Calendar of State Papers, Domestic Series, of the Reign of James I (1603–1610)*. London: HMSO, 1857.

——, 'Nath Brent to [Carleton]', 19 November 1616, *Calendar of State Papers, Domestic Series, of the Reign of James I (1611–1618)*. London: HMSO, 1858.

——, 'Lord Henry Percy to his brother-[in-law] James, Earl of Carlisle, at Venice', 3 September 1628, *Calendar of State Papers, Domestic Series, of the Reign of Charles I (Addendum 1625–1649)*. London: HMSO, 1897.

——, 'Alvise Contarini, Venetian Ambassador to the Congress of Munster, to the Doge and Senate', 19 and 26 February 1649, *Calendar of State Papers, Venetian Series (1647–1652)*. London: HMSO, 1927.

——, 'Alvise Valaresso, Venetian Ambassador in England, to the Doge and Senate', *Calendar of State Papers, Venetian Series, of the Reign of James I*. London: HMSO, 1900, 567.

——, 'Pietro Mocensio, Venetian Ambassador in England, to the Doge and Senate', 14 June 1669, *Calendar of State Papers, Venetian Series, of the Reign of Charles II (March 1676–February 1677)*. London: HMSO, 1937.

——, 'Secretary Covington to Williamson', 7 October 1767, *Calendar of State Papers, Domestic Series, of the Reign of Charles II*. London: HMSO, 1909.

——, 'The Earl of Ranleigh to Viscount Conway', 4 March 1679, *Calendar of State Papers, Domestic Series, of the Reign of Charles II*. London: HMSO, 1909.

——, 'The Earl of Sunderland to the Lord Mayor', 6 p.m., 25 August 1679, *Calendar of State Papers, Domestic Series, of the Reign of Charles II*. London: HMSO, 1909.

——, 'The Duke of Monmouth to the Lord Mayor', 25 August 1679, *Calendar of State Papers, Domestic Series, of the Reign of Charles II*. London: HMSO, 1909.

——, 'The Earl of Ranelagh to Viscount Conway', 12 o'clock, 27

August 1679, *Calendar of State Papers, Domestic Series, of the Reign of Charles II*. London: HMSO, 1909.

——, 'The Earl of Sunderland to the Lord Mayor', 27 August 1679, *Calendar of State Papers, Domestic Series, of the Reign of Charles II*. London: HMSO, 1909.

——, 'The Earl of Sunderland to the Lord Mayor', 2 September 1679, *Calendar of State Papers, Domestic Series, of the Reign of Charles II*. London: HMSO, 1909.

——, '[Robert Yard] to Lady [?O'Brien]', 25 September 1679, *Calendar of State Papers, Domestic Series, of the Reign of Charles II*. London: HMSO, 1909.

——, 'Newsletter to John Squire, Newcastle', 3 February 1685, *Calendar of State Papers, Domestic Series, of the Reign of Charles II*. London: HMSO, 1938.

——, 'The Earl of Sunderland to the Lord Mayor', 4 February 1685, *Calendar of State Papers, Domestic Series, of the Reign of Charles II*. London: HMSO, 1909.

——, 'Newsletter to John Squire, Newcastle', 5 February 1685, *Calendar of State Papers, Domestic Series, of the Reign of Charles II*. London: HMSO, 1909.

——, 'Warrant for erecting an office of chemical physician to the King', 7 May 1669, *Calendar of State Papers, Domestic Series, of the Reign of Charles II*. London: HMSO, 1894.

——, 'A Memorial of the Protestants of the Church of England', June or July 1688, *Calendar of State Papers, Domestic Series, of the Reign of James II*. London: HMSO, 1972, 226.

——, 'Council Chamber. The Birth of the Prince of Wales', *Calendar of State Papers, Domestic Series, of the Reign of James II* (22 October [1688]). London: HMSO, 1972, 327.

——, 'The Earl of Devonshire, Earl of Darby, Earl of Shrewsbury, Lord Lumley, the Bishop of London, Admiral Russell and Henry Sidney to the Prince of Orange', *Calendar of State Papers, Domestic Series, of the Reign of James II*. London: HMSO, 1972, 223–5.

——, Several dispatches from the front at Salisbury, *Calendar of State Papers, Domestic Series, of the Reign of James II* (9 June 1687–February 1689). London: HMSO, 1972, 358–61.

Saltmarsh, John, *A Letter From the Army, Concerning the peaceable temper of the same*. London: Giles Calvert, 1647 (Microform E. 393, British Library, London).

Sanderson, William, *The Compleat History of the Life and Reigne of King Charles From His Cradle to his Grave*. London: Humphrey Moseley, Richard Tomlins, and George Sawbridge, 1658.

Scotland, Lords Commissioners of His Majesty's Treasury, 'Drury to Burghley', 23 May 1573, *Calendar of the State Papers Relating to Scotland and Mary, Queen of Scots (1547–1603)*. Edinburgh: HM General Register House, 1905.

Scott, Walter, ed., 'An Exact Account of the Sickness and Death of the late King James II. As also of the Proceedings at St. Germains thereupon, 1701. In a Letter from an English Gentleman in France, to his Friend in London', in *A Collection of Scarce and Valuable Tracts (The Somers Collection of Tracts, in Sion Library)*, vol. XI. London: T. Cadell and W. Davies, 1814, 339–42.

Seton, Alexander, *Memoirs of Alexander Seton*. London: William Blackwood and Sons, 1882.

Sloane, Hans, 'Sir Hans Sloane's Account of Queen Anne's Illness in December 1713–January 1714', Sloane MSS, 4034 ff., 46–50, British Library, London.

Turner, E. in a letter to Brand, J., *A Declaration of the Diet and Particular Fare of K. Charles the First, When Duke of York*. London: Society of Antiquaries of London, 1802.

Weldon, Anthony, *Court and Character of King James the First*. London: John Wright, 1650.

——, *A Perfect Description of the People and Country of Scotland*. 1659.

Welwood, James, *An Answer to the Late King James's Declaration*. London: Dorman Newman, 1689.

SECONDARY SOURCE MATERIAL

Abbott, Jacob, *History of King Charles The First*. London: Thomas Allman, 1850.

Akrigg, G.P.V., *Jacobean Pageant*. London: Hamish Hamilton, 1962.

American Psychiatric Association, *Diagnostic and Statistical Manual of Mental Disorders*, fourth edition. Washington, DC: American Psychiatric Association, 1994.

Anderson, Maurice, 'Queen Anne's Children', *British Medical Journal*, vol. 1 (9 March 1963), 684.

Ashdown, Dulcie, *Royal Children*. London: Robert Hale, 1979.

Bibliography

Ashton, Robert, *James I By His Contemporaries*. London: Hutchison of London, 1969.

Bergeron, David, *Royal Family, Royal Lovers*. Columbia: University of Missouri Press, 1991.

Black, Jeremy, *Convergence or Divergence? Britain and the Continent*. London: Macmillan, 1994.

Bloch, Marc, *The Royal Touch: Sacred Monarchy and Scrofula in England and France*. London: Routledge and Kegan Paul, 1973.

Bloom, H.J.G., Richardson, W.W. and Harries, E.J., 'Natural History of Untreated Breast Cancer – 1805–1933', *British Medical Journal*, II (28 July 1962), 213–21.

Bonney, Richard, *The European Dynastic States: 1494–1660*. Oxford: Oxford University Press, 1991.

Bowen, Marjorie, *The Third Mary Stuart. Mary of York, Orange and England. Being a Character Study With Memoirs and Letters of Queen Mary II of England, 1662–1694*. London: John Lane, Bodley Head Ltd, 1929.

Bowle, John, *Charles I*. London: Weidenfeld and Nicholson, 1975.

Brewer, Clifford, *The Death of Kings: A Medical History of the Kings and Queens of England*. London: Abson, 2000.

British Medical Journal, 'Some Royal Death Beds: James I' I (4 June 1910), 1363.

——, 'Some Royal Death Beds: Charles II' I (25 June 1910), 1557–60.

——, 'Some Royal Death Beds: Mary II' II (16 July 1910), 148.

——, 'Some Royal Death Beds: William III' II (20 August 1910), 461–2.

——, 'Some Royal Death Beds: Queen Anne' II (12 November 1910), 1530–32.

Brockliss, Laurence, 'The Literary Image of the Medecins du Roi in the Literature of the Grand Siecle', in *Medicine at the Courts of Europe, 1500–1837*, ed. Vivian Nutton, 117 ff., London: Routledge, 1990.

Bruce, J., ed., 'Charles I', in 1646, *Letters of King Charles The First to Queen Henrietta Maria*. London: Camden Society, 1856.

Bruce-Chwatt, ed., *The Rise and Fall of Malaria in Europe: A Historico-epidemiological Study*. Oxford: Oxford University Press, 1980.

Bucholz, R.O., *The Augustan Court: Queen Anne and the Decline of Court Culture.* Stanford: Stanford University Press, 1993.

Burke, Bernard, *Genealogical History of the Dormant, Abeyant, Forfeited and Extinct Peerages of the British Empire.* London: Burke's Peerage/Genealogical Publishing Co., 1985.

Bynum, W.F., 'Medicine at the English Court, 1688–1837', in *Medicine at the Courts of Europe, 1500–1837,* ed. Vivian Nutton, 262 ff. London: Routledge, 1990.

Carlton, Charles, *Charles I, The Personal Monarch,* second edition. London: Routledge, 1995.

——, *Royal Childhoods.* London: Routledge, 1986.

——, *Royal Mistresses.* London: Routledge, 1990.

——, 'Three British Revolutions and the Personality of Kingship', in *Three British Revolutions: 1641, 1688, 1776,* ed. J.G.A. Pocock, 195. Princeton: Princeton University Press, 1980.

Cartland, Barbara, *The Private Life of Charles II: The Women He Loved.* London: Frederick Muller, Ltd, 1958.

Chapman, Hester, *Mary II Queen of England.* London: Jonathan Cape, 1953.

Charles, Richard and Corrigan, Elizabeth, 'Epistaxis and Hypertension', *Postgraduate Medical Journal,* 53 (May 1977), 260–1.

Chevers, Norman, *An Enquiry Into the Death of King Charles the Second of England.* London: R.C. Lepage & Co., 1861.

Clayton, J.W., *Personal Memoirs of Charles the Second,* vol. 2. London: Charles J. Skeet, 1859.

Crawfurd, R., *The Last Days of Charles II.* Oxford: Clarendon Press, 1909.

Creighton, Charles, *A History of Epidemics in Britain,* vol. 2. London: Frank Cass, 1965.

Cumston, Charles Greene, 'Some Medical Gossip Pertaining to the Last Illness of Queen Anne of England', *New York Medical Journal,* 94 (22 July 1911), 179–81.

Cunningham, F.G., MacDonald, P.C., Leveno, K.J., Grant, N.F. and Gilstrap, L.C., III *William's Obstetrics,* nineteenth edition. New York: Prentice-Hall International, Inc., 1993: 1234–6.

Dean, Geoffrey, *The Porphyrias: A Story of Inheritance and Environment,* second edition. London: Pitman Medical, 1971.

Dewhurst, Jack, *Royal Confinements: A Gynaecological History of Britain's Royal Family.* New York: St Martin's Press, 1980.

Bibliography

Disraeli, Isaac, *Commentaries on the Life and Reign of Charles the First, King of England*. London: Henry Colburn, 1851.

Ellenhorn, Matthew J. and Barceloux, Donald G., *Medical Toxicology: Diagnosis and Treatment of Human Poisoning*. London: Elsevier, 1988.

Emson, H.E., 'For the Want of an Heir: the Obstetrical History of Queen Anne', *British Medical Journal*, 304 (23 May 1992), 1365–6.

Fenner F., Henderson D.A., Arita I., Jezek, Z. and Ladnyi, I.D., *Smallpox and Its Eradication*. Geneva: World Health Organization, 1988.

Fraser, Antonia, *King Charles II*. London: Weidenfeld and Nicholson, 1979.

——, *King James*. New York: Alfred Knopf, 1975.

——, *Mary Queen of Scots*. London: Weidenfeld and Nicholson, 1969.

Fritze, R.H. and Robison, W.B., eds, *Historical Dictionary of Stuart England, 1603–1689*. London: Greenwood Press, 1996.

Furdell, E.L., *The Royal Doctors 1485–1714: Medical Personnel at the Tudor and Stuart Courts*. Rochester: University of Rochester Press, 2001.

Goodall, Archibald L., 'The Health of James the Sixth of Scotland and First of England', *Medical History*, 1 (January 1957), 17–27.

Green, David, *Queen Anne*. London: Collins, 1970.

Gregg, Pauline, *King Charles I*. London: JM Dent & Sons Ltd, 1981.

Haley, K.H.D., 'Charles II', in *The Historical Association Book of the Stuarts*, ed. K.H.D. Haley, 153. New York: St Martin's Press, 1973.

Hamilton, Elizabeth, *William's Mary: A Biography of Mary II*. London: Hamish Hamilton, 1972.

Hara, James, 'Severe Epistaxis', *Archives of Otolargyngology*, 75 (March 1962), 84–94.

Hay, Malcolm, *Winston Churchill and James II of England*. London: Harding and More, Ltd, 1934.

Hill, Brian, 'Queen Anne's Favorite Physician', *The Practitioner*, 198 (May 1967), 717–22.

Hill, C., *The World Turned Upside Down*. London: Penguin Books, 1991.

Holger, J., 'Epistaxis: a Clinical Study of 1,724 Patients', *Journal of Largyngology and Otology*, 88 (1974), 317–27.

Hollingsworth, T.H., 'Demography of the British Peerage', *Population Studies* (supplement), 18 (no. 2).

——, *Historical Demography*. London: Sources of History Ltd, with Hodder and Stoughton Ltd, 1969.

Holmes, F.F., 'Anne Boleyn, the Sweating Sickness and the Hantavirus: a Review of an Old Disease with a New Interpretation', *Journal of Medical Biography*, 6 (1998), 43–8.

Hopkinson, Maria Ruan, *Anne of England: the Biography of a Great Queen*. New York: Macmillan Co., 1935.

Jesse, John Heneage, *Memoirs of the Court of England from the Revolution in 1688 to the Death of George the Second*. London: Richard Bentley, 1843.

Jones, Colin, 'The Medecins du Roi at the End of the Ancien Regime and in the French Revolution', in *Medicine at the Courts of Europe, 1500–1837*, ed. Vivian Nutton, 209 ff. London: Routledge, 1990.

Kenyon, John, *Robert Spencer, Earl of Sunderland, 1641–1702*. Aldershot: Gregg Revivals, 1992.

——, *Stuart England*, second edition. London: Allen Lane, Penguin Books Ltd, 1978.

Kenyon, J. and Ohlmeyer, J., *The Civil Wars: A Military History of England, Scotland and Ireland, 1638–1660*. Oxford: Oxford University Press, 1998.

Keynes, Geoffrey, *The Life of William Harvey*. Oxford: Clarendon Press, 1966.

Keynes, Milo, 'Smallpox and Queen Anne', *Journal of the Royal Society of Medicine*, 90 (January 1997), 60.

Kishlansky, Mark, *A Monarchy Transformed: Britain 1603–1714*. London: Allen Lane, Penguin Press, 1996.

Klippel, J.H., ed., *Primer on the Rheumatic Diseases*, eleventh edition. Atlanta: Arthritis Foundation, 1997, 234–5.

Koenigsberger, Helmut Georg, *The Habsburgs and Europe, 1516–1660*. Ithaca: Cornell University Press, 1971.

Krumbhaar, E.B., 'Two contemporary manuscripts bearing on the death of Charles II of England', *Transactions and Studies of the College of Physicians of Philadelphia*, 6 (1938), 51–9.

Kummel, Werner Friedrich, 'Diseases Found at Court', in *Medicine at the Courts of Europe, 1500–1837.*, ed. Vivian Nutton, 15 ff. London: Routledge, 1990.

Bibliography

Lamont-Brown, R., *Royal Poxes and Potions: The Lives of Court Physicians, Surgeons and Apothecaries.* Stroud: Sutton, 2001.

Lenihan, J.M.A. and Smith, H., 'Activation Analysis and Public Health', *Nuclear Activation Techniques in the Life Sciences.* Vienna: International Atomic Energy Agency, 1967.

Levine, J.S., Branch, D.W. and Rauch, J., 'The Antiphospholipid Antibody Syndrome', *New England Journal of Medicine,* 346 (2002), 752–63.

Linklater, Eric, *Mary Queen of Scots.* Edinburgh: Peter Davies, 1934.

Longueville, Thomas, *The Adventures of King James II of England.* London: Longmans, Green and Co., 1904.

Louria, Donald B., 'Trace Metal Poisoning', in *Cecil Textbook of Medicine,* ed. James Wyngaarden and Lloyd H. Smith, Jr. Philadelphia: W.B. Saunders Company, 1982.

Luttrell, Narcissus, *A Brief Historical Relation of State Affairs From September 1678 to April 1714,* vol. I. Oxford: at the University Press, 1857.

Macalpine, Ida and Hunter, Richard, *George III and the Mad-Business.* London: Allen Lane, Penguin Press, 1969.

——, 'The "Insanity" of King George III: A Classic Case of Porphyria', *British Medical Journal,* vol. 1 (8 January 1966), 65–71.

Macalpine, Ida, Hunter, Richard and Rimington, C., 'Porphyria in the Royal Houses of Stuart, Hanover and Prussia: A Follow-up Study of George III's Illness', *British Medical Journal,* vol. 1 (6 January 1968), 7–18.

Macaulay, Lord, *History of England From the Access of James II.* London: Longman, Brown, Guern, Longmans & Roberts, 1858.

Macpherson, James, *Original Papers: Containing the Secret History of Great Britain, From the Restoration to the Accession of the House of Hannover. To Which Are Affixed Extracts From the Life of James II, As Written by Himself.* London: W. Strachan and T. Cadell, 1775.

Major, R.H., *Classical Descriptions of Disease.* Springfield: Charles C. Thomas, 1945.

Masters, Brian, *The Mistresses of Charles II.* London: Blond and Briggs, Ltd, 1979.

Maxwell, J. (Baron Herries), *Historical Memories of the Reign of Mary Queen of Scots.* Abbotsford Club, no. 6, ed. R. Pitcairn, Edinburgh, 1836.

McElwee, William Lloyd, *The Wisest Fool in Christendom: the Reign of King James I and VI*. London: Faber and Faber, 1958.

McLynn, F., *Charles Edward Stuart: A Tragedy in Many Acts*. London: Routledge, 1988.

Miller, John, *The Life and Times of William and Mary*. London: Weidenfeld and Nicholson, 1974.

Mitchell, J.R.A., 'Nose-Bleeding and High Blood Pressure', *British Medical Journal*, vol. 1 (3 January 1959), 25–7.

Moore, Norman, *The History of the Study of Medicine in the British Isles*. Oxford: Clarendon Press, 1908.

——, 'An Historical Case of Typhoid Fever', in, *St Bart's Hospital Reports*. XVII, 1881.

Morrison, Nancy Brysson, *Mary Queen of Scots*. New York: Vanguard Press, 1960.

Munk, William, *The Roll of the Royal College of Physicians of London: Comprising Biographical Sketches. Vol. 1 and Vol. II*. London: published for the College by Harrisons & Sons, 1878.

Nenner, Howard, *The Right to be King: the Succession to the Crown of England, 1603–1714*. Chapel Hill: University of North Carolina Press, 1995.

Nicholson, Harold, *Kings, Courts and Monarchy*. New York: Simon and Schuster, 1962.

Nutton, Vivian, ed., *Medicine at the Courts of Europe, 1500–1837*, a volume in the series, Porter, Roy and Bynum W.F., eds, *The Wellcome Institute Series in the History of Medicine*. London: Routledge, 1990.

Oxford Dictionary of Quotations, second edition. Oxford: Oxford University Press, 1955.

Paine, Thomas, *Rights of Man: Being an Answer to Mr. Burke's Attack on the French Revolution*. London: J.S. Jordon, 1791.

Palmer, Richard, 'Medicine at the Papal Court in the 16th Century', in, *Medicine at the Courts of Europe, 1500–1837*, ed. Vivian Nutton, 49 ff. London: Routledge, 1990.

Petruson, Bjorn, 'Epistaxis: a Clinical Study with Special Reference to Fibrinolysis', *Acta Oto-Laryngologica, supplementum 317* (1974), 1–72.

Phillips, Virginia, 'Queen Anne's Seventeen Disappointments', *Medical Journal of Australia*, 156 (2 March 1992), 341–2.

Bibliography

Pittis, William, *Some Memoirs of the Life of John Radcliffe, M.D.*, second edition. London: E. Curll, 1715.

Porter, Roy, 'Gout Framing and Fantasizing Disease', *Bulletin of the History of Medicine*, 68 (spring 1994), 6 ff.

Post, Jerrold and Robins, Robert S., *When Illness Strikes the Leader: The Dilemma of the Captive King*. New Haven: Yale University Press, 1993.

Princess of Orange and Princess Anne of Denmark, 'Questions Sent by the Princess of Orange to the Princess Anne of Denmark', and 'The Princess Anne of Denmark's Answer', in *Memoirs of Great Britain and Ireland*, vol. II, ed. John Dalrymple. London: W. Strachan and T. Cadell, 1773.

Reeve, John, 'Britain and the World Under the Stuarts, 1603–1689', in *The Oxford Illustrated History of Tudor and Stuart Britain*, ed. John Morrill, 419–22. Oxford: Oxford University Press, 1996.

Robb, Nesca Adeline, *William of Orange: A Personal Portrait*, vol. II. London: Heineman, 1966.

Savile, George, *A Character of King Charles the Second*. Dublin: James Edsall, 1750.

Schumacher, Ralph, Jr., Klippel, John H. and Keepmans, William J., eds, *Primer on Rheumatic Diseases*. Atlanta: Arthritis Foundation, 1993, 213.

Scott, Otto, *James I*. New York: Mason/Charter, 1976.

Scott, Walter, *Secret History of the Court of King James the First*. Edinburgh: James Ballentyne and Co., 1811.

Sharpe, Kevin, *The Personal Rule of Charles I*. New Haven: Yale University Press, 1992.

Smith, J.R., *The Speckled Monster: Smallpox in England, 1670–1970, with Particular Reference to Essex*. Chelmsford: Essex Record Office, 1987.

Snyder, Henry L., 'The Last Days of Queen Anne: The Account of Sir John Evelyn Examined', *Huntingdon Library Quarterly*, 34 (1970–1), 261–76.

Spedding, James, *An Account of the Life and Times of Francis Bacon*. Boston: Houghton, Mifflin, and Company, 1880.

Stephen, L., ed., 'Charles I', *Dictionary of National Biography*. Oxford: Oxford University Press, 1968.

——, 'Charles II'.

——, 'Anne Hyde, Duchess of York'.

——, 'Queen Anne'.

Stevenson, Scott, *Famous Illnesses in History*. London: Eyre & Spottiswoode, 1962.

Stone, Lawrence, 'Results of the English Revolutions', in *Three British Revolutions: 1641, 1688, 1776*, ed. J.G.A. Pocock, 92–3. Princeton: Princeton University Press, 1980.

Strickland, Agnes, *Lives of the Queens of England*. Philadelphia: Blanchard and Lea, 1853 and (subsequent edition) Philadelphia: Blanchard and Lea, 1853.

Sutton, H. Manners, ed., *The Lexington Papers, or Some Account of the Courts of London and Vienna: at the Conclusion of the Seventeenth Century*. London: John Murray, 1851.

Thompson, Charles John Samuel, *The Lure and Romance of Alchemy*. London: George Harrup & Co., Ltd, 1932.

Thorndike, Lynn, 'Alchemy and Chemistry After 1650', in *A History of Magic and Experimental Science, The Seventeenth Century*, vols vii and viii. New York: Columbia University Press, 1958.

Trevelyan, George, *England Under Queen Anne: the Peace and the Protestant Succession*, vol. 3. London: Longmans, Green and Co., 1934.

Trevor-Roper, Hugh, 'The Court Physician and Paracelsianism', in *Medicine at the Courts of Europe, 1500–1837*, ed. Vivian Nutton, 79 ff. London: Routledge, 1990.

Tudor, Vasile and Strati, Ioan, *Smallpox: Cholera*. Tunbridge Wells: Abacus Press, 1977.

Turner, F.C., *James II*. London: Eyre & Spottiswoode, 1948.

Wahl, Francis X., *The Matrimonial Impediments of Consanguinity and Affinity: an Historical Synopsis and Commentary*. Washington, DC: Catholic University of America, 1934.

Waterson, Nellie M., *Mary II Queen of England 1689–1694*. Durham: Duke University Press, 1928.

Weiss, Noel, 'Relation of High Blood Pressure to Headache, Epistaxis and Selected Other Symptoms', *New England Journal of Medicine*, 287 (28 September 1972), 631–3.

Williams, K., Holmes F., Kemper, S. and Marquis, J., 'Written language clues to cognitive changes of ageing: an analysis of the letters of King James VI/I', *Journal of Gerontology: Psychological Sciences*, 58B, 2003, 42–4.

Bibliography

Willson, David Harris, *King James VI and I*. London: Jonathan Cape, 1956.

Wilson, E. (Lord Moran), *Churchill, Taken From the Diaries of Lord Moran*. Boston: Houghton Mifflin Co., 1966.

Wolbarsht, M.L. and Sax, D.S., 'Charles II, a Royal Martyr', *Notes and Records of the Royal Society of London*, 16 (November 1961), 154–7.

Index

Index